THE REACH OF POLITICS

The Reach of Politics

A NEW LOOK AT GOVERNMENT

James K. Feibleman

HORIZON PRESS / NEW YORK

To
Andrew J. Reck

PREFACE

This book represents one more attempt to find out what the political structure is. The analysis will not begin with a blueprint for good government but will cut under such sophisticated suggestions in a sustained effort to determine the nature of politics, a speculative field in which many studies have been undertaken already. The problem is admittedly an old one, but there are new facts to be adduced; and whenever there are new facts there is apt to be a new theory lurking somewhere in the background needing to be brought forward for examination.

In the following pages I owe much to contemporary studies in political theory as well as to the journalistic presentation of political events. I have also obtained many facts and theories from other sources, such as the recent work on human aggression. My thanks are due chiefly to Mr. Huntington Cairns, to Dr. David R. Deener, and to my wife, for their numerous suggestions. The more an author owes, the richer his work is likely to be, provided, of course, he has something comprehensive of his own to contribute. But in any case he alone is responsible for the final product.

CONTENTS

ix

Part One

THE LOGICAL POSSIBILITIES

Chapter I

THE STUDY OF POLITICS

Section 1. A Reason for This Work

A man who would write a book about politics these days should stop and think twice. A great many articles and books on nearly every topic get published. Indeed modern life is hedged about with what has aptly been called "paper work," so much so that whole-sale methods of dealing with the flood of research have had to be devised. Complex computerized methods of centralizing the vast amounts of information to make it available for decision-making are being suggested.

New and important ideas, however, are rare enough, but now even if they are discovered, there is more than an even chance of their being lost, for the machines to evaluate the relative worth of the results of investigations are not yet available. As things stand now, who will be lucky enough to run across the seed-thought in all that data processing?

Since most activities in a modern scientific-industrial culture take place within the confines of one institution or another where every-thing has to be executed in triplicate, the pile-up of records is in-evitable, though many who are occupied with more substantive in-terests deplore it. There are good reasons why they do so, for no doubt much paper work is obstructive, legalistic and bureaucratic

3

beyond the immediate needs of the occasions which give rise to them. But other paper work is facilitative and necessary, and smooths the way for cooperation.

In a positivistically oriented culture, only what leads directly to practical effects is taken seriously. Currently, writings about politics are judged by the same standards as writings about science, that is, does the work produce immediate applications? It has been recently stated that the days of theoretical speculation in political theory which produced such classics as Plato's *Republic*, Aristotle's *Politics*, Machiavelli's *The Prince*, and Marx's *Capital*, are over forever. We have moved on, it is claimed, to a situation where there is only the practice of politics on the one hand and a verbal clarification of the language of politics on the other.

That verbal clarification was needed cannot be denied, but there are no closed situations in human affairs, and the most disappointing recital in the world must be the monotonous account of how things initially declared impossible were accomplished almost immediately thereafter. A list could be made of these instructive prohibitions and of how they were contradicted by events, but this would constitute a digression. The delay in improving practice that the development of an adequate theory often requires is more than made up by the size of the consequent improvement. The need for constructive theories remains. It is sufficient to say that there is nothing morally wrong in aiming as high as a thinker can, especially with the best of the past as his models, and as his aim the hope that his influence upon the future might be what all men of good will desire.

One thing we can be sure, then, is that the greatest practical benefits are to be derived from withdrawing from practical issues and problems to the areas of detached theoretical speculation. The aims of the humanist must often take him away from the immediate consideration of humanity. Much progress has been accomplished without having humanity in direct view. Pure mathematics, pure physics, pure biology have resulted in knowledge whose applications have been of immense benefit. If this were not the case we would not have atomic powered water purification plants, antibiotics, or the medical use of X-ray machines. And the same can be said of politics. We want to know the nature of the state as such, and, if possible, something about the ideal political system without regard to the immediate problems of government. For in this way governments of the future might be rendered better and more serviceable.

Good government and good administration may come from improvements made on the spot; but they will have more permanent value and more widespread application if they are combined with the work of those few abstract thinkers who withdrew from what-is to consider what-ought-to-be. Then, what ought government to be? This is the question which motivates the political theorist. In the hands of Locke and Montesquieu, it produced democracy, and, in the hands of Marx and Engels, it produced communism. No doubt still others will produce more far-reaching political theories which will in turn be applied in practice.

The more advanced the human species becomes the more it is inclined to design its own future. The Greeks began the tradition of planning in politics. The idea that behind each political program there lies a political philosophy and that behind each political philosophy there lies a theoretical metaphysics seems to have originated with Plato. But the idea that such a program can be deliberately put into effect in a country with a very large population originated in the Soviet Union. This is not the end of the development of theory but only the beginning. Now that we have such a vivid and dramatic illustration of the power of ideas in practice, the pursuit of the best ideas is likely to be accelerated.

One point in favor of this ambition must be made, and can be stated as a theorem: *There are no inapplicable true theories.*

Examined carefully, this statement turns out to be a truism. For truth suggests a connection with facts that has already been shown; that others will follow might have been logically expected. Yet, there is an important purpose derived from establishing and defending the position. For a time lag does exist between the statement of a truth and the discovery of significant and important ways in which it can be applied to human affairs.

Many examples spring to mind. For instance, some two thousand years elapsed between the discovery of conic sections by Appolonius of Perga and their application to practical engineering problems. Often the time is shorter. Early in the twentieth century, Rutherford said he was sure that no practical results could come out of atomic theory. He did not live to see the many peacetime uses of atomic energy, such as the manufacture of electric power and the treatment of cancer which followed so quickly after his discoveries.

It is distressing that the theoretical investigator is uncomfortable with the facts, particularly when these tend to be ugly. For the cogency of a pure theory depends upon its not going against the facts, upon its being able to account for them. A knowledge of facts is essential to the theorist, and in the case of politics they are more apt to be found in the marketplace rather than buried in the library. It is not for nothing that Plato engaged in politics in Syracuse and Machiavelli in Italy, and if both were unsuccessful in a practical way, what they learned in the course of their adventures stood them in good stead when they undertook to think and write about the problems.

An assumption upon which the body of this work depends, then, is that there is no such thing as useless knowledge. The more general a truth the greater its potential for practicality.

There is of course in the case of any abstract truth the problem of finding out where it applies and how it can be used, a problem which admittedly is not always simple. If the statement—"there is an abstract truth"—is true, then the statement—"there are concrete situations to which it can be applied"—is an analytic truth; that is to say, the truth of the second is contained in the truth of the first. The electrical engineer who collected obscure languages as a hobby at the outbreak of World War II proved to be the only one of his profession in the country who also knew Swahili, a combination of talents the army needed very badly.

Cultures which rise to great heights always exceed their political accomplishments. The prime example is the ancient Greeks, whose achievements in the arts were unparalleled and in the sciences originative; yet despite the fact that they held the state to be above all else, they were failures at its successful management. If there is one consistent theme in human history it is that people everywhere and at all times are incapable of governing themselves. Why should this be so? Even those who think the best about what they do, their judgments are apt to exceed practice. I propose to look for the source of this difficulty in the effort to find a remedy.

No one would claim that nationally or internationally governments are structured so well and are so well run that there is no need or room for improvement. Therefore political speculation is almost a necessity and may be construed as society's investment in its own future. I make no greater claim for my work than that it is pointed in this direction.

These are the general difficulties confronting the contemporary political theorist. If there are special difficulties as, for instance, the rise of the great populations and the rapid advance of technology, it is because the conditions which exist are so different from those which prevailed earlier; some reflection on this very fact and its causes would seem to be a necessary part of any attempt to understand either social man or his political history. In any case, a renewed interest in theory is essential.

Section 2. Political Theory

Here is a new study of politics. Like all studies in which ideas have been advanced for the first time, this one contains many theories which are offered without proof and only for their use in explanation, as though this would be enough to lead to the examination of their claims and not to the discovery of a truth. No worker in the field of politics can hope to shake the world again so soon after the impact of the followers of Marx and Engels in the first half of the twentieth century. But Marx brought a new kind of conflict with his justification of the class war. It resulted in old countries identifying their nationalism with the triumph of the masses, through an elite which professed to represent them but which, in fact, has exercised a rigid dictatorship, even though this was hardly what Marx had intended. Since him, few have dared advance a well-defined theory of the state. But anyone bringing even the hope of peace would have more than justified the effort.

The pure theory of politics suffers from the disability that holds up all investigations in social fields. There has been little or no success in the attempt to penetrate lower levels of analysis in political subject matter. It is still treated at the level of enlightened common sense even though political relations are known to be both subtle and complex. Whatever is holding up the development of experimental social science is also retarding political theory; one can advance no faster than the other. Statistical journalism is hardly the best way around the problem. The answer may lie in the very fact that there are too many variables.

Any serious study of politics would have to assume that objective laws of behavior based on human needs exist and can be discovered, or else there would be little point. And yet the extreme simplicity of all social analyses would seem to argue for their falsity or at least for some degree of distortion. The integrative levels of the social fields, according to which the social and the cultural are complications of lower organizations, are a clear indication that the higher a structure is the more complex it must be. Thus, a human society must be far more complex than an organic cell. But the facts as we know them are just the reverse, for we know so much more about the complexities of the cell. This would seem to indicate that what we have uncovered so far about the nature of society is less than adequate. However, there is no reason why informed guesses should have to wait until matters improve.

Men are complex and they lead lives involving complex social relations, yet they govern themselves by means of comparatively simple systems. Their governments are the best they know how to construct, and, if these are inadequate, it is because the elaborate structure of social relations exceeds man's social knowledge. The analysis of cultures is not on a par with the complexity of cultures. For if the elements of cultures are, among other things, human individuals, as well as, say, institutions and artifacts, then the analysis is insufficient.

The human brain is presently considered the most complex of organizations, containing as it does some nine billion neurons. And social relations contain, among other elements, those between individuals which are greater in number than the sum of the individuals themselves. If on this level alone the complexity exceeds our present knowledge, what must it be like when all levels of culture are considered? The political structure is a poor organization indeed to modulate, contain and rule over such an intricate network of relationships, especially since each such relation has its corresponding quality, force, or value.

According to Arthur F. Bentley, there is nothing to the state except that process of government whereby some people succeed in determining the behavior of others. Like so many theories, Bentley's is true in what it affirms and false in what it denies. No doubt in politics some people do succeed in determining the behavior of others; this is true, but it is just as true when the people doing the determining are artists, scientists, and theologians, for they also determine to some extent the behavior of others. The important questions are: how is the determination made effective, and what kind of behavior is involved?

It is precisely here that we are brought back to the necessity of discovering the nature of political power. So we find that we have been nowhere at all: we still must find out how the state works and what government is.

These are the problems to which I address my inquiry. The political theorist experiences more difficulty than the physicist, say, or the philosopher, in getting beyond current events in order to grasp the essentially abstract nature of politics. I assume that the truth about politics would apply equally to every time and place. The political theorist is a "social scientist" and, like all whose subject matter comprises an aspect of human society, the difficulty of avoiding what is local and peculiar in favor of what is widespread and common seems insuperable. Civilization cannot be allowed to mean only the western civilization of Europe, nor can political development be equated solely with the problems of the emerging nations of Asia and Africa. Western civilization, with its applied science and technology, its industry, improved transportation and communication, may be the best today, but that does not mean it is the best for all time, or even, the last. Nor does it entirely replace what others may have lost by accepting it.

The political theorist's problem must consider what can be found in history to exemplify theories which are constructed for the primary purpose of exploring possibilities. His task is to use his knowledge in order to find the direction in which the greatest improvements in existing political arrangements will lie.

The study of politics must undergo a long apprenticeship before it can claim to be part of social science. The search for invariants need not be endorsed by such an honorific classification until it has met with some measure of success. Of course, it will not succeed at all unless one assumes there is a subject matter to be discovered and political regularities to be found and isolated.

Meanwhile, many points of view oppose such a conception. Those who subscribe to a relative or an absolute position with respect to political values may be equally in error even though the error is not shared.

The relativists are convinced there are no universal political values, political value as such being relative to a given society at a particular time and place. There is a deep pessimism in such a contention for it assumes that mankind is forever condemned to be divided by personal or social values, each in opposition to the other. If this be the case, there is no hope for the harmony of mankind, no possibility that a world government and with it a world at peace could ever be established and maintained. It assumes that people are divided in some fundamental but irreparable way.

The absolutists, on the other hand, commit the error of saying, not that universal political values exist but that they have found them. Each group thus justifies to itself at least the effort to impose its own ideas upon others. If this be true then the Stalins, the Mussolinis and the Hitlers will have their inevitable successors, and people will be hopelessly divided.

Both relativism and some fashionable variety of captive absolutism—constituting the chief choices up to the present among political theorists—are deeply pessimistic and irretrievably divisive. Either peace will be based upon a broken world in which one nation cannot have commerce with another, or a hegemony will be imposed by force so that all nations except the strongest will exist in some degree of slavery.

Fortunately there is a third choice. In contrast with the false alternatives which assert either that there is no political absolute truth or that the absolute political truth is known and owned, there is the alternative that the absolute political truth exists but as yet is not known. This possibility is what inspires the speculator in political theory to pioneer new ground. It will guide the investigations which I present in this book.

Therefore, again the ideas must be general if they are to count at all. If what I write here is to mean anything, it must apply in a basic way to all countries, governments, and states. If it is false for one, it is false for all according to the strict logical truth which I have chosen to employ. The aim, then, is to make a political analysis which will stand the test of those major changes which occur in time. The examples and illustrations are drawn, for the most part, from the contemporary world, and these will inevitably be outdated. I can only hope that the theory itself does not perish with them.

An original thinker is one who is in a more or less continual state of violent interaction with his times. To make matters worse, ours are among the times when political changes are occurring so fast that it is all but impossible to ignore them even temporarily. The atmosphere surrounding the patient investigator therefore must seem more like a pause in the fighting. Everyone lives a life of crisis in which steps taken today to survive have nothing to do with the character of his actions tomorrow, for we live in a period when systems of ideas compete in the arena of practice more obviously than ever before.

A theorem of actuality states that no claim can be made for the reality of any principle for which there is not some evidence in existence. A corresponding theorem of possibility states that no claim can be made for the reality of anything in existence which cannot be read as the evidence for some principle. Outside the boundaries of one school of philosophy, the two theorems would be found equally objectionable. Nevertheless, they furnish the justification for endeavoring to weave theory and practice together.

Practice is not in want of advocates; but theory, in such exigent times, goes begging. There comes a time in the affairs of men when any theory is better than none if it serves to keep speculation alive. Though the discovery of truth is the aim of every theorist, a new theory is judged not by its truth but by its boldness.

There is one danger which threatens truth in every investigation. There is always the possibility that what-ought-to-be will be misread for what-is. Then, too, what-ought-to-be is often formulated in terms of personal preference, individual advantage, or prejudice. When a man refers to "the ideal," he often means *his* ideal, and he might be shocked were he to learn that it is not necessarily everyone else's. The safeguard in such a case is to apply the counter-principle of wishful self-aggrandizement. If when examining a statement a thinker can see that he stands to gain personally from a certain interpretation, then the truth of that interpretation, for him and for the time being at least, should be suspect. Ideals are not self-validating, and statements of ideals ought to be viewed with the utmost suspicion by those advancing them.

Political theorists need to be realists with respect to conditions as they are, and idealists with respect to conditions as they ought to be. The political realists like Machiavelli were describing things as they are, and must be distinguished from others like Plato who undertook to describe how things ought to be. But we need both, remembering always, of course, that the one must not be confused with the other. Generally it might be said that idealists are more plentiful than realists. Men love to indulge in political speculation, especially when they are not actively engaged politicians, yet both groups shrink from admitting the ugly facts. And it is just these ugly facts which are the prerequisite of ideals, for how can we move toward goals unless we know from where we are starting?

The man of action is always uncomfortable with pure theory on the grounds that it gets nothing done. That this often has been and still is true of some pure theories is no doubt the case. Not many theories ever live to be applied, and many when applied are found wanting. But this is no argument against the cogency of pure theory. The power of theories which are true has been demonstrated over and over, and the power of theories which are believed to be true has been demonstrated even more often. Whitehead once pointed out a relation of theory to practice: the more abstract the theory the more powerful its effects on practice. This has certainly been tested in the applications of quantum theory to atomic energy, on the truth side; and on the side of theories believed to be true, in the power of an outdated Marxism to continue to influence human societies.

There are, of course, other reasons for wanting to know the truth; I might say other forms of application. Knowledge increases both the intensity and the range of human life. One of the most important of all practical uses of truth is its aid to understanding. The more one knows the more deeply one feels, and to increase feeling through knowledge seems the best way to intensify life. But it also happens that the extent of the world we understand defines the limits of the world in which we live. Therefore knowledge increases the range of our involvement.

Since the wants of individual man are now so many and so varied, participation in political life is hardly an option. Each of us takes some part in politics merely by being a citizen of a state. Yet our ignorance of what this means often makes us passive victims of other wills. It is too late to change what is already upon us, but to affect practice in the future requires approaching it from a particular theory. Hence the study of politics is a necessity for the individual who would hope to influence his increment of the collective destiny.

Section 3. The State as a Partially-Ordered System

A study of politics may properly begin with a theory of the state. Every state contains some kind of political order, and, since order is a rational affair, it is legitimate to argue that the state is reason applied to human society, just as political thinkers from Plato to Hegel have said it was. Their insistence that the state is by that account necessarily inflexible does not, however, follow. Systems as such are not inflexible; only inflexible systems are. An open system is a possibility and in logic is often described as a partially-ordered system. The state as a political order could also be a partially-ordered system.

A partially-ordered system for our purposes will be one which contains only a primitive vocabulary of the principal terms, a definition of which will include a formula and some principles of interpretation. The terms will be the familiar ones, though more precise definitions are given in the Appendix. The formula is shortly to be provided, while the principles will be offered from time to time throughout the book where each will be indicated by the use of italics and usually labelled *"political rule."*

In so far as there are laws, the state is partially-ordered; in so far as there are conflicts, it is not. The partially-ordered system may be understood here as a loose arrangement of propositions about a specific general topic, in this case politics. The effective criterion for deciding whether or not a statement is part of the political system is to ask if it describes a need-reduction of the individual citizen without interfering with the future improvement of the state. Both the outlines of a political system and a theory of politics should emerge from a reading of the whole book.

Every political system has to reckon with the two most powerful elements in human nature and in the world: first, its rationality, and, second, its irrationality. The former makes any concrete order, including law, possible; the latter makes it necessary. (I assume that "law and order" here include the force to back them up.)

It may be that nature is through and through rational, and that what we call "irrational" is simply the evidence that our laws are insufficiently inclusive; but if there is any such thing as objective chance then rationality itself has limits. In any case we need to find a wider order which could include what now appears to be the evidence for man's aberrant behavior.

The point is that it ought to be possible to construct a political theory which is independent of contingent differences. Political relations ought to be fundamentally the same whether they hold between the few citizens of a small state, such as Luxemburg, or the vast population of a modern great nation, such as the United States. The principles involved ought to be the same, also, the mode of economic production. A man's political duties and obligations should be the same—fundamentally the same—in an agricultural economy and in a highly mechanized and industrialized technical and scientific community. There would be differences of course, but the differences would not be material with respect to the nature of politics.

If we were to begin with the blueprints for an ideal society the presentation would be vastly different. But we are not. We are only asking about the conditions for political rule. If we assume that the state is to contain a large population, then it should be theoretically possible to give abstract rules for the relation and operation of its parts: institutions, interest-groups and individuals, properties and regions, under the aegis of the whole state. The outlines of a logical state would be a kind of prolegomena to any government at all.

Every state is founded on two principles: the establishment of order and the controlled use of violence on behalf of that order. The order established follows closely into practice the outlines of some chosen utopian ideology, and the controlled violence rests on a standing arrangement where it is held in reserve pending appeal. In addition, there are the usual elements of any actual practice which is sufficiently formal to be able to last: a phenomenology and a technology. Or, in other words, the peculiar view it takes of the rest of the world, the way it is *faced*, and the means it is able to employ to produce its power.

Two elements combine to make up the political history of a people: abstract ideas and physical forces. The ideas lay down the lines along which the forces develop. In the course of a sufficient number of successive practical events, the ideas become modified and the forces channeled and restrained, so that it may sometimes be difficult to recognize the original form in the present intention. The ideas and the exigencies produced by the forces interact in unpredictable ways. Looking back from the present always produces a view of development that is logical but not inevitable, changes qualitatively different yet at the same time not unrelated. Suppose, for instance, that the founding fathers of the United States government, men like John Adams, Thomas Jefferson and Alexander Hamilton, were to return in the middle of the twentieth century to examine the disposition which had been made of their principles!

Otherwise, the requirements of a political system, or government, would be the same as those for any system. They are: consistency—that the elements in the state, human individuals, interest-groups, institutions, properties, regions, hold together without conflict; completeness—that the government be sufficiently broad to provide rules for any one of a pair of contrary but relevant decisions; independence—that each of the elements of the state is able to retain a requisite degree of autonomy; and, finally, economy—that there be in the state no more government than is necessary.

Some form of contract is implicit in society. It may or it may not be explicit as well. The contract is an open agreement among a people who have decided, or who have had it decided for them, to live in a certain way, and it is their announced testament to that agreement. If a society has in its government a social contract, then it is, as Burke pointed out, a contract that includes the dead and the unborn as well as the living. The government is, of course, in the hands of the living, and in times of crisis it would seem to be entirely theirs. But do they not have in mind their descendants for whom they would like to make things better, as well as their ancestors to whom they owe some sort of obligation for what they themselves are? The existence of a contract which may be only implicit but which may extend to absent persons suggests a larger conception of the state, and one is given here in the promised formula.

Formula: *The political entity sui generis is the interposition between any elements in the state of the presence of an overriding order, having available as part of its resources not only a contractual obligation but also what is needed for any final appeal to physical force.*

Interposition is a political confrontation: a reminder of the conditions of limited order represented by the relation of rules between ruler and ruled, and conditioning any lesser order, as, for instance, a formal or informal arrangement between elements. The theory of confrontation in individual morality states that "good behavior may be defined as conduct toward another, in consideration of all others." In social morality it becomes "conduct toward an element of the society, in consideration of the whole society." Forceful relations are thus always qualitative at the interface where the political entity as a third party is encountered. Government is the generic presence, operating on the principle of interposition.

The essential function of government, then, is interposition, in the sense defined above, which can be employed to settle disagreements between elements and to enforce laws when infracted, and to proportionately relate the same political elements as, for example, by means of taxation, military defense, or the conservation of natural resources. The activity of interposition is the politically functioning government, an established moral theory implemented.

The state is the official presence by virtue of its function of interposition. It lends a needed measure of stability to the society so that the ongoing processes, which are necessarily dynamic, do not overbalance the social structure. The state exists so that the forces engaged in the struggles of day to day intercourse remain in equilibrium. The task of government is to see either that interests do not conflict or that, when they do, ground-rules are set for limiting the conflict by providing proper channels for it, so that it shall not destroy political order.

Individual encounters are marked by amity or enmity, by co-operation or competition. In the cases of amity and cooperation, it is the business of the state to formalize the arrangement so that it can be to some extent perpetuated. In the cases of enmity and competition, it is the business of the state to see that nothing is done to disrupt the social order and to mark down for punishment any citizens responsible for violence which borders on the illegal. Apart from the interest of groups there is a general interest: the survival of a state-wide order which shall facilitate the functioning of all lesser relationships. The alternative is anarchy; and since anarchy is always possible, a government of some sort is the only alternative under which it is practical for individuals to live in peace and security. Where anarchy prevails, it has always been found that citizens yearn for order—any order rather than none—and long for the police—or for death.

The mob is the primitive raw material upon which a political order is imposed by political arrangement; not arbitrarily, though, but by nurturing the potential for order which has already existed between individual members themselves. The members of the mob are aggressive, impulsive, irrational and merciless. They would rather do anything than nothing, and would rather do something violent than something nonviolent.

Radical empiricists in political theory, men like Bentley, Truman and Easton, deny the existence of the state as an entity, insisting that its existence is confined to its function as the process of government. But it is in the legitimate nature of the force exercised by the government that we find the evidence which justifies the assertion that the state exists.

The government functions as a partially-ordered system, a logical structure which, if merely logical, would be vertical and linear but which, because it is incorporated in an actual social organization, is horizontal and interwoven, and laid down along a time-line, more like a musical theme-and-variations, only in this case one which is interrupted by contingencies which it can support provided they do not become large enough to be totally disruptive.

In the established morality we have guidelines along which the society is henceforth to be conducted, from whence laws are deduced to contain the savagery of the conflict in the struggle for power. The predatory human animal is to be allowed to do whatever he can to gain his ends provided he does not contravene the rules delimiting procedure.

It has been the business of the state to survive as a state without regard to the service of any other principles, such as truth or justice; for without the existence of the state there can be no functioning government and hence no social order. But it should also be the business of the state to contribute to the larger political organization, such as the prospective global superstate, even though the achievement of this end might mean its dissolution as a power. It is possible to argue that the existence of parts as themselves wholes need not cease when it becomes clear that as wholes they are parts of still larger wholes.

Some political order is necessary, then, but the kind of political order to be selected is perhaps a secondary question. The sad thing is that almost any order which has been accepted by a majority or which can be successfully imposed will work for a while: tyrannies as well as democracies, monarchies as well as oligarchies. The only important requirement is that the order which has been adopted be regarded as inevitable and inescapable and that everyone accept it as the nature of things. Anyway, although good government is preferable to bad, no government lasts very long because no culture does. Only in terms of individual human lives, may a social order seem permanent. But what survives the lives of many will not survive the lives of some; and there will come that day for a generation of citizens when they will see the failure of the government on which they had counted so heavily, when they see it replaced first by a temporary anarchy and then by another kind of government.

The strength of a state is contained in its ability to shelter and promote differences among its citizens in every domain. The state is regulative, not constitutive; governments are established to maintain social order. Anarchy and revolution, both of which represent disorder, are sometimes necessary so that one order replace another, and justifiable in the long run if, and only if, a worse order is replaced by a better.

The goodness of a political order is defined by the degree to which that order does what it was designed to do: to provide the greatest number of need-reductions for the greatest number of citizens, such as the minimal materials necessary for food, clothing, shelter, medical attention, work, protection against enemies, security against defectors. In the case of defectors, delicate decisions are sometimes involved, for instance, a defector under the Nazis might have been a patriotic German who wished to restore democracy; but then what about a patriotic Tibetan under the Communist Chinese? The list is deliberately shorter and simpler than it ought to be. Some needs are more complex and, as we shall see, can be reduced only by drives which extend beyond the state. I am thinking of arts, sciences, religions and philosophies, which can seldom be limited to political boundaries.

It can be seen, then, that under the principle of interposition no more than a partial ordering is possible. The need for flexibility would not allow any stricter order, and flexibility is required of any order which contains the diverse elements of the political state. There are always individuals, often very many of them; there are interest groups, each with demands on the whole; and there are inevitably those successful institutions which tend to be preemptive of the whole. And so, as we have seen, what is needed is a generic political presence introduced from above which at the same time does not prevent a people from electing themselves into a body by the votes of existing members.

Chapter II

ORIGINS OF THE STATE IN
HUMAN NEEDS

In this chapter I plan to trace the origins of the state on the assumption that these are to be found in the organ-specific needs of man as he must have existed in prehistory. This will give us the necessary background for the understanding of the state in its relations to the autonomous human individual. In the next chapter I will examine the relations of the state to other institutions and to society and culture. But these last exist at organizational levels higher than the state, and the entire story of its relations to them will await a still later treatment when they are connected with a theory of its future history.

Section 1. *The Human Individual*

Before giving an account of the way in which organic needs lead to the formation of the state, it will be well to describe the human individual himself in the most basic terms, for it is on the collection of individuals that the political structure properly rests. I begin, then, with the human individual understood as an absolute political minimum. It is he who must constitute the starting-point for all considerations of the state. We shall be most interested in features which the individual shares with all other concrete things, those

which are merely material as well as those which are actual, for they
are fundamental. I shall be talking, then, about the human individual,
but in terms which could as well apply merely to a material entity.
Paradoxically, this approach will lead us to a view of human nature
which will prove useful in the following pages when we try to understand the political alternatives and limitations which follow from
it.

I shall look quickly at seven of his characteristics. They are:
*historicity, infinity, improbability, privation, discontinuity, inequal-
ity,* and *intolerance of opposition.*

The individual has the characteristic of *historicity.* That is to
say, he occupies a position of his own in some segment of history.
He has lived through a succession of personal states and has become
to some extent formed by them. He has received both habits and
memories from them. Indeed he may be said to have inherited his
own past. Thus each individual is different and each lives in a present made up somewhat of his own selection.

The individual is *infinite,* and he is so in two ways. In one sense
he is infinite as a product of history. What has happened to him can
never be changed; he lives forever in a kind of immortality which
he shares with all other human individuals and things which have
had the privilege of existing. To be part of the past is to be infinite
in the sense of always having been.

In a second sense he is infinite in the dimension of intensity. He
has depth. No one has ever probed the ultimate reaches of any
finite individual, be he an electron or a man. The human individual
possesses a complex organization with no known limits.

The existence of the individual is highly *improbable.* If we
reckon with the number of circumstances which must have had to
occur, and occur together, in order that an individual could exist
precisely as he does, such concurrence, and consequently the individual himself, is, on any calculation, unpredictable. Yet the fact
is he does exist. And so we are justified in saying of him that one of
his properties is a high improbability.

Privation, fourth of the individual's characteristics, is the absence of value where value could legitimately have been expected.
Instead of fullness in this regard there is emptiness; instead of
perfection, want. A complete individual, one having all the char-

acteristics possible in such an instance, does not exist, and so privation is common and to be expected. The position of privilege which
anything actual enjoys by virtue of existing rather than by not existing—a situation which is rare enough in view of all the possibilities
—entails limitation which causes disadvantage and accounts for disvalues. Because of privation, the individual has a tendency to act
for himself in every way, legitimate or otherwise.

Discontinuity is the absence of continuity. For an individual,
the process of enduring involves the breaking of some connections as
well as the making of others. The immediately surrounding environment of the individual puts him into contact with the brute fact of
difference: most of the material things in his environment differ
from him to this extent and demand of him a particular reckoning.
His sheer survival as a separate entity requires that he come to terms
with the things around him. They serve as plain marks of the limits
which he must acknowledge through their effects.

Inequality is a fact of existence and derives obviously enough
from the absence of equality. No two individuals have exactly the
same set of characteristics. But they come into contact on the same
level. This leads to the insistence of inequality and the always threatened outcome in conflict. Inequality would not come so forcibly
into evidence were there no encounters of individuals on the same
level. But such encounters do exist and are frequent, so some kind
of adjustment must be made beyond the individual level.

Lastly, the individual is inherently *intolerant of opposition*. This
follows from the fact that he has a partly blind and somewhat un-
governable will. Opposites cannot join together in total harmony.
There are many activities in which the individual can engage but
he must engage in them one at a time; and for each of them there is
always present and ready some variety of opposition. The intolerance leads directly to conflict, and this situation can be resolved
only at a higher level of organization.

We are now in a position to sum up the political implications of
the possession of the seven characteristics by the individual. As a
result of the first three characteristics, namely, historicity, infinity
and improbability, the human individual may be said to be *authentic*.
The individual as the minimal unit of political organization is inherently irreducible in any absolute terms. He remains stubborn be-

cause he stands above all for himself. He belongs to existence and he belongs to history in an unalterable way.

As a result of the second three characteristics, namely, privation, discontinuity, and inequality, the human individual can be said to be *incomplete*. No individual has all the properties he is capable of having. That he is what he is, is as much the result of what does *not* constitute him as of what *does*.

As a result of the last of the seven characteristics, specifically, *intolerance of opposition*, the human individual may be said to be aggressive.

We have at last accumulated a comprehensive view of human nature. It is a genuine account even if not a flattering one, and it explains many of the facts which have hitherto been omitted because they are disparate. And we can see now the proper place of the above two properties, authenticity and incompleteness. The individual is intolerant of opposition and hence aggressive because his authenticity gives him the right to be so and his incompleteness, the necessity.

Our next task is to see how this view of human nature leads him to act in terms of more specific needs.

Section 2. The Organ-Specific Needs

Man's nature is incomplete and therefore aggressive. I define aggression broadly, as the effort to alter the material environment, usually to reduce his many needs. His responses are appetitive and his behavior, dictated by his needs. The stimulus to his activity comes from the available environment in the form of an element which is in short supply. Aggression is either violent or peaceful. The violent variety is destructive, the peaceful, constructive. For the individual this means competition with his fellows, and the resultant social relations have their destructive side. There is plenty of evidence from South Africa to California that prehistoric man was a cannibal, and even stronger evidence that cannibalism survived in many parts of the world well into the nineteenth century, in the Caribbean, among the Fiji islanders of the South Pacific, and among the Tupinamba on the coast of Brazil, to name just three. Slavery is indeed an ancient institution, no one knows how old; it survived until 1865, in the United States, and is said to exist still on the North African coast and among the Trucial States of the Persian Gulf. Serfdom was the mainstay of the feudal system in Europe as late as the eighteenth century and in Asia much later. The view of human nature which follows from such an analysis has never been popular.

For many centuries man's exalted view of himself and his virtues has prevented students from making an honest and detached analysis of human nature. No doubt there is much to admire in him, but some of the facts point otherwise, and we have accumulated a picture that is at best mixed.

Hobbes conceived of an early "state of nature" in which men were in a continual "condition of war." This can now be dated back to what is called prehistory, measured in just under two million years when humanoid types first appeared, and in hundreds of thousands of years during which man first evolved from lower forms. Civilization, the condition of settled communities which began some ten thousand years ago, arrived with a rush, so to speak, and found the human species in many ways unprepared. Governments were political organizations by means of which men tried to cope with the new situation brought about by the fact that they had begun to live together in considerable numbers in small spaces. They have not yet solved this problem.

Given the disparity between the hundreds of thousands of years of the human species and the ten thousand years of civilization, it becomes clear that in human terms civilization is an experiment. It may be too early to judge whether it will work or not. The success of politics is of course a question inextricably connected with the success of civilization. Obviously, politics must somehow contain the answer to the question of whether or not men are able to live together in settled communities. However, the political question antedates civilization and indeed has made it possible.

What we are going to attempt to trace here are the physiological origins of political ideas. The explanation will be made in terms of needs that can be traced to particular organs and of excessive behavior. The need to live is so fundamental and the action from it so immediate that there is practically no difference between the need and the drive it produces. After that, there is the need to live better in material terms; but here a distinction can be made, for alterations in segments of the environment are involved. The human organism, like all others, acts as a unit, and so only one organ at a time drives the organism to action. The organ-specific needs begin with a primary group: water for the kidneys and tissues, food for the stomach, mates for the sexual organs. A secondary group includes: information for the brain, activity for the musculature, and security for the skin.

The first law of nature is immediate survival, and the second is ultimate survival. Man works for the former in terms of his primary needs, and for the latter in terms of secondary needs. What Aristotle called "livelihood," I am calling ultimate survival. The activities of man can be considered as extensions into motion of one or more of the needs, expressed as drives. Some are organismic activities, in which man is moved by the needs of his organism as a whole, as for instance when he seeks safety from threats in the environment, builds a house, and obtains clothing and weapons. Usually, however, the motivation is organ-specific.

One characteristically human feature is that drives exhibit a tendency to extend beyond the needs and to continue when the needs are reduced. That is what I have called "excessive behavior." So too when the needs are combined in the generic need of aggression, which is extended in the drive to dominate the entire environment.

What every individual wants is the absolute domination of his entire environment, and he wants this for a good reason: nothing less holds out to him the prospect of total need-reduction. There are two reasons for this: the reduction of his needs in the indefinite future combined with excessive behavior calls for such domination; secondly, the need to be continues indefinitely, which means a kind of super-identification of the individual with the whole of the cosmic universe or with its cause, which likewise calls for such domination. Since the need to continue to be means an appetite for the control of the entire environment, the acquisitive drive is bound to be unlimited.

As it happens, however, there are inevitable difficulties under a scheme which relies on the basic physiological needs and the consequent drives. Man comes into inevitable conflict with his fellows, and when he does so he proves himself the most violent of all ani-

mals. Anyone who has watched unsupervised school children in-
discriminately fighting amongst themselves in the back of a school
bus must know man as a ferocious animal; anyone who has witnessed
the murderous effects of a gang war must recognize him as an animal that must be trained to kill only on command.

Given the frequency and the prevalence of wars in human affairs, it is not sufficient to describe violence as a product of subcul-
tures. It is typical of human social behavior in what might be called
the normal or average range. The biological human individual with
his anatomical structure was clearly made to function through activity. All activity involves alterations in the immediate environment, for all effort is directed at overcoming resistance; indiffer-
ently as to whether it is the resistance offered by inert materials, the
resistance of a stone to carving for instance; botanical materials, the
resistance of a tree to felling; or organic materials, the resistance of a
wild animal to capture; or of one human individual to another, the
resistance to slavery. Violence is necessarily involved in activity
when resistance is overcome. It is channeled when used construc-
tively but usually not when used destructively. Construction is slow
and reduces the need for aggression slowly, whereas destruction is
swift and effective, and reduces the need for aggression quickly.
Hence the tendency in human life toward destructive aggression.

Now, men cannot live together in an atmosphere of violence.
Under law and order, which can be imposed only by a government,
need-reductions are maximized by setting up social conditions which
prevent conflict between drive-motivated individuals. There are no
peoples without government, yet it is possible to see something resembling such a situation. Apathy, interrupted by aimless violence,
is the characteristic of the political raw material of the population.
In low material cultures—either primitive ones, like some tribes of
the interior of New Guinea, or those which result from the decay
of some great civilization, like the Iranian peasant villagers of today
—it is possible to see the nature of the human detritus which an established morality and its political arm must somehow mold into a
cultured nation.

Just as government is established to make the reduction of needs
possible, so there are effects back on the state from these. Primary
needs preempt the government when they are considered important

as well as importunate, but secondary needs are more in evidence in this connection: information not so much, but activity in the short run and ultimate survival, or security, in the long run. A sufficient amount of frustrated activity can lead to forms of violent need-reduction, such as war. In the case of ultimate survival and of super-identification the desperate efforts of the individual to live forever means that the state to which social power has been handed is accountable for the domination by the individual of his entire environment which he must have in order to secure his ultimate survival.

There is another important factor in the situation. For many of the individual's need-reductions, cooperation with his fellows to some extent is essential. For just as game animals were at one time too large for a single hunter to kill and his enemies too numerous to defend himself against, so now he needs help in obtaining the more elaborate materials with which to reduce his needs, and he needs allies in order to defend his fixed territory. Therefore, in addition to material goods we shall have to add services, for in terms of the help he must have from others, he needs both goods and services.

The state of nature for man was the condition in which he would help those who would help him, the family, for instance, and help or harm those who would help or harm him, such as other individuals or interest groups. Thus an ambivalence of motivation was rendered by the necessity to engage in both cooperation and competition as a matter of sheer survival. Social organizations must have emerged from individual needs when individuals discovered the necessity of cooperating with others in obtaining need-reductions. From this arose the recognition that others shared not only the same needs and need-reductions but in much the same way—in contrast with foreigners who seemed to have quite different means even though they were for similar need-reductions. Thereby antipathy and sympathy arose, "*odi et amo*," and it seems strangely true that one should strengthen the other.

The extent of ambivalence of motivation has been greatly underestimated. For instance, people have been known to engage in almost unbelievable sacrifices to save others from pain. But they have also been known to invent instruments of torture to inflict pain. As a result, when one human being meets another, he cannot always tell whether to embrace him in fellowship or run away in terror. These are the conditions under which an arrangement to live together must be made, a development with serious political overtones.

There was a further development which bears on political organization. The evidence of prehistory points to the fact that the transition from primitive man to civilized man was largely effected through his ability to alter the materials in his immediate environment into tools which could aid him in facilitating his need-reductions. Everything by way of artifacts was called into service, from machines to symbolic communication systems (i.e., languages). Evidently, civilization is externalization, for tools not only aid man to do things more efficiently outside the body than he had formerly done inside, such as cooking food, which is a form of predigestion, or mentally calculating by means of machine computers, but they enable him to do more than he had been able to do and to perpetuate the effort by passing the accomplishments on to successive generations. We are bound to the past by the artifacts our predecessors have left us: everything from the science of physics to the art of poetry, from buildings and what they house, to books and what is in them. Thus the civilized effort is a social effort involving material culture; for the artifacts, inseparable from the men who made them, are intrinsic to the political organization.

It is easy to see why this must be. For the reductions of future needs some stable arrangements have to be made with other individuals to insure that what they have done together in the past and what they are doing together in the present will be repeated to their mutual satisfaction. Hence the existence of society as such, and its political arm, the state. Politics, too, is a kind of division of labor, and does not become sharply demarked until the population is of sufficient size. Then, too, there is the question of the possession of artifacts, more often, in this connection, called "properties."

Indeed government is the repository of all those drives which do not entail the competence of the individual. Men organize themselves into states to obtain mutual protection, to provide cooperation, to insure an orderly succession of the generations, to continue an inheritance, to avoid internecine conflicts which could be paralyzing or fatal, to deal with other states, and, as we shall see later in this chapter, to exercise the kind of large-scale aggression which states specifically prohibit to the individual.

Thus domination over the entire environment would have been unmanageable had there not been some kind of order. Order made use possible, for only where there was some kind of order could men stop fighting with one another long enough to collectively extract from their environment the materials necessary for need-reductions. This situation called for some kind of centralized control. Hence the state, which is the rule or order in the midst of an environment, since it presides over natural resources and "property" as well as over populations, was essential to man.

The ambitious individual could not have failed at this stage to recognize that he who controls the state may avail himself best of all its opportunities for need-reduction. Political ambition was developed as a subclass of the drive to control the environment under the generic drive of aggression. Every man wanted supreme political power for himself in the interest of absolute domination. He could not get it and so he settled for participation in it by means of the compromise which is the social contract. In this way the theory advanced here goes behind the social contract theory to show its historic roots.

Section 3. The State as a Compromise

Society is autonomous; it exists because of the enormous opportunities it affords the individual for his need-reductions. From a continuous supply of food and water to the production of the fine arts and pure sciences and the religious hope for an indefinitely prolonged personal security, the needs of the individual are made available socially where they would not have been individually. But men cannot organize themselves into societies, cannot provide the continuity of need-reductions, without some sort of prevailing order to sort out the various elements and activities in such a way that they do not interfere with one another. And this is the task of government, provided by politics.

Politics as such is urban, a fact recognized by Ibn Khaldûn as early as the fourteenth century. The community of law by means of which an accepted morality is established and maintained is possible only in a settled culture. Civilization and government in our sense began when men ceased to adapt themselves to their environment and instead adapted their environment to themselves.

From the point of view of the individual, then, the state is that order of society which is intended to substitute the facilitation of a maximum amount of need-reduction for the alternative of continual fighting, and the consequent absence of all specific need-reduction in favor of the reduction of the generic drive of aggression, which by itself cannot provide the requisite maintenance. Man cannot live by war alone; he also needs to drink and eat, to make love and learn, to construct things and perpetuate his own existence. But since individuals hold their entire environment in common, serious conflict is inevitable. The avoidance of such conflict can be accomplished only through an established agreement to renounce total control in order to obtain partial control and a measure of need-reduction. There have grown up inadvertent social moralities as the result of the exigent needs of interest-groups. It is not so with political organizations which have always had to be planned.

The human species, in small family groups, in *gens*, clans and tribes, has existed for hundreds of thousands of years, but politics began with settled communities which do not date back more than ten thousand years. Settled communities may be regarded as new and experimental, and politics an uneasy arrangement which has yet to be learned.

The transition from the nomadic hunters of the desert to the citizens of the settled community has always been marked by the formal adoption of a charter. Moses gave the Jews the Ten Commandments and Genghis Khan early in the thirteenth century gave the Mongols the "Yassa"; in both instances, the respective Code was henceforth to be law; both also shrewdly combined tribal customs with a rigid monotheism in documents which could order their newly settled lives.

The hypothesis is that precisely at the point in the history of the human species when men fenced in their herds and bred them for food, cultivated edible plants, and established orderly avenues of communication by means of written records as well as spoken language, they also handed over to the state their individual right to unrestricted aggression and the use of unlimited violence, which henceforth was at the disposal of federal authority in virtue of an established agreement. This, in effect, is my theory of the origins of the state.

Remember, that there is the phenomenon of excessive behavior, in which the drives do not stop when the needs are reduced. Again conflict is inevitable and again compromise is expedient. The political establishment provides the vigilance necessary for the permanent representation of an interposed presence between any conflict of interests, as these occur in so many social confrontations. In short, what is political is the effect of the interposition of order at every confrontation in which disorder is threatened.

The state has the negative task of maintaining order and the positive task of facilitating need-reductions. The struggle of the unaided individual for the control of the entire environment proves too much for him and so is transferred to the state. Territoriality is the established compromise consequent upon the renunciation of the individual's generic need for aggression against his entire environment and in favor of holding his drives to reduce his needs within accepted limits. The transference of the legitimacy of total and unlimited aggression from the individual to the state explains why the individual's expression of power is sharply curtailed while the state's is not. Many observers have noted that the behavior of states answers only to the law of the jungle: to destroy or be destroyed without restriction, a kind of behavior which those same states deny to their individual citizens. The previous transference of aggression is the answer.

All activity involves the exercise of power, and political activity is no exception. The power-drive of entire man can now be tied up with the political entity *sui generis*, which is nothing less than the drive to dominate the environment translated into the relations between ruler and ruled. In these terms any establishment is an acknowledgment of the status of government, and any splitting of power, as in the democratic "separation of powers," is a truce based on the tacit agreement that no one man can have what every man wants. Government is established in order to provide a maximum of need-reductions for every individual citizen. That is the basis on which it is founded, and there is no getting away from it. Rights and duties issue from it.

Politics treats men as equal although, on the whole, they are unequal. The equality is related to a basic humanity and to primary needs. Inequalities, while not political, may, however, be politically recognized as they often are. Plato's victory of persuasion over force is not to be read as the unity of peace and reason. Conflicts of interest and ambition are natural and necessary. Only where there is effort is there energy; and an inert society would not be a vigorous one.

Many observers have thought that the morality of states is so much worse than the morality of individuals—at least by some standards—and they have been able to think so because they have taken a peculiarly charitable view of the morality of individuals. But if we agree that the individual's need to dominate his entire environment in order to reduce all of his needs leads him into a permanent attitude of intended total aggression, and if further we agree that his excessive behavior leads him to continue his drives after his needs have been effectively reduced, then it is clear that the expansive ambitions of states are nothing but those of the individual writ large.

Most men who have speculated on political ideals have held too flattering a conception of human nature. The violence and ferocity of mankind have not been sufficiently taken into account in the strategy of moving toward ideals through gradual improvement. Thus, in 1899, thirty-two years after the appearance of the first volume of *Capital*, Bernard Bosanquet was able to publish his *Philosophical Theory of the State* with only a footnote reference to Marx's materialism and no mention of Engels at all. It is to the credit of the Marxists that they at least understood the violent side of human nature, but it is to their shame that they endorsed it and endeavored to use it.

It has been said that for every man cannibalism is no more than ten meals away. In the same spirit, an honest man can be described as one who would never steal less than a million dollars. Due to the exigencies of actual life in which competition is more importunate than cooperation and hostility more familiar than friendliness, the resistance to temptation is not easy and is chiefly the virtue of those who have never had the opportunity to be dishonest without detection or penalty.

The surrender of the individual's sovereignty has been responsible for several developments. It has been assumed that by giving it up he has lost it. But the sovereignty of the individual is inalienable, as Rousseau correctly saw. In so far as the individual has needs and the drives to reduce those needs are activated, the sovereignty continues to be his. Rousseau was wrong in supposing that he cannot delegate it. The fact that he *can* delegate it indicates where it resides, and this residence is permanent. The sovereignty of individual man is as much a part of him as his organs.

It has been assumed also that the state which takes up sovereignty inevitably owns it. True, the state carries out acts of aggression on a large scale and against other states which would be far beyond the physical power of the solitary individual. Yet the state, as we have already noted, is not only the recipient of super-identification but often the nearby surrogate of those faraway large-scale objects with which the individual could not hope to come into personal contact and, given his limited intellectual powers, could not expect to comprehend. Exaggerated nationalism or patriotism, the worship of the state, however, is a misplaced attachment to an object which is unworthy of it and in the end unable to carry it. That many who gave their lives for their country made sacrifices for an object of veneration which could not stand up to its evaluation was certainly true of the citizens of Napoleon's France, of Mussolini's Italy, and of Hitler's Germany.

The politically disaffected individual may look beyond the state as much as that other individual who is seeking a more permanent and a larger object to which he may give his undying allegiance. In this too he may be helped by the state. The aim of government should be to aid its citizens—as many as possible—in working toward the reduction of all their needs, including both primary needs, which contribute to immediate material welfare, and secondary needs, for which it may be necessary to reach out beyond the culture.

This leads us to our first Political Rule:

Given that the generic need of the individual for ultimate sur-

*vival drives him to work for the domination of his entire environ-
ment in order to continue his existence on a permanent basis, then
the recognition of this need by an interest-group and its establishment within a society means that the state has the task of containing
an institution whose legitimate aims extend beyond the state.*

The solution of this problem will itself constitute a lemma for
the solution of further problems we will encounter before we have
done with our comprehensive examination of politics.

Section 4. The State as the Repository of Individual Aggression

We have noted that the ultimate aim of every individual is the
absolute domination of his total environment, because with nothing
less could he hope to reduce all of his needs. If, for example, we were
to accept the religious aim as a kind of super-identification: the
identification of the individual with the universe or its cause, as
the only method whereby he could hope to achieve his ultimate goal
of eternal survival, then nothing less than the absolute domination
of the total environment would do. He has a need for total aggression.

As we have noted earlier in this chapter, every man has a ferocious ambition to dominate his entire environment as the only possible means for reducing all of his drives, from the hunger drive at
the most importunate end of the scale to the drive to achieve
eternal security ("immortality") at the other and most important
end. It is this ambition which makes of each the enemy of all. And
it is the impossibility of its succeeding, the innumerable conflicts
which would have as their result the frustration of all of the drives,
that lead men to compromise. They turn over to the state the aggression they cannot themselves afford, and live within it in the effort to be successful through other more tractable ambitions.

Total aggression directed against the entire environment is not
only beyond the powers of the individual, it is also, needless to add,
beyond the powers of the state. But the state is recognized by the
individual as more powerful than himself. Thus his need for total
aggression is handed over by him to the state for execution. The
need is not reduced, but something in the same direction which is

still beyond the powers of the individual is accomplished. It is called war. How else can one account for the fact that in international relations one finds released man's most destructive aggression? The conduct of war by the state serves the purpose of reducing individual needs for aggression beyond what the individual could accomplish by himself in an unorganized fashion.

The political system—the state—has to reckon at all times with the native and natural tendency of man toward violence. This is the direct expression of his drive to dominate his environment—all of it—in order to be able to reduce all of his needs. To this end he has a specific organ: the musculature, which demands its own unlimited exercise. There are very few exceptions to the rule that the state acts as aggressively against other states as its own powers permit. By leaving nothing undone that naked power could do, the state serves to absolve the citizen of responsibility for aggressive actions involving brute force which, if individually performed, could only be regarded as inexcusable.

The state as such works in two directions with the violence that is an integral part of each of its citizens. First of all, it reserves the use of violence and prohibits it to its citizens. Inside, the state may resort to legal execution; outside it may resort to war. In both instances, of course, the violence is carried out by citizens, but they are acting for the state and not themselves. This does sometimes call out an ambivalence on the part of the individual whose identical actions may be condemned when committed for the state and equally condemned when not. The man who commits murder is branded a criminal; the man who refuses to do so in battle, say, is also branded a criminal; and both are liable to punishment.

Government has to do with aggression, as Herbert Spencer correctly saw. It holds in its very nature the control of aggression: to employ it or prevent it; the modulation of aggression, you might say. The ambivalent nature of human aggression—man's loving and constructive side, and his hating and destructive side—means that if he is to be a good citizen the government must be prepared both to encourage and discourage him; the former through transparent facilitation, the latter through brute force and even violence but only as authorized under the rule of law. The state has become the repository of individual aggression, and as such is in a position not only to order it or prevent it, but also—a third choice—to endeavor to transform it into a structure that will promote the state's own welfare.

Thus part of the aggression which the state siphons off from the individual is used to maintain the state itself, a fee, so to speak, which it charges in order to give what the individual needs. But there is no check on the state, and so it too develops a tendency to exceed itself, a tendency which some extra-national force will have to limit. We will look at this question again in the last Part of this book.

Chapter III

THE STATE AS AN INSTITUTION

Section 1. Aims of the State

The test of a political system is what it is able to promote by way of constructions. Transparent facilitation is the mechanism. It is the supreme task of the state to maintain social order with a minimum of political interference; to the extent that it finds interference necessary, it fails. But the state also aims to grow, inwardly as well as outwardly; inwardly through the prosperity and progress of its citizens in their efforts as individuals, as interest-groups, and as members of institutions; outwardly through its expansionist policies, in the effort to gain territory and to influence other states, in the understanding that such gains could be constructive, too.

The second story of the two-story world of logic over matter, which characterizes everything in existence, nonhuman as well as human, is in political theory represented by the fact that government is "of laws, not of men"; and this is no less true because it is the men who make the laws. Government, as we shall presently see, is the largest institution within the society to be faced inward; it becomes extended from politics into economics and indeed into all other institutions under the provision that it shall at all times be more conducive than coercive, more facilitative than restrictive. The prestige of the politician should simultaneously be increased and decreased,

37

but not for the same reasons. That is, it should be increased because the citizen must learn to value government, and decreased because he must at the same time learn to value other things more.

Presumably, the things that he values more than government should be those at which the government aims. Goals of this sort are not set, they exist already in the theory of reality assumed by the people as their fundamental beliefs. The near-term goals are of course security and prosperity, goals, incidentally, which may often be at odds, as when either depends upon conquest when the other does not, while the long-term goals may be growth and progress. The United States under the Presidency of Eisenhower sought only to enjoy its own development in a period of economic prosperity. The Soviet Union under Stalin sacrificed the comfort and freedom of individual citizens to the transition from a feudal-agricultural to a scientific-industrial economy.

The citizen must learn, in other words, that what he lives *by* is not necessarily what he lives *for*, that the facilitative institutions are also the most importunate ones and that consequently nothing else can be accomplished until their claims are settled; moreover, the facilitative institutions have as their end the service of the others, and in a country which does not feature the fine arts, the pure sciences or speculative philosophy, there is no particular point in having a good government or anything like it unless the citizens are to suppose that mere existence is sufficient. And so it is, but only in the hope that living men may acquire something else, that missing values may be restored on the grounds that what lives but does poorly may with time and effort do better, whereas the dead are forever dead.

It is possible both to reject the notion that the sum of the citizens of a state is the state and to accept the idea that the state belongs to the citizens and should therefore be responsive to their judgments. The existence of artifacts, meaning "properties," and of institutions is clear evidence that the state is more than the sum of its citizens. But since one aim of the state is the welfare of its citizens, it ought to be sensitive to their wishes. When this is said, it becomes apparent that something is missing, for the wishes of citizens differ, to some extent, at least, from state to state.

There are, in fact, such things as national characteristics. They do exist even though they are only cultural and undergo change from time to time. Consider current descriptions of the "phleg-matic" English and the "excitable" French, and compare them with the exact opposite descriptions brought back by travellers during the sixteenth and seventeenth centuries. Stability is certainly typical of the citizens of some nations while absent from others. The Japa-nese were able to effect the transition from a feudal society without any violence. The Spanish firmly rejected the same alternative but with the accompaniment of violence in the Civil War of 1937.

Whether a state is to be considered successful depends in large part on the national purpose and this is connected to national char-acter. What is the aim of the average citizen? What does he want in life? Where exactly does he want events to take him? The over-whelmingly general answer would be a large, fat zero. For most citizens look forward first to surviving and secondly to having a little pleasure even though it be very little indeed. Beyond them, however, even in them despite themselves and certainly despite their conscious knowledge which is strictly limited, there lurk other forces. For they participate willy-nilly in the quality of the internal environment of a culture, and every state is a part of some culture.

There is no simple mechanism for national goal-setting. The ambitions of a nation are determined by its own past, by what its citizens find wanting, and by what they have and value most. The expanding state surely does not have the same goals as the contract-ing state. The ambitions of the Roman Empire were not the same in the third century A.D. as they had been in the first century B.C. The state as an instrument of aggression does not have the same emphasis or the same adventures as the state functioning primarily as a secu-rity-system. A player will not win a chess game by overturning the table, but he will change the character of the game. And yet revolu-tion can never be more than an exchange of types of stability.

Section 2. The Dunami

I can find no word to stand for the dynamic quality of a culture, so for this purpose I will borrow a Greek term. *Dunamis* is a conven-ient term meaning strength, might, ability. Dunamis will here signify the dynamic quality of a culture. I will use it chiefly to refer to the strongly directed power-drive of a state, its tendency to increase its range and control by extending its effects as far as possible into its environment in every direction, intensively as well as extensively.

Nations acquire dunamis when an idea, of which its citizens may not be even half aware, takes hold through feeling and dominates unconsciously held beliefs in such a way that it emerges as the only sort of action which the citizens themselves regard as "logical" or "natural" or under the circumstances inevitable because the only possible alternative. Ibn Khaldûn tried to describe it as "social solidarity" or group feeling. There is strong reinforcement for an individual belief when the individual takes it for granted that those around him do also. For then the belief is not a belief, not anything special, only a nearby segment of the nature of things. Ibn Khaldûn thought that the dynamic quality was occasioned by the transference of the feeling of solidarity from a kinship group to an abstract ideology. This is occasioned either by a religion or by a newly formed nation-state.

The central questions in the history of a nation are: how was its dunamis acquired, how was it maintained, and how did it get lost? For every historical culture which rose there is one which fell. They blaze up after a long silence, then fade out, like the supernovae observed by astronomers. Many suggested explanations have been offered, from theories of the fourteenth century Ibn Khaldûn to those of the contemporary Arnold Toynbee, but none is altogether acceptable. Thus far no one has given a satisfactory answer to these questions. They remain important, for they alone perhaps hold the key to the future control of cultures.

The fate of nations can hardly be considered, then, without looking at that large issue which consists in the rise, the growth, the decline and death of cultures. What makes a nation strong at one period and weak at another? The spectacle of history which, as we have earlier defined it, is after all only a kind of developmental culturology (despite the awkwardness of the term), discloses sharp declines: Spain in the seventeenth century, England in the twentieth. And just as giants suddenly fall asleep in the midst of great successes —the Ottoman Empire in the eighteenth century after the defeat before Vienna in 1683, for example—so sleeping giants just as suddenly awaken and become formidable forces, as Russia has just done and as China is trying to do in the first half of the twentieth century.

Dunamis manifests itself as power. "Power" in connection with politics means control over the thoughts, feelings and actions of men, acting either alone or in concert.

What we call politics is the power structure of the state, and we consider also as political the power structure of any political organization larger than the state, such as cultures or institutions. Politics is the attempt to comprehend in the short run what manifests itself only in the long run. We look at cross sections of social changes and try to understand them on their own, when as it happens they are only fragments of a much larger picture.

From the point of view of the individual citizen such events are reflected in him as he is heartened or discouraged, often in ways of which he is unaware. Certainly it is true that the state is more dynamic when the citizens look to it for their own self-aggrandizement. They are made to feel that they participate in its power only when it makes continual gains for them, and the process is an accelerating one.

When the citizens of a state sit down to enjoy the privileges they have gained through the accession of power, they are already in the process of losing it. Perhaps that very fact holds the key to its loss, but we do not know. There is here evidently a political rule: *the benefits of political power can be either gained or enjoyed but not both.*

No doubt this rule is related to and influenced by the ultimate questions which split the state and for which there seems no reconciliation possible. "How can man solve his immediate problem?" And "what can be done about the eternity which confronts him?" In another version this dilemma is presented as the choice between living for present enjoyment and planning improvement through future populations.

Section 3. The Ethos

The ethos is the prevailing quality of a culture. It is the effect of the dunamis and is as passive as the dunamis is active. The ethos is an emotional attachment to the national spirit, a whole fused by the feelings of a number of components, such as ideology, customs, traditions and iconography. It functions as the prevailing tone of a community when there is a sufficient history of shared experiences to constitute a kind of cohesion. The ethos changes with the condition of the state, aggressive or regressive, expansive or contractive.

The most intense expression of the ethos is that of the sense of style. Style may be defined as the quality of unicity, expressed through the dominance of form in action. That is to say, when the form of action becomes more important than the action, we tend to recognize the existence of style. It is felt by individuals because it is a quality, and so though not itself a material thing it is a property of material things. But it is capable of exercising action at a distance, too, and the action in this case is promoted by attraction. Individuals are attracted where there is style because they take pleasure in the sense of form. The ethos cements society and reenforces the authenticity of the state. Patriotism and all other emotional expressions of the state, its myths and its symbols, are inextricably bound up with the ethos through style.

In brief, there certainly is such a thing as the spirit of a nation, and nothing mystical need be meant by it, the imponderable items all being imaginary. The spirit of a nation is its ethos, the prevailing emotional tone of the society, felt through the quality of its institutions. The ebb and flow of the gap between capability and intentions is not determined by the ethos but is evident in it. The quality of a people is not the same when as a powerful nation they are on the way up as it is when defeated they are on the way down.

But the controls of such large cultural forces and movements are not in the hands of its leaders or even its citizens. At the present time it is not possible to say where they are. A greater study of the functioning of qualities will first have to be made. Societies live a life of their own irrespective of the general will and of all considerations that we are able to estimate now. Government goes the way it is led from within or pushed from without. It acts in conformity with the sum of the influences brought to bear upon it. Thus any absolute plan, such as the Soviet Union's "Five Year Plan," has had to undergo many modifications, for no such plan can be executed rigidly without disastrous effects on the society. There are too many coordinates making up the direction of any institution as large as a state is likely to be.

In politics the principle of multiple causation mentioned earlier must always be borne in mind, as indeed it must in all social and cultural considerations. Almost nothing that happens in human society may be said to have had only one cause. Too many factors are brought to bear upon any single point for a simple cause and effect to have any meaning.

Cultures have centers and peripheries, and multiple causation acts directly in proportion to its proximity to the center. There is something important but as yet unanalyzed about the intensity of a culture at its center in the land in which it first flourished. English culture does not have the intensity in its colonies that it has at home. Canada, New Zealand and Australia are culturally conservative; their spiritual life has remained that of its people in the period in which they first emigrated. Evidently, it must always be so. The same is true of the French Canadians in Quebec *vis à vis* the inhabitants of modern France. A traveler to a colony is always made to feel that he is traveling backward in time. The United States owes its vigor in all probability to the fact that it was not only English in origin but equally German, with many other national strains in the mixture. The result was not anything specifically European but something different.

Section 4. The State and Other Institutions

Institutions are of two kinds: constitutive and regulative. Constitutive institutions furnish a society with its goods; regulative institutions with its services. One of the most important services is to provide an order which is society-wide.

Politics is institutional order conducted by a single institution, that of government. It is the instrument which guarantees, through the assignment to it of all legitimate use of force, that the established morality and the chosen technology shall be operated as planned. The state therefore is always one institution among many, though the dominant one. If another institution wishes to dominate the society, it has first to capture the state. This at times has been managed by one institution or another: by the church, by business, and, more recently, by applied science. The state can be captured also, and sometimes has been by its own subdivisions. The military is part of government but has often run the government. Marx was anxious to show that economic classes dominate the state, that the state is, in fact, an instrument of oppression in the hands of the ruling class.

It is certainly true in any case that the state is the most powerful institution in the society. It dominates the others, while they in turn dominate interest-groups and individuals. The state as an institution also dominates both interest-groups and individuals and in the same two ways: by being larger and more powerful, and by lasting longer. It is possible for an interest-group, or even an individual, to gain control of an institution and to run it for private ends, but usually not for very long. The institution *qua* institution tends to outlast any misuse of it, chiefly because of the existence of a group of men whose peculiar charge is the institution itself in distinction from the ends it serves. Something essentially impersonal, detached and objective, because material, is included in the makeup of an institution which enables it eventually to wrest free of any special domination.

There seems to be no way to handle large masses of human individuals and the manipulation of highly specialized knowledge, to say nothing of the large-scale instruments developed by technology, except through the medium of institutions. Politics is organization and the politician an "organization man," for paradoxically there is no subject matter. The state is not a substance and its managers do not deal with anything substantive. They deal instead with political relations and these are real, but they constitute a service, not a stuff, a service more like what the lawyer performs than the architect. All other institutions presuppose the service of the political, for it provides the unseen freedom under which they operate.

The special business of institutions—all of them—is administration. This is as true for a church as for an industry, for each has its own administrative hierarchy and its own rivalries and struggles. Politics is administration *sui generis*. It is that institution which has as its business the control of the state.

The modern problem which threatens to defeat all efforts in this direction is the control of institutions. The factors which affect the direction of institutions are many and varied. They may come from any and every activity within the society, from other societies, or from the vast expanse of the environing nonhuman natural world.

Just to see how enormous the number of such factors is, we have only to note two domains into which knowledge has been extended through the aid of the physical sciences from which information affecting all institutions often comes. These are the microcosmic and the macrocosmic levels. The microcosmic level is the level of the minute: of the cell, molecule, atom and its nucleus. The macrocosmic level is the level of the very large: of stars and planets, galaxies and metagalaxy. The principle of humanity states that the applications of the knowledge of these two domains other than the domain in which the human species is found, the mesocosmic level, must be somehow accommodated at that level.

No matter how specialized the knowledge, some of its effects will be felt at the level of developments affecting the state in terms of human individuals and gross material objects; it is at this level that the politician operates and conducts his professional affairs. Information affecting the state feeds into him from areas in which he has no competence, but it is still his task to evaluate such information and, if need be, to employ it in his decision-making.

To add to the principle of multiple causation, then, there is the principle of coordinate direction. Consider that the individual exists at all levels: physical, chemical, biological, psychological and cultural, and that any social organization, such as an institution, consists in a number of individuals, and it becomes possible to see how many and how complex the interrelations must be. If we knew all of the factors involved in determining the direction taken by an institution, we could predict it; but we never do. And of course any of the factors could influence it. The worst error is to suppose that men fully understand and wholly control the forces they have discovered and the systems under which they function. Institutions are not organisms, they are not alive; but they do have their own logic and inevitably operate by it. This occurs in ways which men do not understand and hence can neither predict nor influence. Coordinate direction means that the future of an institution in terms of our present information is unpredictable. Kafka's novels, *The Trial* and *The Castle,* are excellent dramatic examples of how unknown even the institution itself is.

As we have noted, the state maintains order in the nation. But it must at the same time be sensitive to other institutions, and particularly to those which stand at the top of the institutional hierarchy. No government in the Middle Ages could afford to neglect the Church. The power of the Church as a political organization, in a condition sometimes to rival the state, was based upon the firmly fixed belief of the population that the Church could bestow or withhold immortality in the form of life beyond the grave. But the struggle between church and state sometimes took ambiguous intermediate forms in which "the things that are Caesar's" seemed to be the concern of both.

When Pippin the Short seized the crown of the Frankish kings, after his father had defeated the Moslems at Tours in 732, and had his usurpation confirmed by the Pope, who poured the oil on his head and thus made him the Lord's anointed, this founder of the Carolingian line was able to pass on to his son, Charlemagne, a power equal to, if not exceeding, that of the Pope himself. The struggle between Pope Pascal II and Henry V, after the latter was crowned Emperor at Mainz in 1106, was not the dispute over investiture that it pretended to be but really a contest for possession of the vast estates left by the Princess Matilda to the Church. Who is to sort out motives responsible for the Thirty Years' War? Was it an attempt on the part of the Roman Catholics to stop the progress of Protestantism, or an outlet for the territorial and political ambitions of the German, Swedish, French and Spanish who were engaged?

One of the most tragic things about human life is that the issues over which men eagerly fight and willingly die are never solved; they are only dropped. Despite the intensity of the religious struggle, with the advent of experimental science and the spread of the empirical criterion to all areas, belief in an after life was largely dissipated, and the Church as a political force rapidly declined.

A society is an indivisible entity, stratified by institutions but not decomposable into them. Whatever the effects, an institution influences the entire society. The higher the institution in the hierarchy, the greater the influence; and this means that the state is more sensitive to the more powerful institutions than to the less powerful. General Eisenhower's warning to the American people at the end of his last term as President—to beware of the growing power of the military-industrial complex—was no idle one. Science rapidly became a major factor in American politics after the explosion of the first atomic bomb over Hiroshima.

In the contemporary world no state can afford to neglect applied science. The value system of the state is one involving power over men and materials in an order determined by the hierarchy of institutions. Obviously this hierarchy varies from society to society, and decisions concerning which institution is to be most influential with the government is one that members of the society or its leaders have to decide for themselves.

The usual way is to make an unconscious commitment, and, because it is crucial, I have named it the unconscious crucial commitment. This is the dunamis, considered from the perspective of its residence in the human individual where it exists as a kind of dedication. Societies given over to single causes, from religious to military societies, are perhaps the most common examples and good ones because they are the extremes of the social spectrum. The commitment to a single cause is usually unconscious and crucial. It can be conscious, too, of course, though usually not.

The Soviet Union under Lenin and Stalin was deliberately dedicated to the industrialization of Russia. Some would argue that applied science is not second but first in the Soviet Union, and that the Soviet state exists in order to promote science. It is too early to decide the question. Certainly the Soviet state goes beyond science in its authority and even in its national goals, for its seeks to promote the communist revolution around the world. But in any case, the state, applied science, and Marxist ideology are certainly the leading three authorities in the Soviet Union with, I should venture to say, the state first, ideology second, and applied science last. But even in this instance which, because it is deliberate, seems to be an exception, there are forces at work which collectively take the nation in the direction of conquest and world domination, in accordance with ancient national ambitions. The principle of coordinate direction is effective here as well.

History is chiefly the record of societies whose citizens have made some sort of self-sacrificing type of unconscious crucial commitment. The higher institutions which gain control of the state involve the society in efforts to penetrate beyond itself and as far as possible into the environment, as far as the limits of the cosmos. In such cases, the commitment is not internal but external, and calls on the society for sacrifices similar to those which are demanded of it when the goal is the aggrandizement of the society for the sake of its own indefinite future. We are here talking about the organization of the state around central aims, but it should be clear that the social instrument in terms of which such aims can be pursued are always political. The order, the organization, and the controls which are necessary all belong to the state.

In our own day we have witnessed the increased influence of government over science, technology and industry. One result is the vast acceleration of communication and transportation, another is Big Science—the science of the large nuclear accelerators—and of Big Government—government by a vastly proliferated bureaucracy. There is as a result of this development a great increase in basic need-reductions, the quality as well as the supply of food, shelter, clothing and medicine. But there is a decline in the intensity of the spirit, which I define as the dominant inner quality, and its manifestations in the fine arts, good manners, and high style.

The unconscious crucial commitment is the outcome of the struggle of institutions for a prominent place in the hierarchy, because of the opportunity it offers to dominate the state, as this struggle affects the allegiance of individuals. National goals, in other words, are decided by the outcome of the competition among institutions for the position of supreme institution, the one just below the state. The cultural relations within a country make its politics to a certain extent dependent on other institutions. The economic potential of India is hampered by its religion, cow worship, which compels the government to appeal to other countries for additional food for its starving millions. The poet, Blake, pointed out that "the priest promotes war, the soldier peace." Paris surrendered to the Germans in World War II as a by-product of the economic class struggle and in order to prevent the bombing of its art treasures.

Perhaps the greatest danger in the domination of the state by other institutions is the tendency it affords to encourage absolutes.

World religions had a monopoly of absolutes until the modern advent of Marxism, which makes a religion of the state and hence endows it with ultimate and supreme value. There is a very short distance from Vatican infallibility to Kremlin infallibility, and it is one which people trained to obedience can traverse without the slightest difficulty. This is particularly true when the technology can be adduced to support the claims.

Instruments to some extent decide policies. What can be done determines what is done. New developments in technology spread their influence all over, extending it even to politics. Marx's claim that the mode of production of material goods determines everything in a society needs to be widened to include all technological advances and not merely economic ones. The new technology of rocketry has occasioned a race between the United States and the Soviet Union to put a man on the moon, involving the outlay of a considerable portion of the revenue of both nations' total resources.

Section 5. The Organization of Space

The state is society-wide and so is politics. The country is the state extended to the organization of space. The politics of a society must therefore reach as far as the space occupied by its members. Spatial occupancy can include the entire surface of the earth and we have found that it can extend a few miles below it as well as many thousands of miles above. There are after all airplanes, rockets and satellites as well as spaceships. Consequently, we must come to an understanding of the range of society. It reaches beyond human populations and artifacts into a territory which comprises a geographical living-space. It is no more possible to ignore the importance of the living-space and the artifacts than to ignore the human population. Thus in the end the central problem of politics is perhaps how to utilize space. The contents must follow because contents is a matter of spatial occupancy.

The human species developed as a response to selective pressures from an environment to which it was compelled to adapt if it was not to perish. But, as we have noted, civilization was the outcome of a new turn that was taken when men adapted the available environment to themselves. It should be possible within limits to manage that environment. But as controls increase with the advance of technology, new problems are presented to management. There is no end in sight though presumably the total environment will never be managed.

The political unit is seldom as wide as the culture or even the society of which it is part. The city-state of ancient Greece was smaller than Greek culture, and modern France is smaller than European culture. The concentrations of immediate power are, however, always vested in the state. The outlines of the organization of space are not so easily discernible, and what affects the state may not be of the same limited size. Thus when cultures move, individuals, interest groups, and even institutions have little choice but to go along; and the state itself sometimes follows, filling in with appropriate legislation. Leadership in these terms consists in being first and foremost in the discovery of what direction is being taken. The leader is one who, it turns out, wants first to do what, because of the culture, must be done eventually.

True, men do sometimes influence the direction taken by the culture; but it is seldom the political leaders who exert such influence. Man can exist for any length of time only in an orderly world, otherwise mutual destruction would end it all; and it is by uniting rather than by dividing that order is increased. Still, it is important to remember that diversity is not disorder: there must be elements to unite. The culture is moved through institutions other than the political establishment, and by originative geniuses, who are only making explicit what has already been implicit. The state, like any other social institution, is an instrument which men operate, and the politician presides over a vast and intricate network of cultural relations many of which he does not understand and only some of which he feels. Those about which he is ignorant do not impinge upon his interests until they emerge through action. Overt action is more limited than its mainsprings but, even so, may lie well beyond his powers of comprehension.

Just as no one understands everything about a long-established institution, so no one understands completely the reach of a nation-state. To show the range of the state involves making an abstract point somewhat ahead of our exposition, but, if we consider cosmic solidarity to be defined by the sense of the unity of the universe and of its stipulation by a specific theory of reality, condensed in the state by means of its identification with the community of right, then the state has no absolute limits.

This condition of unlimited influence exists only in a special connection. It is important, therefore, to understand not only where the state reaches but also where the state does not reach. It does not reach within the texture of interests and experiences which lie either intensively inside the state or outside the state extensively. Intensive experiences could come from exposure to works of art, discoveries in science, philosophical insights, religious emotions. Extensive experiences could too; only the former group is within the person, whereas the latter reaches outward toward extra-political goals. Viewed from this perspective, states and governments can be said correctly to be neither artificial nor conventional merely, but natural, in the sense that they are the only possible arrangements allowed by all of the circumstances.

Chapter IV

THE ESTABLISHMENT OF
MORALITY

Section 1. Assumptions of Moral Establishment

Everyone lives in a state of some sort, so that in examining the nature of politics we do not find ourselves faced with the problem of preconditions but in the middle of things. No one knows what human life is for, and this makes the task of facilitating it very difficult. All that any government can do is to order society toward one or more ends, but in which direction is a citizen to turn when the ends are not known? It happens that, looking up the series of assumptions, we encounter first a set of codified laws, then a morality, next a theory of being, or an ontology, and, beyond that, a whole philosophy. The metaphysics necessary to establish a morality and by this means to found a state is assumed, but it is genuine and functions most effectively in supporting and sustaining a government.

Cultures may be ill-defined entities, but they do exist; and because of their pervasive nature they may cut very deeply without being specifically noticed. Even those who are aware of the power of concrete philosophy may sometimes be its victims, those who are unaware of it are almost always its victims. The state only formalizes the status quo for the community, which must first exist. No one notices a culture when he is immersed in it unless he happens to be put temporarily in the position of encountering its differences with other cultures.

Thus cultures appear as the properties of ethnic groups, including skin color, body movements, traditional ways of doing things, as particular constructions of artifacts, and as peculiar kinds of government. To the peoples themselves these always seem innate and irrevocable, because they tend to persist for so very many generations. But the experience of the swift transition from monarchy to democracy in France and from "Holy Mother Russia" to the Soviet Union was so abrupt and successful that evident changes of a radical nature in structures ordinarily regarded as unchangeable do occur.

In the long run it is neither geography nor race that determines the dunamis of a people but the driving force of their ideas, and their ability to exemplify such ideas in material constructions—the ideas and the hardware. People with a large success are generally those with a powerful set of ideas. Energy and material resources are of course necessary, but these could certainly be a function of health and favorable environment. What is needed and unavailable could be as powerful an incentive as any. Rules respecting behavior —"rules of conduct"—which have been rightly said to constitute the essence of civilization are only half the story, for they neglect the glaring fact that there are material things, artifacts, which the behavior is about and which constitute another aspect of it.

All behavior, all conduct, all action, is taken to effect energy interchanges with men or with their artifacts, and usually the interchange with the men is through the artifacts. I mean to include here among artifacts of course any written instruments. The Romans had the force to obliterate Carthage but it required the addition of Roman law to give them the strength to establish a republic. The Arabs were nothing but desert nomads in the sixth century. By the eighth century, thanks to the ideals of Islam as set forth in the Koran, they had founded a vast and successful civilization, occupying and ruling the land and the peoples throughout a large area at the eastern end of the Mediterranean.

In short, the foundation of a state is usually metaphysical in nature, as much when implicit in ideas as when explicit in artifacts. The principles formally adopted, whether written or unwritten, have usually some basis in a belief about what is primarily real. The mechanism is qualitative, and so the theory of reality is established in the society as a set of values, which are thenceforth regarded as absolute, as though other societies had had no choice but had adopted the same values.

The values are expressed as self-evident principles which are then incorporated in the founding document: a charter or a constitution. After that, as Burke and Bentham were at such pains to point out, every action is taken on the basis of interest and advantage. But what is interest if not the individual's conception of what will further his advantage according to the ideas he holds in common with his fellows about what is primarily real? Weber was wrong in conceiving an opposition between ideas and interest. Advantage is a short range affair, interest a long range one. Interest determines the direction of activity—whether churches or launching pads are to be built. And interest, in turn, is determined by conviction, while advantage is dictated by more basic needs.

This duality of interest and advantage indicates the presence of a double aim. For every society needs to survive and strives toward an end which lies well beyond it. Here we shall have no trouble in recognizing Aristotelian concepts regarding efficient and final causes. The efficient cause is a simple one, the same in every society, and it motivates most exigent behavior. The final cause is more nebulous and varies from society to society. For the moment we will only say in this connection that for every organized society there is an ultimate aim which lies beyond the competence of its concerted efforts. Just what that aim ought to be will take us into a discussion of political ideals and of ideology, and this must wait for a later chapter.

But there is one situation which arises as a result of the fact that there exist such ultimate aims which can be found operating in every society, which I will now mention. As will be noted from time to time throughout this book, politics, like all endeavors, will have to be explained on the basis of the tensions between ideals and actualities, between essence and existence, between logic and fact. These tensions come into play with the driving force of aims at goals.

There are three ontological dimensions of which we shall have to take proper account: the dimension of essences, the dimension of existence, and the dimension of the drive from existence toward essence, or, in other words, actuality, possibility and destiny.

Here, then, we have the bare skeleton of a philosophy presented as a set of assumptions behind the morality by means of which that philosophy could be established politically in a going society. The core of the matter is the metaphysics which for this purpose I have named the implicit dominant ontology. It is an ontology because it is a theory of reality; it is dominant because it determines the choice of morality as well as many other features of the society; and, it is implicit because, although powerful and determinative, its presence and force are seldom recognized as such.

The implicit dominant ontology, then, is the accepted and established belief by the individuals in a society of what is primarily real. It does not operate directly. It is placed in action for the first recognizable level of elements by the basic value system which consists in ethical actions, esthetic tastes, and religious preferences. These decide which needs shall be reduced, how, and in what order. We shall be concerned in this book only with the first, since morality is the direct charge of politics.

Everything there is carries with it as part of itself its own ontological commitment in virtue of merely being what it is. This is the position which justifies the existence of concrete ontology. Culture, in so far as it is organized or has an organization of its own, makes its own ontological commitments, and it is the business of the philosopher of culture to sort these out. The same can be said of any society within the culture and of any institution within the society, and particularly of that institution upon which the organization of the culture depends; its political institution, the state and then the leading institution. The ontological commitment of a political system depends upon the peculiar properties of that system. The philosophy of the state is to be found in the myth of its leading institution. Usually, such a philosophy is expressed indirectly and qualitatively, and this seems to assume its absolute truth and to put it forever beyond argument or question. Consider the "Sayings of Chairman Mao" of Communist China, and before him the edicts of Stalin in the Soviet Union.

The assumptions of moral establishment are made possible by metaphysics, the implicit dominant ontology, as a set of back-up principles, justifying in real terms the particular structure of government. Since the Greeks it has often been the fashion for theoretical philosophy to stand behind practical politics. The man of action seems to need principles to which he can appeal for purposes of justification. The instruments of political power consist of a bureaucracy, a professional army, including the police, a division of taxation, and an endorsement of sovereignty, whereby the bureaucracy is able to argue that it rightly should be in the position of supreme power which it holds over the army and over property because it has always issued from some absolute claim: a divine authority, the General Will, or a metaphysics contained in a constitution. In every instance metaphysics is involved, whether it lies behind the reason for the divine right of kings, for popular support, or for a socio-economic philosophy like Marxism.

Section 2. The State as Moral Custodian

According to the demands of the exigencies of any social aggregate, man's moral nature is fulfilled in the state. The political may be considered the lowest grade of the good. Basic values have to be established in a society through acceptance by more than one generation of citizens if such values are to be effective. This includes, of course, the establishment of moral values for political purposes. Politics exists in order to convey the established morality into law. The state may then be considered a community of law.

Political problems are, as Burke saw, very much concerned with good and bad. The state is the custodian of the established morality and performs this function by building an institution around it. The morality itself may have been supplied by the leading institution, whichever that is, but it is implemented by the state. For it is the state which determines what are the limits of permissible behavior: how individuals and social groups may act toward each other without transgressing the law; and the circumstances under which it is permissible for material goods as property to be produced, owned and used. A social morality is what is needed to supply a society with survival and its individual members with full development. Politics is therefore the effective arm of social morality. It guarantees the strength of the establishment of the morality and lends support to its practical continuance.

It is important to note that the state does not in most cases determine morality. The state is usually neutral with respect to values, and administers whatever values the society acting through its leading institution wishes to establish. Usually such values are confined to the moral section of the basic value system; but not always. The state has the power to control whatever the moral values call for. If the morality itself is spread all over the values, as it is in the Soviet Union, then esthetic and theological values come under its aegis. The result in that particular nation is that works of art have to have a bias in favor of the struggle of economic classes, and official atheism is substituted for religion—perhaps is the religion.

As a rule, however, the morality which is established and for which the state acts as custodian is more narrowly conceived. Political entities and processes in such instances are bound variables and as such are operated within well-defined limits. Traditional practices and politics, customary procedures, special interest-groups, all are involved and often silently. If the establishment has endured for any appreciable length of time, then the facilitation is transparent and no one would dream of calling it into question. Two generations will suffice to bring about this situation. Not until the 1960's did a small group of young artists and intellectuals in the Soviet Union begin to realize that things had ever been otherwise than as they had known them. Political systems are in a constant state of gradual change even when there is no violent revolution, but people seldom notice.

While politics is based on morality, at the same time it is not morality. The unwillingness of the United States to recognize the government of Communist China because it does not approve of the actions of that government confuses political recognition with moral approval. To deal with a government through diplomatic channels does not imply an endorsement of anything except its stability. The United States at the very moment when it was withholding recognition from China on these grounds was recognizing other governments it did not approve, notably the Soviet Union, Franco's fascist Spain, Kwame Nkrumah's Ghanaian dictatorship, and many others.

Section 3. Establishment and Change

Politics is the theory of how to get done what according to ethics ought to be done. Government is the effort to carry out what the established morality dictates. But societies are fluid, and so there always are in effect three public moralities: the outgoing, the established and the incoming. The problem is to establish and keep functioning the administration of a chosen social morality. The morality may be one deliberately chosen and intended to replace another already in existence, as with the government of France immediately after the French Revolution of 1789, or it may have grown up where there has been none firmly established, as was the case with Moses' Ten Commandments. In any event, moral values must always precede political structure and help determine it.

Governments are established by means of contracts (Hobbes), as affairs of fiduciary trust (Locke), or as the outcome of an accretion of exigencies. The last eventuality has not been examined with sufficient care. A government actually begins when the life of a people becomes sufficiently social for a morality to inhere and emerge. It often has happened that wandering or hunting families combine into tribes and the tribes in turn into societies, the latter usually under the influence and direction of a strong leader. At this stage the leader often becomes a law-giver. Government actually begins with the implicit morality of a people which they wish to establish through enactment into law. It exists to promulgate and defend the law and to execute its edicts.

How societies exist and function through their government on a maintenance basis is another matter. The work of consolidation brings about its own changes, for an organized state presents conditions which may differ subtly from the original ones from which it originated. Lines are more rigidly reinforced, rules more strictly interpreted, and as often by the literal meaning as by the original intention. Maintenance, I am here arguing, is a serious form of slow change with its own somewhat different design. It calls into existence a bureaucracy which had not been counted in the original establishment, an interest group which is concerned with its own survival more than with the well-being of the state and its citizens. The center of gravity of the state is thus shifted, and a new focus alters the old direction if even in barely recognizable form.

The morality of a society constitutes a pool into which the government can dip in carrying on its work, as, for instance, in the making of new laws to meet new situations. Such a morality is more general than politics because it touches upon individual and social life at more points and penetrates them more deeply. Consider for instance the force of social disapproval which is apt to exert more pressure than laws in some instances because it operates on a wider front. It is activated by nearby citizens who need no official standing. The government and its overt machinery, which is political, has a covert justification and widespread moral backing.

The source of change in the state is more often than not the result of competition. This can occur at almost any level. Competition between states is perhaps the most common source, but institutional competition is not unknown. Consider the struggle between religions toward the end of ancient Rome, or between science and religion in our own day. It usually occurs on the level of the economically depressed, the ignorant, or the generally underprivileged, or in their name as was the case with the American Civil War. With culture there occur weaknesses, and the strong who have been pressing from below or from outside may increase their efforts and achieve success.

Social organizations usually outgrow their original base and so do states. But mere chronology can be misleading in politics as much as it can in biology, where it would never have been possible to argue from the chrysalis to the butterfly or from the acorn to the oak. The original shape of the state may be retained in its broad outlines or altered beyond recognition, and this could come about slowly through peaceful evolution and "the path of due process," or through violent revolution with the murder of those who had formerly been in power and their replacement by a different group with another base of authority.

Machiavelli was right in asserting that the statesman seeks the acquisition, the retention and expansion of power, but what he did not note was that the same efforts are to be found outside the establishment. The greatest political changes began as doctrinally activated movements for recognition of the lowest class of citizens, the Christians leading the *proletarius* of ancient Rome, the communists leading the proletariat of imperial Russia.

In every case of change, a stated morality is involved and the establishment of another sought. If one already exists, then it must be exchanged, and the struggle over alternative courses of action may cost many lives. To alter an established order which is non-violent may involve a violent procedure. But sometimes the political order itself may call for war as a permanent state of affairs, as we shall see in a later chapter.

Political changes in any case are usually the work of a vigorous and determined minority of citizens acting with the tacit consent or passive indifference of the majority. The consent is bolstered by the claims of the minority that it is acting in the name of the majority. There is one monotonous and often sickening similarity which is that whatever is done is always done for "the good of the people." It is odd and perhaps merely adventitious that what serves the good of the people usually serves even more that small group which is so anxious to act on its behalf.

Section 4. Justice and "Power Politics"

The task of government, we have seen, is to administer the established morality, to conduct confrontations in terms of the interposition of the stated terms which condition all informal as well as formal arrangements. But where moral confrontation was concerned with the quality, political confrontation is concerned with the fact. Government lends to the established morality the resources of the use of superior force. It insures that the moral decisions shall be accepted or else imposed.

Political justice has the task of minimizing inequalities of power or of making them seem part of the nature of things, and often new constitutions are drawn up with this end in view. But only too often the practice is to solidify, reinforce or defend such inequalities. The power referred to could of course come from any institution. It has been recognized for some time that among the arch offenders are to be found the politicians themselves or some division of the state, such as the military. But religious institutions have at times been equally guilty of reinforcing inequalities, and, as the Marxists are so fond of reminding us, economically dominant classes have been signally offensive in this regard.

Justice is conformity to the good. It may be informal or formal. Informal justice is justice in the broad sense, the conformity of things and events to the good. Formal justice, or justice in the narrow sense, is the conformity of law to morality. Formal justice is social but informal justice goes beyond society to the meaning of the ethical. Thus doing justice in the broad sense could be the same as acting immorally in the narrow sense. A law which was just at one time may have become unjust at another due to changing circumstances or to an alteration in material conditions. It is even possible that an entire established morality could be unjust. We shall be concerned chiefly with formal justice, which may call either for changing the laws through due process or for enforcing them.

Formal justice is not a leading principle but a secondary one, although necessary. For it requires adherence to the established morality and therefore in a sense depends upon it. What is just under one set of laws would not be under another. Therefore justice in the narrow sense merely calls for adherence to law. To consider justice primary, as Plato did, assumes that there is one and only one correct morality, further, that precisely the laws it calls for have been correctly established. But this is, culturally speaking, not always the case. The relativity of morality and hence of states and governments prevents justice from being as fundamental as morality.

There is a sense of course in which we speak of justice in a wider connection, but this is to imply that there is a morality above the morality in question. Under an established morality, it may appear that informal justice is not being achieved. This is the ground for supposing that the established morality of a state may not be the highest appeal of humanity. But this question, involving the existence of an international morality with its international law, will have to wait until a later chapter.

The term, immoral, is often, though not always, reserved for those who subscribe to a different morality. But the fact is that there are no nonmoral systems of behavior. Every consistent program of action assumes a morality even where none was formally adopted.

The so-called practice of "power politics," where no agreement is adhered to and no promises are kept unless some advantage is to be gained thereby, is after all a consistent position. The morality involved may not be the one that men of good will prefer, but it is a mistake to see as immoral what is after all merely not the morality they approve.

Moreover, men of good will are not always in a mood of good will. We have noted in an earlier chapter that all members of the human species are at some time capable of the kind of aggressive destruction which at another time they would neither recognize nor approve. The ambivalence of motivation suggests that legislation enacted by men of good will in a mood of good will is unrealistic unless it anticipates and can provide for the effects of men in a different mood. And this remains true despite the recognition that what is at stake in politics generally is the selection of that morality which when carried into practice through the exercise of some political system will extend the greatest benefit to the largest number of citizens. It is the political task to operate in that narrow passage between pity and terror—pity for others and terror for oneself —to make life as bearable as possible, to regulate social life in order to maximize the need-reductions in the order set down by the established morality.

Chapter V

THE COMMUNITY OF LAW

Section 1. The State as a Community of Law

We have noted in the last chapter how a community of law becomes established. Now we shall want to know something more about its nature and how it functions. It is the law and nothing else that formally makes a community. The laws establishing the state define the reach as well as the limits of legitimate action available to the working politician and his ability to frame the laws administered by the state. Thus rules make action possible as well as curb excesses. Men may indicate their willingness to work together, but that is not enough. When they agree about the guidelines along which they propose to cooperate, through the establishment of a body of law, then it is enough. The state is a product of the community of law, through the objective act of establishment.

Of course laws cannot be established in a community until there is a community, and usually the way in which there comes to be a community would never have been possible by any law that could have been established. The laws of a community come into existence with the community, and they change as the community changes. Those who live in accordance with justice and demand it of others are usually the direct descendents of those who carved out the community in defiance of the going retribution for injustice. Laws are the possession of a people and what they have made of the land they have gotten as part of their efforts to maintain and develop it.

Both Plato and Hegel were correct in seeing in the state the objectification of reason. For only with objectification is there progress, and the rule of law is better than the rule of men. We have noted that the body of the law is a codified rendering of the accepted social morality. The morality may be implicit and the rendering only approximate; but it is as faithful as possible under the circumstances, even though what is expressed is not always what was intended, and the implicit morality itself undergoes constant change and development.

A state is an organization of individuals sharing an established method of settling disputes arising over material differences, and politics is what governs conduct toward others within the limits allowed by the enacted laws. Bodin was correct in asserting that the essence of sovereignty consists in the making of general laws. But behind that is the residence of power. For violence is native to human nature but is possible with any persistence only to individuals living in isolation. The moment it becomes necessary for them to live together it becomes imperative for them to restrain their own violence. For this purpose laws were invented, and states brought into existence to be the custodians of laws. In the absence of the requisite instinct, intra-specific relations having any continuity are possible only under the conditions imposed by the establishment of a system of laws.

The threat of the outbreak of violence is never far below the surface in human affairs and can erupt almost without warning at any time and in any connection. Domestic riots, anarchy and civil wars are ever present dangers. The only insurance is the state itself —the coercive agency of the community. It has a mandate to maintain law and order. Its laws express the manner in which its citizens wish their lives to be conducted, and the enforcement of the laws maintains such conduct. Uprisings within the state call for continual vigil, for there is always hope that order can be protected and preserved.

There is a tacit agreement on the part of all those living in a state to obey its laws and so to help provide that harmony by means of which the need-reductions of all citizens can be accomplished or at the very least approximated. Men tend to lapse, however, because of self-interest from adherence to any contract they may have made hitherto, and so the force of law is a necessary part of it. For this reason penalties and sanctions exist, and the state reserves the necessary force to impose them.

We do not need the Hobbesian conception of the "state of nature" to know that without law social life becomes impossible. The reason for law is that it makes society possible. For societies are not constituted merely of men. A society of men without laws would not be a society any more than a society of laws without men. A society is a group of men who agree to live within the limits allowed by a set of laws.

The state, then, is based on law, and involves as part of the machinery of the law a law-making body, or legislature, an executive to put the laws into effect, courts to settle disputes in accordance with the laws, a police force to see that laws are not successfully infracted or violated, and a majority of citizens content to live within the law.

Hobbes was right in supposing that the law was made necessary by that vulnerability of individuals which makes it possible for the weakest to murder the strongest, a vulnerability at the source of their equality. A mutual resolution to refrain from doing harm to others results in a social security on which, he thought, the law rests. So far, so good. But there are other needs besides security, and society can provide them. As we noted in the second chapter, cooperation promises not only the reduction of some needs but the continual reduction of all, and these promises, too, are the source of the state and its laws. Hobbes in a way saw this but only in terms of the economics of scarcity; whereas an economy of abundance would still require a social order and the consequent regulations which are provided by law.

If the good is what is needed, so is the law. The law must exist in any given instance to provide and preserve the order by means of which individual human needs can be reduced. Hobbes understood that the source of the law is the need of individuals and the social cooperation requisite for reducing them. Without the law one supreme need might still be reduced: the need for aggression; but it could be reduced one time only, and after that there would be not only no society but perhaps also no more men. Thus law like morality is rooted in the very nature of community.

Section 2. From Social Morality to the State

The essential human components of a society are individuals, interest groups and institutions. But there are other essential components, for instance, the artifactual and technological material structures. The law reaches out over all of these to modulate their interrelations in such a way as to preserve the fundamental order on which the state rests. There must be a set of laws to regulate the relations between each of these divisions, for example, between individuals, between individuals and interest groups, between individuals and institutions, between individuals and the state itself, between individuals and artifacts (property relations). And the same *mutatis mutandis* for each of the others.

The structure of cultures contains its own laws. It is possible to organize a society only in one direction, given all of the factors which influence it, such as the particular stage of technology, the available materials, the human environment, and the genetic and cultural inheritance. The theory of law advanced here is a variant of the natural law theory, the "nature" being not some arbitrary decision with regard to what God has ordained, which varies from religion to religion, but the condition of man and his material culture in which the laws are to be established and operated.

To consider the law "divine" or God-given is to seek for a higher authority for the law and therefore a more dread sanction with which to enforce compliance. But the laws which are considered divine vary from culture to culture as does divinity itself. Were the connection genuine, no one would quarrel with it; but more and more it becomes plain that we are dealing with a set of man-made laws for which a supernatural authority is spuriously claimed. To consider the law positive, on the other hand, is to insist that there is no higher authority for the law than exigency. But here again there are difficulties, for such a claim does away with the continuity that establishment makes possible and for the legitimacy of enforcement based on a superior authority. The morality of society is less than the first but more than the second; less than divine but more than merely practical in any immediate and temporary sense.

The morality of a society is discovered, not made. It comes into existence covertly and implicitly when the society is formed. It is stated overtly and explicitly in the enacted laws. Based on the established morality, the government by means of legal regulations provides the legitimacy and maintains the equilibrium of the state throughout the lifetime of the internecine struggle of individuals and interest groups for the control of power. The problem of founding a state would involve settling the moral question first; after that, and only after that, could its enactment into law be considered. The laws conform to the morality, but the morality does not conform to anything less than the structure of the society itself; it is an essential ingredient of the society, inherent in the way in which the individual citizens think they should behave toward one another.

The established social morality is the foundation of the state and the law its expression. The morality emerges logically from natural conditions and the law is the attempt to approximate the morality. But the morality changes faster than its expression through the law, so the relation is never one to one. There is always some lag in the enactment of the law as it endeavors to follow the shifting morality.

The theory of the minimum state would deny the legitimacy of any morality beyond that which could be maintained by the individual. No people has as yet worked out an efficient system for getting no more government than is needed, though the British have come close. With them it has issued chiefly from the restraining influence of institutions on statesmen. There are no inalienable individual rights which exist whatever the society. Rights issue from governments, more specifically from their constitutions, and do not have any standing apart from these.

Admittedly, it would be a poor sort of government which did not guarantee rights for its citizens, and we think more highly of a government which ensures a maximum number of rights. But the fact remains that individuals—citizens—must look to the political order for the rights to which they are entitled. Nature does not provide, only governments do; but when governments provide, they do so the way nature does. At least this is true of those governments which are peculiar to the situation, for governments are as natural as

individuals. The idea of natural human rights which only governments recognize and enforce has no evidence to offer, and is based
most likely on historical instances in which it was assumed. Among
the political integrative levels, each has its own peculiar properties,
and human rights belong to the political order of society; they are
provided by governments or not at all.

On the minimum theory rigidly applied there could be no coercive social morality but only voluntary associations of individuals.
But with such limitations could there be a state recognizable and
able to function in the international order? Presumably, if any
voluntary association of individuals achieved the dimensions of a
nation, it would constitute a minimal state. But how would it be
maintained? It is one thing to reach an agreement and quite another to support it. The hidden nominalism which assumes that individuals have a reality greater than the reality of the state is as misleading as the objective idealism which assumes the converse. Reality is in fact not involved, only order. The reality of each level has
a genuineness which cannot be contravened except at the peril to
order.

The state exists by virtue of the agreement of individuals. Law
is the forefront of consensus, as Cicero said; the law merely recognizes the consensus. When there is a dispute, the law governs; which
means that the majority agreement holds sway over the minority
disagreement. A law which is not accepted by the majority cannot
be enforced, as those who defended the Eighteenth Amendment to
the American Constitution discovered before it was repealed.
Those who obey the laws accept the state in so doing. The laws, as
enacted, indicate what kind of state the citizens plan to have. For
the laws represent the kind of morality the citizens expect of their
state. The minimum state is one which is held down not to an atyp-
ically individual morality but rather to one sensitive to the values of
a society. It is both a logical and an empirical error to suppose that
there is no more system to an organization of individuals than there
is to their aggregate.

What laws does a given morality embody? Not the positive laws
arbitrarily made by men, not the natural laws revealed by God; but
instead those which make a particular society possible under the

circumstances and which members are therefore bound to adopt. Laws embody the morality suitable to those general conditions— traditional and environmental—under which a society is compelled for practical reasons to operate. Custom and tradition modified by environing exigencies can so make themselves felt in current events that to enact them into law is only to follow the dictates of a people. It is the "unwritten law" that becomes a law under the rule of consensus.

The law is the way in which a government implements morality. When a custom becomes a law, a morality becomes established. The law is constituted of the morality which it represents in a society, for it is in essence the establishment of morality.

The theory of law as implementing the established morality, and of that morality itself as being the only one practical under the material circumstances of tradition and environment, is a variant of the natural law theory, not as God-given or even as scientifically discovered but as empirically-urged through the ramifications of exigency. I do not recognize the distinction which has been traditionally accepted between natural law and positive law, the former as universal law binding all peoples, the latter as enacted by constituted authorities in a particular state. There are laws prevailing at every political integrative level, and they are all equally "natural." Exigencies illustrate the conditions which must be taken care of in the framing of laws, and, in a sense, serve as guides to what the natural laws ought to be under those particular circumstances. That is to say, they are guides only, not infallible indicators. Exigency is as productive of morality as any system imposed from on high and attributed to the will of God or of some other absolute *a priori* authority.

To consider that we are dealing with actual people and their immediate problems of breeding and feeding is not to suppose that we have exhausted all moral considerations. For such needs are at the source of any morality that has a chance to survive in a particular society. Men in the grip of drives interact, and there must be rules governing such interaction if they are to sustain a continuing set of interrelationships. Laws which should be made are those best suited to the circumstances, and these will vary for many reasons.

There would be no point in laws prohibiting nudity among Eskimos or Finns. In Caribbean countries there would be no sense in laws governing the fur trade.

The political picture is both richer and more complex than most theorists have thought. Marx left out the essential element of morality, but moralists leave out the exigent element of economics. There is a problem in the question of how to reconcile the struggle for economic power among interest groups when the state consists in the establishment and administration of a particular morality. I think the answer lies in the fact that morality sets the rules of the game but not its prizes. The rules are given, the prizes are not; and the rules vary from culture to culture, while the prizes do not.

Given a state with a particular social structure, any law governing a certain kind of situation is not arbitrary but an approximation of the nature of things as brought about by that kind of situation. A different law presumably would not fit, or, at the very least, would not fit as well. In this sense a law can only be amended or substituted by altering the particular social structure accordingly. The goodness of fit which such a situation engenders belongs to what I have called earlier the lowest grade of goodness, the grade on which the legal validity in any state rests. Thus laws respecting the liberty of the person, *habeas corpus* and so forth, are germane to the democracy, which would not be the same without them.

Even though law is established and enforced by the state, it does not issue from the state and the state is therefore not the highest authority except within the law. That there is a higher law than the state follows from the fact that there is a law which establishes the state, based on the implicit and covert social morality. It follows also from the empirical nature of the political structure in accordance with which the laws are descriptions of the regularities inherent in the material conditions of societies. I have tried to make it clear that for every state there would have to be a range of possible laws of which the actual laws would be a selection.

Eventually the size of a state is determined by the organization made by its people, and, the more the people are able to organize themselves and their artifacts, the greater the state. The ideal global state would embrace all humanity. As we shall see later, this is one of the inevitable goals of the future; but meanwhile it exists only as a possibility, and this is enough to insure that the state which establishes and enforces a system of law shall not be the final word or in any way absolute.

In all instances of law in operation, the prevailing morality exercises final determination. The legislator approximates as closely as possible to the changing morality in framing new legislation to meet new conditions. The judge makes the same kind of approximation when he makes decisions concerning types of infractions of the criminal law not encountered before or when he passes judgment on novel conflicts of interest in civil law. Positive laws are enacted in the spirit of natural laws where these are conceived to be laws germane to the morality by which the society was founded and on which it has prospered.

To say that the law implements a morality is not to say that they are the same. For the social morality which gives rise to the law changes faster than the law, and, when the morality the law implements is compared with the morality it gave rise to, there is a temporal lag. The one follows the other at a respectful distance in time and attempts to change in conformity with it.

John Austin's conception of law as the command of the sovereign is not wrong. Laws do issue from the commands of the sovereign and they carry the threat of sanctions. Only, he was construing law as its enforcement. This is what the obligation to obey the law comes to, but not what it is or where it comes from. But Austin's point is no less well taken because the law comes from the morality of the community. Why are these laws commanded rather than any other? Presumably, because they will enable a society to maintain the kind of order it wants. This would point to the choice of a particular morality about which society has already agreed.

There is nothing misleading, then, in the view that law is the command of the sovereign, especially if by the sovereign we mean the people themselves and if their command is the morality they would like to see established. If the law is, as Austin says, an order backed by threats, this must be understood correctly. What is ordered is obedience to law, and the law is the attempt to establish the morality about which the members of a society have agreed. The laws of a state are, indeed, the accepted social morality of its people reduced to rules backed by threats. The law is simply a reminder of an agreement to conform, and the threats are intended to be reminders of penalties, also agreed upon, in the case of those who change their minds sufficiently to commit infractions not intended in the original agreement.

Section 3. Constitutional Law and "The Law of the Land"

Two kinds of laws are recognized to exist within the state. There are laws by which the state is established and laws established by the state. The state is a rule-determining structure, defining the set of laws which it legitimately promulgates. The state is both the product and source of law; the product in so far as the laws concerning reality give it its foundation in charter and constitution; and the source in so far as the laws laid down are based upon its support and enforcement.

The laws by which the state is established are called constitutional laws, laws addressed to the state itself in accordance with the way in which the state is to be constructed and maintained.

The laws established by the state are called "the law of the land," the enacted laws governing the conduct of citizens and laying down the limits within which the citizens are expected to act. They tend to be divided into three categories: laws which enjoin certain kinds of behavior, permit certain kinds, and prohibit others.

Laws which enjoin describe actions which must be obeyed by every citizen to whom they apply, such as laws affecting the payment of taxes, the military draft, and the flow of vehicular traffic. Laws which permit describe actions which may be performed but do not have to be, such as laws affecting passports, interstate commerce, and agricultural allotments. Laws which prohibit describe actions which may not be performed, such as the crimes of murder, treason, and, in England, arson in royal dockyards.

Constitutional laws are in effect axiomatic laws, while the laws of the land are theorematic. The former must be broad enough to permit the framing of the latter. The axiomatic laws set the conditions from which the theorematic laws derive their legality and should, therefore, be the weakest set possible. Constitutional law is the law which establishes the state and determines the range of the "laws of the land." No individual or social action is possible merely on the basis of constitutional law, for it is seldom specific enough; but it does determine what laws shall govern in the land.

Once there is a state, the question of constitutional law does not arise until there is a constitutional crisis; that is to say, until the question is raised as to whether the state, as established, is the kind that citizens want to maintain unaltered. But the laws established by the state are the daily concern of its citizens. Laws should govern their conduct, and be intended to hold for the entire society until repealed. This is not always the case, however, for laws which are not wanted may remain on the books and simply not be invoked, so that they are as good as nonexistent.

Then, too, the actions of citizens are particular occurrences. There is always the question of what laws apply to them. Hence the inclusion of any singular happening under the generality of law always raises the question of relevance. Laws should be so stated and events so described that so far as application is concerned there can be no question of interpretation. Such an ideal is seldom actualized, and the issues involved are continually debated.

Law provides the rules under which all of the people of a state consent to live, and not, as with the Marxists, just those members of the dominant class. In a Marxist state, the proletariat is "the people," the capitalists having long been got rid of; but the communists do not seem to recognize that having only one legitimate party makes it an aristocracy, even an oligarchy of a new kind, because its members are allowed to enjoy exclusive economic privileges even if they do not have large economic possessions. The Marxist state does avoid the paradox involved in the double ownership which comes about when the citizens own some of the land while the state owns all of the land owned by the citizens. For in the Marxist state only the state can own land.

The flexibility of the legal system ought to mediate and modulate between conservation and progress, the protection of order allowing for the improvement of order.

Section 4. The Character of Law

Equality before the law, equality in the application of the law, equity, and distributive justice—these are the foundations of a community of law. How to establish laws based on something firmer than credence yet leave them open to revision as the exigencies of a developing society require it—this is the essence of the political problem *par excellence*. The rule of law, equity, is the first law of any state, and applies to axiomatic as well as theorematic laws; in so far as a state has an orderly government, it must itself be responsive to the rule of law.

The body of law in a state is an attempt not only to preserve order but, more specifically, to preserve a certain order. For the kind of order in one state is not the same as it is in another, though both are maintained by the enactment and enforcement of laws. The function of law is always the same though the laws are not. They always accomplish the same end but not always in the same way.

To say of a particular law that it is just or to recognize the fairness inherent in any instance of its application is to recognize the congruence between the enacted statute and the social morality which originally gave rise to it and which it still represents. The judgment is the recognition of a degree of goodness, and always refers to a criterion of value which is never openly expressed but by which it is measured. It is a just law to incarcerate persons dangerous to the state, but when such a decision is suddenly made on the basis of race or religion, as it was in Nazi Germany, such an action may be unjust because the law interpreted in this way is immoral.

The covertly accepted social morality only comes into play once laws representing it are established: either when a comparison between the morality and the laws is made under the suspicion that the morality has changed and the relevant laws no longer adequately represent it, or when the social morality is invoked around the law and brought to bear instead on the instance of its application, on the assumption that there is reason to suspect that the result is not wholly in accord with the law itself as it was framed to agree with the morality. It can even happen that a particular legal case is not a moral one; then the state is under an obligation to support the legal case. For the state's connection with morality is political and has to be shown on the side of the law, at least until it is changed to agree with morality through the legal process laid down for use in such an instance, provided there is such a process.

To exist in a society, either by being born into it or by becoming a citizen through immigration, is to accept its laws as they stand on the books and are administered. If a citizen has an objection to a law, he is offered legal remedy; there are legitimate channels whereby he can try to get it repealed or changed; otherwise, in most countries though not in all, he has the right to emigrate. Meanwhile, he is expected to obey.

This puts the criminal in a practically advantageous but morally untenable position. He is sheltered by a law to which he does not subscribe and he breaks out of it whenever it is to his advantage to do so. It gives him the protection he needs when he is not busily engaged in making unlawful sallies. The thief would be the first to make legal objection to anyone found stealing from him and would seek remedy at law if that were at all possible.

It is necessary to remember that the aggressive nature of men is held in check only by the fear of social reprisal and that the wish of each to dominate others is not eliminated, only repressed. Third party disputes always involve material conflicts of interest. Laws exist to settle disputes but also to offer guidelines and to correct any inadmissible behavior. The force of law is merely that which puts law into practice and renders it effective, not that which constitutes it. A law without sanctions is a law without force, and a law without force is a law in name only; it is not a law in effect.

Chapter VI

THE ECONOMICS OF TECHNOLOGY

There is no point in writing about politics as though it were a completed affair, as though all that men needed now was to do perfectly what they had been doing imperfectly. For, as history has demonstrated over and over, there are always new elements in the picture which effect drastic changes and with which societies surely have to reckon, and new political systems which have to be devised in order to cope with the changes.

I am thinking in particular of the new importance of technology and artifacts of all kinds. These have always been present but of a magnitude that left them in a socially subordinate position. Marxism was the public recognition of their first great victory, and no doubt there will be others. Now, because of the increase not only in size but in relative independence and complexity, artifacts have moved up appreciably in the social hierarchy and threaten to take over if men are not careful.

If what I said earlier is true, namely, that politics is the institutional moralization of man, then government waits on morality and is involved with its establishment and maintenance. But there is something prior to the concrete social morality which is what the state establishes, and this is theoretical ethics. It must first be decided not what the social morality of a society is but what it ought

76

to be. The state of the future, the possibly perfect state, depends upon present speculation concerning theoretical ethics.

It is clear that the technology of a society defines what that society *can* do. But who is to decide what it *ought* to do? Just now, with the great advances that have been made in technology, it might seem that man ought to do whatever he can do, but that is hardly the answer to the question of guidance. In short, the direction which politics should take has to be decided in some prior fashion and that decision has to be reached in the field of speculative ethics.

This does not mean only by philosophers. It happens that other institutions take up the challenge and step into the breach. An ethic is chosen before anyone is aware that a problem exists, and it is made by a few who are aware at the expense of the many who are not. The crucial nature of the choice affects every activity of the society, and is capable of determining what sort of technology is to be encouraged and utilized and how much is to be sacrificed. It is not one that technology itself should be allowed to make. The ends chosen by the society on the basis of the facility of the means will not necessarily be the right ones.

In a sense artifacts always did matter. Weapons often have determined not only that there would be wars but even the outcome of battles; methods of agriculture have made the difference between famine and plenty. But the effects of technology are more powerful now, and more is affected by them. The situation is indeed serious now that there is an element with its own degree of power in the state.

Section 1. The Relation of Politics to Economics

"Political economy" is an old term, one strongly supported by Marxism and still alive today. It has other adherents like Michael Oakeshott; I think it is erroneous.

Political economy confuses two things which should be distinguished. Politics, as we have seen, is the institution of morality. Economics is the use of material resources. Economics is concerned with the exchange of goods, and politics with how the exchange of goods is administered. Neither can exist without the other and every state has both, but that is not to say that they are the same or that they can be merged. For any given economic system can be combined with a number of political systems. It would be possible to combine an agrarian economy with communism; it has been possible to combine a scientific-industrial economy both with democracy and with communism. Capitalism was developed under monarchies and continued under democracies. To assume that any particular combination is a necessary one which must thenceforth occur because of a logical interdependence that makes them inseparable is to perpetuate one of the mistakes of Marxist theory. Things that occur together by accident may or may not exist together from necessity, and this holds true of politics and economics.

Although politics can be pursued independently of economics, economics cannot be pursued independently of politics. The dependence is that of economics on politics. All economic arrangements, such as contracts, types of ownership, and the creation of corporate entities, are dependent upon the support of governments which guarantee and reenforce their legitimacy.

Politically constructed societies are no doubt all of a piece and give the same ring wherever they are struck. They can be viewed from many aspects, one being the economic. That there is progress in recognizing political responsibilities for correcting economic disequilibrium, no one can deny. In the two decades following the fall in the price of wheat to forty cents a bushel in 1870, the English did nothing to aid the million agricultural workers who were impoverished as a result. Such indifference could not occur today. But there are maladjustments as the result of the governmental supervision of economic events. Producers are encouraged to increase the volume of their goods and services, and then penalized with higher taxes when they do so.

That a hungry man cannot reason clearly is no evidence that, once he has eaten and arranged for securing his meals for the future, he should continue thinking about nothing but food. We have grown accustomed to regarding economics only in connection with the materials requisite for the reduction of primary needs. It is certainly true that offices for government, studios for art, laboratories for science and even material articles for religion, need to be manufactured and sold. The economic alone is not a valid isolate, for too many other considerations influence it. The meaning of economics has to be widened from "the exchange of goods" to "the production and exchange of goods and services providing for all of the needs of culture on its material side."

Cultures are institutionally stratified affairs, and when a disturbance, such as a deformation or a new element, is introduced at one level, it reverberates to the others. It is rarely possible to predict with any accuracy just what the effects of an action will be. It is true also that economics may be culture-wide while politics is not. The Soviets kept the Russian gold mines working, and, when in the 1950's there was a series of bad wheat harvests, the Soviet Union was able to buy wheat from the west and pay for it with gold; moreover, the gold arrived there just at a time when it was sorely needed to shore up the international monetary system. In this way, communism and capitalism were able to keep each other going, a service that surely neither wished to perform.

When we look at economics and politics more narrowly, as they exist in a particular state, for instance, the picture is somewhat different. A political system is always wider than the economic system which accompanies it in the state. No economic system can ever be as large as the political system which controls it. Any temporary dislocation whereby some other institution grows larger or more powerful than government will tend to become corrected as the forces within the state shift and, in so doing, make the necessary adjustments. Economics determines what materials are available, but only politics can say how they are to be used, for use must be in accordance with the dictates of the established morality, and politics is the custodian of that morality.

The state undertakes to preside over the economic arrangements, whatever they are. The only power in the state allowed to be stronger than the state is the morality it exists to administer.

Here we have another political rule: *except for the established morality, the power of the state must be at least stronger than the strongest other power within it.*

The growth of a part of the state can be to the whole state a challenge which it must meet in some adequate way. Industrial corporate giants of the size of some of those at present in the United States, such as General Motors, duPont, or the Metropolitan Life Insurance Company, are country-wide and some even extend into overseas operations. The effect is to force the central government to increase its regulatory functions. The separation of church and state which was written into the American Constitution was an effort to insure that no religious organization could get control of the state. The plan was to hold the state power inviolable, with sovereignty remaining in the hands of individual citizens.

What was true of the church is no less true of the institution of economics; of what, in our modern industrial cultures is more specifically called "business." The extension of the economic beyond the political signals a coming extension of the political. There simply have to be political controls over trade however widespread. The development in recent decades of an international money market, with its consequence of the interdependence of nations within the Western bloc, has meant not only an increase in the integration of economic institutions across political boundaries but also through the instrument of international credit a diminution of political control over domestic economic policies.

Here there is evidence against what I have been maintaining, namely, that politics is the strongest of social forces. But this topic belongs in a later chapter. The recent developments referred to here only indicate the growing necessity for the overt recognition of a larger political unit than has been recognized. We take too simple and naive a view of politics, seeing in it only what has been established.

No doubt economics is a strong force in the state; it can be, in fact, though it has not always been, the strongest next to politics. But that still does not make it as strong as politics or identical with it. It is necessary to distinguish, in particular between the ownership of raw materials and means of production and distribution on the one hand, and the control of such resources on the other. Much depends upon overall aim. Ownership or control could be employed for many different reasons, and so it is aim that affects the final determination.

The dominance of the state over economics is evident in the struggle for the control of material resources. Both the less and more privileged economic classes threaten the social order even though they do so in different ways. The less privileged threaten to overthrow it and the more privileged to control it. Humanity has learned how to cope with both threats and to do so in the same way: by smoothing out inequalities of income or earnings without interfering with individual initiative and enterprise. This has been accomplished by capitalistic democracies in which social welfare has become an important governmental function, as in the United States and Great Britain, and it may be accomplished though more slowly in communist states, as in the Soviet Union. Individuals should be allowed to acquire such property as will be adequate for their most ample needs without enabling them to manipulate it in order to dominate others.

Property, strictly speaking, is a name for the ownership of artifacts. It should mean their use as well: the right to the exclusive use of artifacts. In this sense of the word even land must be included, for there is seldom land which has not been altered through human agency: the ground levelled or filled, trees cut down, soil improved. There are allowable inequalities of ownership, particularly when they are legalized and controlled through federal regulation. The material issue is much larger than the economic, for what there is available by way of material resources must be reckoned along with the questions of who owns and controls them and for what ends.

We will always have with us the problems which the inequalities of men and consequently of their properties present to the fundamental equality of politics. Inequalities of property within limits must be preserved, for the contributions of gifted individuals to the culture is surely worth more. But "within limits" must be precisely defined. The limits are prescribed by the total available resources and so kept in proportion to what the minimum living standard has to be. After a decent minimum for everyone, then something well above that in token of recognition of superior contribution ought to be permissible.

Politics may be considered the cause and economics the occasion. Everything political has an economic occasion. But the struggle is more than an economic one; it is a total cultural struggle for the control of the society and beyond it for the control of the entire environment. In this struggle the economic is only one factor.

It will help to distinguish here between the importunate and the important. The importunate may have to include the economic as a matter of immediate survival, but there is also the drive for ultimate survival and it depends upon total control for purposes, as we noted much earlier, of super-identification. But what is first in importunateness is not also first in importance. An occurrence of multiple causation follows from the nature of the cultural struggle. Multiple causation means that in the state there are many forces at work: individual, social, institutional, which together determine the direction the state shall take. No one has yet worked out how to calculate the effect of the sum of these many variables, but a statistical trend no doubt emerges.

A state is an organization of men and materials built around a central government. Its available materials, its geographical situation, are as much a part of it as its people. We must therefore consider the notion of recognized material resources and the techniques of their alteration for reducing human needs. Those not recognized for all practical purposes might as well not exist; for example, the prevalence of oil under the surface of Texas in 1860 or of uranium deposits in Canada in 1920. The wealth of a nation as calculated at any one time is a combination of its knowledge, or "know-how," and its available supply of raw materials.

Many observers have shown that not only has ownership and control become separate in the new corporate structure but it is often impossible to determine just where ownership resides. The managerial revolution has placed the control in the hands of those who direct the destinies of large corporations without owning them, and ownership is distributed in many cases over millions of shareholders. A new conception of ownership is obviously called for.

Settling the problem of ownership becomes a fresh necessity, when the rise of large economic units due to an advancing technology occurs at the same time that ideas of social justice have been growing in western countries, and they have occasion to meet. Industries are now too large for individual ownership and perhaps even for individual control. But central ownership opens the question of a differentiation of individual rewards in accordance with the difference in individual talents and consequent social contribution.

The contest takes the form of a struggle for the control of the government and with it the decision as to what form that government shall take. The changes and adjustments requisite for maximum efficiency may be the result of a short and violent effort, i.e., the Soviet Union, or of a long and slow one, i.e., the United States. If exigencies are permitted to be the determining forces, the issues can be settled peacefully. A strong government can avoid disaster in supervising such a transition, but the strong government itself could prove to be an equal and more far reaching disaster.

Section 2. Artifacts and Skills

What has been discussed hitherto under the name of economics might be better increased in function and called technology. Since no two human individuals can have any relation, except one, that does not involve artifacts, the place and function of artifacts in a society is of the utmost importance to politics. Marx recognized this in his conception of the relations of production. But the facts extend further, for all material goods are artifacts and so are languages.

The topic is too complex to be amplified here, but suffice it to say that even though there is no way in which a language can be owned, it is still a material tool: combinations of signs carried by modulated sound waves or by marks on flat surfaces pointing to other materials. We must consider, then, not only the role of property and other economic aspects but also the role of material goods. And we must consider them, moreover, not only in economic connections but in all interpersonal relations under the theory of interposition, and indeed in all cultural connections.

The political confrontation is never face-to-face but always mediated by means of a material which has been altered through human agency, in essence, by means of an artifact. Interposition involves an effect conveyed by means of some instrument: a material tool, a document, a verbal statement or set of statements. Laws are codified and enforced, which implies nothing less than that the state resorts to material tools to compel compliance. Governmental regulation is never introduced except as a third party, and then only when reinforced by the threat of appeal to superior force, i.e., actions backed by instruments superior to what the other two parties might be able to call on.

There are no two party relationships which are insusceptible to political intervention and regulation. Thus we encounter in our theory the basic and minimal factor of material technology, understanding by this the construction and use of artifacts in every political interposition. The smallest political relationship comprises two human individuals and one artifact, say a dispute which has to be decided by an appeal to a written law, or a barroom brawl broken up by a policeman.

The view I have been giving is the one from the state; from the view of each individual involved, it looks more like a mediated confrontation. In all his dealings, the individual can count on having to work through a transparent screen separating what is permitted under the existing body of law from what is not. If what he is doing is permitted, he works directly without interference; but the law is always there so long as he is in the state, ready to interpose itself through its agencies in order, if possible, to right a wrong, or, if not, to stop it from spreading.

Let us look at the prevalence of technology from another perspective, that of culture considered as a whole. Economics is chiefly concerned with the ownership of artifacts and the control of technology. The available resources are hardly the crucial part of the story which involves the decision concerning what can be made of them and how. For what are served are not merely narrow economic arrangements but the individuals, interest groups and institutions of the entire culture. If economics has traditionally been concerned with the exchange of goods, this is a small segment of the part played by artifacts and technology in the culture. For by means of the appropriate technologies, special artifacts must be devised for each specialized use.

There are a number of technological functions, plus the employment of artifacts and the special skills making these possible that are not specifically economic. If I buy a violin and play it for my own pleasure, then the exchange of cash for the musical instrument is the only economic function involved. But technology was involved in making it and skill in playing it. And if my neighbor should not like what he hears and if he were to devise a soundproof room in which to take refuge, this would not be economic, either, though paying for it would be. Many specially designed artifacts and technologies are needed to make up the equipment of a modern army, but only their purchase is economic.

We shall be compelled to conclude, then, that the culture reaches out in a state beyond the economic, and that artifacts and technology are as extensive as the culture and required for its every aspect. Indeed, what we shall especially consider is that now, for the first time, there is a serious new factor in politics. Every important technological advance makes necessary a rearrangement of the economic structure within the state, with respect to both class alignments and property relations. Technology has always been present in the political life of the state, under the name of property, but recently it has developed a new and crucial character. It has grown so tremendously that it has developed large-scale mechanisms which are themselves capable of a certain measure of self-determined action, and therefore needing domination in a different way.

I find myself obliged to formulate a new political rule at this point, which reads as follows: *the given stage of technology determines the form of the state.*

This rule is in a sense an expansion of Marx's mode of material production. He was considering the economic aspects, which certainly are fundamental. But the large-scale technology of the state is capable of being importantly extended beyond the economic. What is now called "big science," exemplified by enormous atom smashers costing millions of dollars, and by the space program with its towering gantries and rockets costing billions, can hardly be put down to economics.

Admittedly, it is sometimes difficult to tell which came first: technology or the form of the state. Put otherwise, does the goal-setting occur before the means are devised, or does an accidental devising of the means bring about its own goal-setting? For the reduction of every need there is a technology which is placed at the disposal of the drive. And for every culture there is a need selected for reduction to which the principal effort of the society is henceforth devoted and for which the appropriate technology is accordingly developed.

In the Middle Ages the need was for ultimate survival, and the drive a religious one. The technology selected was the one appropriate to the drive: not much of a material nature was required since the goal was immortality of the soul. The production of consumer goods was not a primary consideration. Economic relations were so secondary that the feudal order of suzerain, lord, vassal and subvassal was never established, not even by decree, but grew up as a result of exigent circumstances. Monasteries and churches provided the meager material background against which holy orders operated. The security of material means was a definite concomitant of the paucity of material ends.

In the modern world of the United States and the Soviet Union, the need is for the material social amenities requisite for the welfare of large populations: food, clothing, shelter, medical services, fast transportation and communication, entertainment. Accordingly, a vast and complex network of industrial technology had to be developed.

At a stage of society when only a few horses and buggies could be produced and distributed, an aristocracy was called into existence to own them exclusively. The vast majority had to find other ends to pursue. But the discovery by Henry Ford and others of the endless belt method of industrial production turned the American society into a producer-consumer type. So far as can be ascertained from the activities, from the expenditure of energy, the degree of concentration, and the consumption of available time, it might be thought that the citizens of the United States exist primarily to produce and consume manufactured products. Instruments of communication and transportation have been vastly improved, but chiefly for the purpose of making more improvements. Since there are no other ends envisaged, it is possible to conclude that what we have described as means are themselves ends. No doubt another technology is to come and with it another set of ends.

If Marx were right in contending that everything in a society is a function of the given mode of material production, then the factory system from which his politics emerged has been replaced by the more advanced technology of the modern industrial plant, with its automation and the rest; and presumably Marxist-Leninsim should be replaced with a more advanced politics. For the mode of material production has made steep progress and is nothing like what it was in Marx's day. Marxist-Leninism provided for its own replacement in a way its founders never envisaged, and that eventuality has occurred sooner than might have been expected. The drift of economics in the Soviet Union in the direction of the profit motive, with some major inequalities in earning power, though certainly not including a return on investment capital, points to the development of a kind of economic structure which the new technology will call into play.

But it is fair to point out that the emphasis of Marxist-Leninism has been slightly off center. For it is not the mode of material production which has such an influence on society but the products which are made available in vast quantities. The mass individual ownership of the products of an advanced industrial technology is what occasions the corresponding political adjustment. As we have seen earlier, the economics of abundance is not the same as the economics of scarcity, not the same in any respect: neither in values nor in activities intended to achieve the values.

Section 3. The Technological Society

At the present time in the most advanced industrial countries, the citizens live entirely in an artificial environment. By this I mean there is nothing in their surroundings not altered through human agency, neither the roads they drive on nor the air they breathe. From having had to adapt to the environment earlier in the history of the species, man has discovered how to adapt the environment to himself. Technology with its artifacts and skills has changed everything, and so it is legitimate to talk about such a society as technological, for that is what characterizes it in all of its phases. That is what keeps it off balance so far as the pattern of the life of its citizens is concerned, and that is the object to which it is plainly dedicated.

Great care must be exercised to be sure that artifacts exist for the benefit of those who use them, and not the reverse. Human survival, as well as human welfare, depends upon the production of artifacts, and it is the business of politics to provide and preserve

the order whereby artifacts can be made and used to the end of individual human integrity as disclosed by the utilization of all of
man's constructive capacities. Yet it is always possible for things
to get so inverted that the state comes to exist for the sake of the
operation of its equipment. There are phenomenological shifts
which indicate that such a danger exists. It is not the *nouveaux
riches* who make all the mistakes in a technological society but the
nouveaux savantes.

Because the technologist believes in the generality of his method,
he accepts the certainty of its results. He is assured by the preci-
sion of his machine and by the mathematics he employs along with
it that the effects of his efforts on political life will have the same
clean-cut lines. But it is a truism now that small causes may have
large effects, and particularly so in a field of innumerable variables.
We know no more now about what we do than we did before the
advent of technological society. We know that we accomplish some
things with far greater efficiency, but we do not know the political
effects.

One of the chief results of the new industrial technology is the
concentration of all effort. The equipment for greater and more
intensified organization is at hand and its employment compelled
both by the new ways of doing things and by the new things that
are being done. We shall for instance have to rethink the whole concept of sovereignty. In loosely organized societies, such as the agricultural, power went with the members of the landed aristocracy
and through them with their king. That was the source even though
his authority was often solidified by a church speaking in the name
of divinity. In early industrial societies of the democratic form,
sovereignty resided with the people. But with the tight organization
now made possible by industrial technology, sovereignty is associated with the control of technology, with the constancy of definite aim. I am not suggesting that large populations are helpless in
the hands of public relations men. The "engineering of consent," as
Bernays has so precisely called it, only operates to initiate a demand
in a direction which already exists or to move preference from one
product to another of the same kind; for it has been a failure with
the larger issues.

J. K. Galbraith is not right to suppose that the giant corporations are able to create desires on the part of the consumer. The wants of the public are headed in a given direction by the nature of the means of production and they cannot be turned round so easily, a few instances to the contrary notwithstanding. We must not confuse that narrow margin of taste which spells the difference between profit and loss with the larger questions of the movement of the society as it is influenced by technology. But he is right in supposing that the size and function of such corporations have now made them into public charges which are threatening to exceed in importunateness much of their importance.

Those who think the machine is dehumanizing individuals have made the mistake of considering man and machine on the same level of analysis. The machine that does the importunate labors for man frees him for what is important. Thus technology, the technology of modern industrialism, can be used properly as a liberating force which will enable him to devote most, if not all his energies, to fine arts, pure sciences and speculative philosophies.

The structure of the society is determined by the established morality and that morality is moved in one direction or another by the technology. But back of the development of the technology was the set of preferences for which the society had assumed it would work with all of the energy and ingenuity at its disposal. Not "every man a king" but "every man a machine-tender," and this on the basis of his own volition as a result of the values that supported him in the first place.

In a technological society, artifacts occupy as large a place as the citizens, including even their interest groups and institutions. Important tools must be taken into limited partnership, for the digital computer and the linear cyclotron are now members of society. No matter that they were made by men and are employed by men for human ends. That was clearly the intention but is no longer the whole story. Things do not sit still because we expect them to, nor do they necessarily go in the direction in which we send them. We start causes but are powerless to predict the manifold effects which may result. A state which has the responsibility of managing a society for the benefit of its citizens must take into consideration all of those materials and energies which influence it.

The artifacts, therefore, will have to have their legitimate representation. This means a federal department of technology with, in the United States, for example, cabinet representation: a secretary of technology. Thus another division has been called for in the separation of powers: executive, legislative, judicial and technological, the latter including a division to regulate decisions concerning the correct design, production and distribution of artifacts, with a bearing on national defense, long-term planning and social welfare, since these all depend upon the future production of new inventions and improvements in the industrial structure. The bureau of research and development should legitimately be a subdivision of this department; for it is not enough to be concerned with encouraging technology: the existing technology will have to be policed. Something resembling this situation already exists in the United States in the form of regulatory agencies, such as the Interstate Commerce Commission or the Federal Aviation Administration.

A great deal of social effort is always placed at the service of plans and investment for the future. This is true of short-terms when crops are planted and animals bred; it is true when machine tools are manufactured and capital accumulated. It is true of long-terms when the growth of societies is made a definite part of present activities, from "five year plans" in the Soviet Union to the founding of new cities in that country, India and Brazil.

The needs of present day consumption have first to be provided for, but in the scientific-industrial cultures this effort uses only a small part of the available energy. That is why it is so easy to engage in other activities, presumably those intended to reduce human needs in the future. The planning of expansion by the state is of this character, and so is the policy which includes future wars of conquest, and no less so when they are called "wars of liberation."

Both short- and long-term aims at expansion, the former usually intranational, the latter international, are expressions of excessive behavior made possible by the efficiency of the scientific-industrial culture. In encouraging excessive behavior, the scientific-industrial culture makes human progress possible but also exposes it to the dangers of self-destruction. That is why the economics of technology becomes so crucial a part of politics. For politics has the task of facilitating the aims of society, but only up to a point; for after that point it must act to preserve that society whose aims may if reached bring about its destruction.

Research and development contain much of the hope for a good life for the citizens of the future. As support for them, there should be a campaign to recognize the place for imagination in the society conceived as an investment for its own future. Speculative thought should be assigned a corner of the society where it may be entertained without limit. Meanwhile—and this is equally important politically—it is necessary to make sure that the existing technology does not run away with the society, that it is kept within bounds. This is the task of politicians also, given the prior decisions of what changes are to be made by those who determine the established morality of the state.

Industrialism, resting on a base of applied science and technology, which in turn is supported by pure science, is an intimate part of the cultural development of Europe. It has spread most effectively to the United States and the Soviet Union and is in process at the present time of spreading to Communist China and to the rest of the inhabited world. As with any cultural development, the gains are immense and perhaps overbalance the losses. Nevertheless, there are losses as well as gains. The assumption behind the phrase, "underdeveloped countries," is that the solely desirable cultural development lies in the direction of industrialism. This may be true but it is far from proved.

The gains are of course obvious: the production of more and better food, shelter, medical services, clothing, transportation, communication, and information. The losses are less obvious: the absence of immediate contact with the elemental entities and forces; the absence of nature undisturbed and unmediated by artifacts in its contacts with the individual; and consequently the absence of all those values which such contacts bestow.

If technology has solved many problems it has also brought about many others. The march of the advance of technology is so rapid that the achievements of yesterday become the obstacles of today. No one wants an old machine when a new one will do the job better. Consider the problem of maintaining machines for which there has been no "planned obsolescence," or, worse still, the problem of their disposal. Consider the graveyards of old automobiles which litter the outskirts of large cities and the "urban renewal" which is sought after by cities with neighborhoods grown prematurely old. Technology develops faster than efficiency in its applications.

An environing world has been produced for man by his technology which enables him to ride upon a sea of constructions of his own invention. And so he rarely comes into contact any more with the concrete nonhuman world of material things as they were before the human species developed. He has indeed been alienated from that larger reality which is the prevalent state of affairs throughout the cosmic universe in which he together with all his works is nothing but an occasional exception. He has learned more, much more, about that universe thanks to the discoveries of pure science, but he has been subtly isolated from it thanks to the great impetus applied science has given to technology. He has become the creature of himself, a product of his own devising, in that larger world whose other influences upon him have remained unnoticed but continue to be powerful.

Individual man in the last analysis is nonpolitical man. It is politics to which he looks to find the security in which he can remain his own master. Government exists in order to provide the maximum desirable conditions for individual citizens. It guards them against enemies from without and against infractions from within, on the theory that a peaceful order is the best opportunity for those citizens to pursue their own goods. But when a society moves in a cultural way to channel its interests, as it does when it turns itself over to the single-minded development of an industrial technology for the sake of the products which are thereby made generally and cheaply available, and when that society pays as a result a certain price of freedom through voluntary self-regimentation, there is nothing that the government can do about it except stand helplessly by. If the scientific-industrial complex with all its preoccupations and controls is what the people want, then it is what the government must see that they get by regulating and otherwise facilitating the procedure to insure that it shall continue to remain orderly.

Chapter VII

THE PROBLEM OF IDEOLOGIES

Section 1. Absolutes vs. Exigencies

The constitutions of states assume metaphysical truths; they are put into effect to implement moralities, but they are framed in terms of ideologies. That is to say, a constitution is what a state hopes to follow in order to actualize a stipulated ideal. Before such a dream can be realized someone must first have dreamed it, and, awake or asleep, the dream is always the same: an attempt to answer in the planning of concrete terms just what a state ought to be.

Unfortunately, concrete political acts never leave things at that, they are always for or against an ideal. A great deal of havoc in the world has been the result of a strong sense of right following from metaphysical theories expressed in nonmetaphysical form and accepted absolutely. In this connection medieval Christianity joins hands with Islam and with contemporary Marxist states, the Soviet Union and Communist China. There is no need for a supernatural or divine authority when absolutes can be derived from the analysis of economic events just as easily. Ideals are, if nothing else, uncompromising, but that is not their chief virtue.

I will not digress about the ideal state. That is reserved for a later chapter. Here I only want to raise the question and point to some of the problems confronting such a formulation. Hence the treatment will be methodological. The understanding of ideals is not an easy matter. For some unknown reason, it is often supposed that men differ with respect to their actual situations but that their ideals are always the same. Just the opposite is the case. For every actual situation, including its limitations, weaknesses and strengths, its compromises, its gaps between pretensions and actions, bears a striking similarity to every other situation; all have the same character of particulars and the same habit of turning into something else. Ideals differ sharply; for men do not agree about what ought to be.

When Plato wrote his *Republic*, he failed to provide any place in it for producing the man of genius. He conceived it as perfect and therefore saw no need for improvement. Ever since, the political theorists have been divided between those who see their ideals in these terms, and those, like Machiavelli, who thought that imperfections of human nature were such that no ideal state was possible. Neither group has given sufficient ground to the twin facts that there always is change and that all change occurs in terms of stipulated ideals.

There will always be those who limit their thoughts to immediate problems and keep their sights on the ground before them. Only a determinative few reach beyond that and look up to the sky which the turning world sweeps out in circles. Society has the necessity of reckoning with both. For ideologies exist at the level of aims at ideals. Actualities are composed of order and disorder, of harmonies and conflicts, of values and disvalues. The discrepancies between ideologies and actualities is a result of the daily dealing which takes place in the midst of actualities and is confronted first by the negative side—by disorders, conflicts and disvalues. The highly individual fact of death—that, as Camus said, we are all condemned to die—must be recognized in any highly integrated society. In this way ideologies are either forgotten or reinterpreted to fit the exigencies of the present moment.

The realist thinks that no goals are needed and that none are attended to in the midst of action; the idealist thinks that every move is toward or away from some remote goal. As a matter of fact, however, neither has hold of more than a half truth. Goal-setting is a first necessity in politics. Without it nothing can be done. After it, everyone goes to work to grapple with day-to-day problems as they arise, for only in this way can a society be maintained. Thus we are under the necessity of balancing forces; we sacrifice ideals, sometimes the better to deal freely with immediate problems, at other times we sacrifice advantage in order to be true to ideals. But the administrations we admire the most in history are those which are most mindful in practice of the ideals toward which they aim.

An ideology is a conception of the rights of man based on a theory of reality. Though often silent, it cannot be ignored, unless men think they exert themselves at random and without goal-setting. Yet as a practical matter this is not the case. For action must have an overall direction. This is what makes prolonged and consistent activity possible and also what brings about difficulties. The distinction between exigency and ideology is also one between power and morality. Might does not make right but it does make winners; and something is missing when those who were right are dead and the others still living.

But that is not the whole story. For while the right may be temporarily lost to the wrong, statistically the right tends to assert itself merely because facts refuse to conform to any false theory. The long-term victory of the right is won, when it is won at all, at the expense of a series of short-term defeats.

To see the connection between ideology and exigency as an ultimate one, it is necessary to remember that mass armies can be conscripted more easily when a lofty ideal is used to motivate citizens. Total war is made possible by absolute idealism. It is not necessary that ideals be followed strictly into practice but only that they be held and that the masses believe that the actions in which they are engaged are applied ideals. The masses never stop to examine the connection or calculate the consistency between plan and action.

Every ideology is in a certain sense also a utopia. There is a plethora of utopias; which one ought to be adopted? All political plans are, so to speak, made in the dark. How are we to decide which form of government is best when we do not even know what human life is for? Each ideal aims at the perfection of the political order. This is the factor which makes it an ideal and arouses in citizens the requisite emotional allegiance. It is simply impossible to become dedicated to a compromise of any sort. The kind of belief on which sacrifices can be based is always absolute belief.

Every human individual has on the average two arms, two legs, and one "absolute truth." Certainty is by any count the world's cheapest and most ordinary commodity. What makes certainty so disastrous is the great number of conflicting certainties. There exist many certainties, and some of them seem to be endorsed by their large capacities for survival. Astrology and divinely authorized monarchy are two of the oldest institutions supported by certainties and both still have their adherents today. The difficulty is that almost any two certainties chosen at random can be found to conflict.

The recognition of this signal fact has been no help to those whose adherence is a condition of sanity. It can be argued further that the tendency to possess absolute truth crosses the line between stupidity and intelligence; it is a claim made equally by the informed and ignorant. An ideology, if it is to succeed in practical applications, will have to contain utopian elements.

All people who hold absolute beliefs behave in some of the same ways despite the differences in their beliefs. All absolutists hold inquisitions and maintain the most inflexible of governments, employing cruelty where necessary, and even resorting to genocide— so much are they under the necessity of convincing others. In addition, action, by its very nature, is always absolute. It is what it is: irrevocable, and focused on perfection. Huntington Cairns has pointed out that the true ideal is necessity, violated by actual states in so far as they fail to work.

That absolutism has over and over been the story of utopian ideologies points to a basic flaw. The very idea of an inflexible ideal contains a contradiction. As an ideal it sets the goal for action but as inflexible it cannot be a goal since actions never conform inflexibly. A compromise is effected by the asymptotic nature of the approach to ideals. Thus, ideologies have succeeded to the extent that aiming at them has made actual governments possible; they have failed to the extent to which, in applying them, actual governments have operated in an uncompromising fashion. Clearly this means that somehow an ideology must be designed that will meet all the usual requirements and yet not be so inflexible as to produce havoc when applied. To that extent it would fail as an ideal.

There is another difficulty. It can happen that in the application of absolutes the effects may be the opposite of those which, strictly speaking, would be consistent with the absolutes. For example, Bertrand Russell is an absolute pacifist. As such he counsels ending resistance to communist aggression, but in so doing he encourages the kind of aggression to which he is in principle opposed. Absolutes in practice tend to be self-contradictory. Total surrender in the face of the threat of war could lead to a violence of subjugation that would, by comparison, make war seem desirable. Imagine what would have happened if England and the United States had taken Bertrand Russell's advice in dealing with Hitler. The German Jews for the most part did not practice forceful resistance against the Nazis, and the only result was their almost total annihilation.

In the face of the number of variables which are always involved in any social situation, in face of mistakes which have been so often made in the past, in face of the scarcity of reliable knowledge—in the face of all this, certainty can only be considered an affirmative and assertive form of ignorance. There is a dilemma involved and it can be stated as a political rule: *since perfection is always absolute, calls for perfection are also calls for absolute action; but action is never perfect even though aimed at absolutes.*

In other words, ideologies, while needed for action, are never appropriate for action. Doing implies certainty. If we are not certain, how could we act? But not to act, to refrain from action, is a form of action since it may have consequences which are comparable. The answer will have to be found in a reformulation of ideologies.

In short, ideologies must be framed in tentative terms and men must learn to live by tentative knowledge, by workable half-truths. An open-ended and flexible ideology is what we may call, paradoxically, the ideological ideal. For we have now come to see that the discovery of ideals is a speculative field which must be explored before it can be explained. We are not ready at this stage of the argument to frame an ideology, only to investigate the nature of the problems involved in it. And, as is usually the case, the more we investigate, the greater the number of problems we uncover. It is the case in every field of investigation that, together with the discovery of new truths, there are always a greater number of unknowns. Our ignorance is never specific enough; we must learn the hard way what it is that we do not know. In what follows, then, we will attempt to back ourselves into the dim outlines of an ideology by moving away from the limitations of actual practice. This will not give us a positive ideology, but it will show something about a negative one: it will teach us at least what ought not to be.

Section 2. Some Primary Requirements of Ideology

In the organization of society, which is to say, the life of the state, the metaphysical categories become renamed. In place of "possibility," "actuality," and "destiny," we now have "ideology," "actual conditions," and "strategy." For an ideology is worse than useless when it does not take into account both how far actual practice falls short of the political ideal and what steps will be necessary to move practice toward that ideal. Thus we shall be wanting to (a) frame an ideology, (b) describe the actual situation at its worst, and (c) design a strategy for changing the situation into something closer to the ideal. I shall undertake none of these in this chapter. For the moment, I will rest content if I can show some of the primary requirements which will have to be met by any political ideal held desirable for practice.

In the establishment and maintenance of a morality which has been accepted, much more is now involved than formerly. The theory of reality underlining a government now counts for as much as its armed forces. Conquests can be and sometimes are made through the force of ideas which often supplement military might. Large populations need to be linked together through the acceptance of common beliefs on a deep psychological level.

The ideal of government may be said to be well on its way to successful practice when all citizens feel most profoundly that public office is the highest honor it is possible for them to attain, and when they continue to venerate the office even though it is occupied by those unworthy of it. For if the individual exists for the service of society, then through his devotion to politics he can find in it one of the preferred ways in which society can be served.

The ideal state should make possible a maximization of all values for individuals collectively. For the ideal individual is one who has great capabilities for good, and the ideal citizen is one who can actualize such capabilities in the state. The measure of the success of a state is contained in the answer to one question: how much diversity, on the part mainly of individuals but also interest groups and institutions, can the government support without loss of national unity? The state can be good as a system even though the individual citizens are not. Yet it should be so constructed as to bring out the best in them.

A state cannot exist without an ideology. The term is well-chosen, for an ideology is a political philosophy formulated in both ideal and applicable terms. Therein lies the inherent difficulty, for once a constitution is adopted formally, the procedures of expediency take hold, and thereafter the process of the taming of the doctrine begins. This consists mainly in modifying its absolute demands as an ideal, in softening it by means of clever interpretation, not excluding downright neglect in every respect except the abstract protestation of faithful adherence.

Philosophy and workability, ideals and practicalities are beautiful dreams of harmony and the stark reality of physical and forceful conflict. This is the heritage of the state which could not be brought into being in the first place without some large-scale plan such as one derived from an ideology; and could not be continued without compromises so serious that they border upon repudiation. Thus the opposition of conservatives and liberals—conservatives who want the ideology preserved at all costs and applied in all its demands, either because they are idealists or because they stand to benefit personally from such a course, and liberals who bow to the practical problems of exigencies because they too are idealists though of another kind or because dealing in ideologies which have not yet been adopted they are humanitarians who see that the already established ideology will work hardships if not adequately modified.

To talk about political systems in the abstract is meaningless unless a theory of implementation be one of its elements. This last must include not only an ideology, which is the political name for the system of philosophy that includes politics and from which the theory of politics can be deduced, but it must also be executed by means of a technology, which is the name for that system of applied science by which the resources of a country can be exploited for the benefit of its citizens.

To insure that the proper ideology is complete, it will be necessary to spell out the requirements of the open society. They are:

(1) expectations accepted that anything in the political structure may be changed;

(2) a sense of security resting on the common good will of all citizens;

(3) beliefs which are always somewhat less strong than absolute certainty yet strong enough to act upon;

(4) ambitions for social planning which are never more than half-devoted to the future, the other half of the resources in energy and materials being reserved for the enjoyment of the present;

(5) decisions involving the whole society made only after taking deliberate thought and never on emotional grounds;

(6) people within a country behaving toward each other in accordance with a predetermined scale of values which has already been incorporated as part of the beliefs of each citizen;

(7) everyone facing in the same direction as the state, with the state maintaining a flat level of importance so that when citizens arrange themselves in any hierarchical order it is on other grounds;

(8) and, finally, politicians functioning as a set of dedicated men willing to serve anonymously when they serve professionally, with the heads of government constituting themselves a hierarchy of obligation.

The ideal of government is excellently illustrated by the performance in recent decades of the United States Public Health Service, which has done indispensable work without applause, credit, recognition or publicity, and even without all the support it needs—a silent, magnificent achievement. Evidently, the rewards in satisfaction to be gained from acting morally can be made to replace the rewards to be gained from stealing, influence-peddling, and other antisocial behavior.

The distinction introduced earlier between the importunate and the important applies also to political goals. The importunate goal of every state is the same, for it is to survive as a state. To this end it must be capable of protecting itself against enemies internally through the use of police powers and externally by means of armed forces. The important goal varies, and again it may be internal or external. In terms of the self-perfection of the state, there can be an internal importunate goal. Many of the citizens of ancient Athens were evidently of this persuasion. In terms of conquest, it may be an external goal, and for ancient Macedonia this was evidently the case.

It may be asked whether one of the two above goals is capable of carrying all of "the national interest." This varies, and the citizens do not always know, unless their chosen goals are recognized and made explicit by a political leader. For there are always goals, stated or unstated. They are stated when there is a constitution; but they are as often unstated, and unstated goals have a way of being very effective.

The ideology contains the national goals. An ideal democracy, for instance, is a state in which every citizen has a share in the making of all those decisions which affect him. But in terms of the large modern populations, this becomes impractical. It is necessary to substitute government by professionals, designating as professionals not the best of the vote-getters but those trained in the profession of government and those whose financial rewards are limited by law.

The function of good government ought to be one of modulation: interference in the affairs of citizens only with a view to facilitating their efforts toward chosen goals in order to benefit them as individuals and at the same time contribute toward the welfare of the whole society—so far as possible; and it ought to be transparent facilitation: aid that is so unobtrusive it almost goes unnoticed. In a word, as little government as is necessary to maintain the established order set forth by the principles upon which the state was founded. But everything depends upon the nature of that order, and on as much government as is necessary.

It will be well to remind ourselves of what we had laid down for the state in an earlier chapter. The aim and direction toward which all political activity tends is to facilitate the reduction in each citizen of all his organ-specific needs, and in the end efforts toward the reduction of those highest needs which cannot be reduced altogether, such as the need of the skin for superidentification with the whole of the material universe or its cause. The lesser needs are reduced by an efficiently functioning political economy, but these

still leave the needs for feeling as such—the fine arts—for knowledge as such—the pure sciences—and for activities as such—the
originative religions—which reach out beyond the state.

Engels' contention that the state is an organization for the protection of the propertied class against the nonpropertied class is in
a sense correct, but it does not go far enough. So long as men have
unequal abilities and the state wishes all of its citizens to benefit
from them, it must protect them in the security of their efforts. Unequal rewards must follow, and in any system of political order if
this is true it will have to be maintained to the extent to which order is preserved. Private capitalism is one such order; none is inevitable. What is inevitable, as we have noted earlier, is the existence
of some order, and this must always rely upon a stable economic
arrangement.

It can be readily seen how global economics outdates national
politics. That economic structure will have to be considered the best
under which there is at least a maximum of production and distribution of goods. Given the contemporary high rate of interchange, it is
doubtful that any economic arrangement which is limited to the
boundaries of a single nation can be considered the best. For raw
materials are not mindful of national boundaries; they are un-
equally distributed over the globe. To organize them into manufactured products and then to get those products to the people who
need to consume them requires an international arrangement of
some sort. Thus a single international economic system is necessary
even though there continue to be local differences with respect to
politics. Now that we recognize that politics is determined by economic factors, a global politics will probably be developed.

To achieve one commensurate with a global economics would
require a degree of cooperation by which the entire human species
on the surface of the earth would have to be considered an in-group.
We shall return toward the end of the book to see how this can be
done. Meanwhile, we must begin to face the obstacles to its
achievement. If we look around us as well as back into history, we
shall be forced to confess that "humanism" is a poor term. In view
of the preponderance of human behavior, we should speak rather of
"inhuman ideals" when we mean "brotherly love," "perpetual
peace," or the like. This disparity between the ideals we espouse

and the aggression we practice shows something of the distance to be travelled and the individual improvements to be made before we can talk in any serious terms of utopian ideologies and their applications.

Section 3. The Limited Ideology

Nothing smaller than a government for the human species as it exists on this earth will prove satisfactory in the long run. And, as we shall see later, to provide such a government may necessitate the extension of human interests still farther. Meanwhile we have the insistent problems which must be dealt with in a concern for what we might best describe as a limited ideology, something better than what we have and consisting of improvements which will serve us while we plan by looking into the future for the largest of utopian ideologies.

The limited ideology because of its half-exigent nature can hardly be spelled out in all its special details here. That would require a separate treatment, which, by the way, it certainly deserves. But what can be done in the meantime is to suggest what is involved by setting up a number of concepts that can be useful as steps toward larger considerations. These concepts are: the welfare state, the size of the state, preventive illegality, and artifactual relation. I have put them down in the order of familiarity.

The aim of "the welfare state" is on the level of animal survival, comfort and longevity. It includes food, clothing, housing, medical services, efficient transportation, communication, and education. It is essentially urban rather than rural, and uniform rather than differentiated. It does not include the production or distribution of the fine arts or the pure sciences; these are neglected in favor of what are considered adequate mass substitutes: entertainments and popular ideas. No one doubts the value of these goods. What may be doubted is the price paid for them, and whether they can in the end be accepted as substitutes for neglected values.

In any theory of politics there ought to be a consideration of the basic size of the ideal state, the question of the proper dimensions for political organizations and social groups: how large ought the ideal country to be? Eventually, such units will be included without being submerged in a larger global state. It is not possible during an interim period to make political units uniform in size because the territories of habitable lands are not uniform. But something of a general estimate can be made and differences in contributions assessed on the basis of current population pressures.

At the present, crimes are dealt with only when they arise. There is little disposition to forestall their occurrence. Yet in any functioning government, there could be a broad effort toward what might be described as "preventive illegality," that is to say, doing outside prison reformatories and in advance of the crimes what is now ordinarily done only on the inside. With proper measures, criminals can be detected and their crimes prevented, and special educational facilities provided for the antisocial. We do this now for infectious diseases; we could do it as well for infectious criminal attitudes.

Finally, among our illustrations, there is the unfamiliar concept of "artifactual relation." To replace the person to person relationship on which both democracy and communism have been built, there is the necessity for constructing a more advanced concept of the person-artifact-person relationship. It would be necessary to redesign government to contain the management of the artifacts as central. For as we have noted, almost all human relations are mediated by artifacts, remembering always that languages are included among the artifacts because of their material nature.

Part Two

THE FACTS OF ACTUALITY

Chapter VIII

THE SMALLEST POLITICS

Section 1. The Public Involvement of the Private Citizen

We have noted already that politics begins historically with the moralization of man. It finds its basis logically in his moral conscience, the feeling he has of being part of a community through the prescriptions regarding behavior which by governing that community make it possible. Yet it is not in the morality he accepts but in his very private acceptance of it that we find the point of origin we are seeking.

The closer one approaches the individual citizen, the smaller the politics becomes, yet this is where all politics rests. For it is also true that the smaller the politics the more local and specific. Generalizing about differentia is a contradiction in terms, and, were it not for the fundamental nature of the lowest membership, the differentia would have no place in a study of this kind. What cannot be said about politics that transcends time and place cannot contribute effectively to political theory.

However, while politics begins at home it does not stay there; its effects are felt all the way up to international levels. "Home" or "local" politics differs greatly not only from country to country but often between a city or town within the same country. In the United States, cities of approximately the same size have varying

city governments: some may have city managers, others city councils with mayors as presiding officers, still others with strong mayors and weak city councils.

The individual becomes a citizen of a state when his readiness
to live in it and his obedience to its laws are formally accepted by
the authorities. For the great preponderance of individuals, citizenship is acquired as a matter of birth, though this is not true for all.
The ground-state of politics, therefore, is to be found in the individual citizen himself, and next above him, in his closest political
contacts. In the United States, for instance, it is the individual voter,
then next his precinct captain and the ward leader. The political
bosses above that level may never be seen and certainly are not
known personally—for example, the mayor of the city or the city
councilman.

Yet it is just here that the political structure is based and where
its vast superstructure rests. It is here too that logic has to mingle
with bad reason, prejudice, and hastily aroused emotions. It is here
that volatile changes are so imminent. But it is here too that stability
is to be found if it exists at all.

This is where politics comes into immediate contact with the
most intimate life of the greatest number of citizens. The average
man is occupied chiefly with his own concerns: with job, family,
friends, and neighbors. He may rely upon his city precinct captain
or his town selectman to make his political decisions for him; but
usually this is as far as he goes with his interests and concerns. He
knows about the local issues. He has opinions about everything including international relations, but he is rarely informed about
them; and it happens that the less he knows the more pronounced
his judgments become.

He learns only remotely about state politics, to say nothing of
national and international politics which are important in direct ratio to the extent of his ignorance: the farther away the greater.
What information reaches him bears little if any resemblance to the
truth. All the more reason for him to be shocked when he finds
that remote political events have a drastic effect upon his life. He
hears distantly of an assassination in Sarajevo, then suddenly he is in
France fighting the Germans. He learns that the Nazis have invaded
Poland, and he assures himself *"they* are always fighting over there,

so what business is it of ours?" when almost immediately he finds that his son has been shipped overseas with the armed forces to take part in the staging of an invasion of continental Europe from a base in England.

The point is that, thanks to gains in transportation and communication, for the first time in the world's social history what happens somewhere, no matter how trivial, might have critical consequences anywhere else. Small politics will always exist because there will always be a local level. But it has now more far-reaching connections, it affects and is effected by more distant social events than ever before. To understand the functioning of politics at the highest level it is necessary to pay attention to politics at the local level.

The large increase in populations means that a different kind of management has become necessary, for the shift from small politics to large is more than a quantitative change. An increase in quantity in any area brings with it a change in quality, and this is as true of the political domain as it is in any other. This was the experience in the United States in the nineteenth century; the political organizations developed then to deal with large metropolitan centers differed radically from the earlier—and quite adequate—forms of government for small towns. Thanks to the huge increases in population, the whole character and responsibility for formal rule turns into something different from what it was.

As cities grow in size, the character of the population which politically dominates also changes. The city-manager plan in the United States prospered in towns under 100,000 and almost never in cities over that amount. In the smaller towns the more capable and energetic members of the upper classes exercise control, while in the larger cities the voters from the lower classes not only predominate, they also find their political champions, and this makes all the difference. Efficiency is a village affair. Small town politics is more likely to produce economical and unwasteful government. In large populations with correspondingly large governments, the considerations shift radically, and issues not necessarily to the state's advantage come more to the fore.

In this way perhaps it is possible to see the growth of the destructive element in the very same properties which indicate prosperity and success. The greater the population and the bigger the government, the more likely the eventual downfall of the state. The terms which will eventually consume the life blood of the state are introduced by the factors which are necessary to its operation in big government. Quality is inverse to quantity, in some aspects at least: the larger the worse, the smaller the better. The "town meeting" that ran the small New England village before the twentieth century, and still does in some places, was run by a better and more dedicated group of leaders than the metropolitan city is today. The qualities which emerge and the elements which intrude themselves into the larger communities are mostly detrimental even though they make possible the material cultures on which all great civilizations depend.

It comes to this, that village life has been better than city life for the development of certain fundamental aspects of the human individual, even though the cultural heights to which he has risen are altogether products of the great cities. Human life is animal life of a particular kind, and depends, as we have noted, largely on artifacts; which means that the village was a stage with no future and with certain virtues which had to be sacrificed in order to attain great advantages provided by the arts and sciences. The "world" religions were all products of village life; the fine arts and, more especially, the pure sciences are city products. Science needs laboratories and large constructions; architecture relies not upon humble dwellings but upon cathedrals and skyscrapers.

The problem is easy to formulate, if not to solve, and is simply this: how can it be arranged so that the governments of great states are operated by men of the same honesty and integrity as the governments of small villages? The difficulty is that direct democracy, in which citizens come to hear the arguments in person and vote on all the important issues, is more effective as democracy than the form in which the voters only elect their representatives who thereafter either guess what the electorate would like them to do or do what they prefer and afterwards try to convince the electorate that this is what was best for them.

Village life in an agricultural state is, however, quite different from what it is in an industrial state. The essential antagonism which always exists between the local community and the national aggregate is intensified. The state always rests on a basis of very many communities in which the citizens feel "local" and resent the interference of rule from afar. Those who know each other and are familiar on a daily basis interact quite differently from those compelled to operate abstractly and at a distance. More knowledge is required to effectively integrate that wide-scale community which is the nation-state. It is not within the reach of the average citizen to comprehend the forces inherent in the formulation of ideal political principles.

Generally speaking, it might be said that such principles belong to large-scale politics. To aim at the ideal, it is necessary to have in mind the largest political units, and we shall consider these in detail in the last chapters of this book: the state, international political bodies, such as the United Nations, and the prospect of a global superstate, and even beyond. But there is after all the local level, and for that level it is nothing so grandiose that we shall have to bear in mind. For the local level, the level of the vote-getter and wardheeler, compromise and concessions are the words of the day. Ideals have to be modified or temporarily forgotten, and perfect programs abandoned as immediate goals in favor of gradual approaches, slowed by temporary cross-actions. The movement toward an ideal, to be effective at the local level, must be a dialectic, like the path of a boat sailing close to the wind: approached at an angle which at times may almost seem off the point, only to be reversed and approached from the contrary angle.

To back and fill, to give and take, to have attention called to politics while immediately afterwards having it withdrawn once the necessary permissions have been granted, these are the reactions of the man in the street. And if he enters professional politics, he takes this training with him. For he will keep it thereafter no matter how high he rises in political life; he will recall how short the memory of the average voter actually is, and that this failing is what makes his own political career possible—makes it possible, in other words, for him to be as much in favor of a decisive action on one occasion as he had been vehemently against it previously.

There is the famous case of the politician who was asked on a local platform how he stood on whiskey.

"If you mean by whiskey," he said, after the briefest of pauses, "the solace of the working man, the comfort of the sick, the refuge of the senior citizen, then I am emphatically for it.

"But, if you mean by whiskey, the activity of the wastrel, the failing of the honest laborer, the corruption of the adolescent, the seducer of our women, then I am uncompromisingly against it.

"That is my stand and I will not withdraw from it one iota."

On most issues the local politician takes the same position as the one who was for whiskey, unless he can find something utterly blameless to advocate, like home or mother. The local politician in the United States is pretty firm in his views that a man's home is his castle and that apple pie is the best American dish and hence the best there is in the world.

The influence of the politician is insidious in any form of government and always threatens to get out of control. Continual vigilance on the part of the private citizen is required if every aspect of his life is not to be regulated and controlled from above by politicians who in so doing exceed their legitimate function. So long as thought control and birth control, to name but two, can be placed at the disposal of the politician, there can be said to be no individually inviolate areas. The limiting of government by the citizen is of the utmost importance to even the least politically aware. No individual, in other words, can afford to forget for very long that he is a citizen.

I have been speaking of conditions as they are in western industrial democracies. In the communist countries it is already too late for such observations. An absolutely rigid political domination exists, and it is possible to watch from the side lines as sections of the population struggle for degrees of freedom. Artists are most active in this endeavor, and, in a less noisy fashion, so probably are the smallest politicians on the local level. From the slave uprisings of ancient Rome and the American southern states in the nineteenth century, to the efforts of the individual situated lowest in the political hierarchy, men have always been working to express their political needs. Political involvement of the private citizen is necessary, but he wants the influence to flow from him as well as to him in his interacting with larger units in the political order.

Section 2. The Citizen as Voter

Politics is rooted in the phenomenology of the solitary citizen and influenced by his stock of beliefs, prejudices, feelings and accidental encounters. He is oriented in a particular direction, and this gives rise to a deference hierarchy, which in turn determines how he will vote in an election. Whatever comes closest to his personal interests and sense of justice will receive his political approval. He acts first for himself, then for society.

The mirror in which he sees himself reflected politically is what may be called the contact order at the local level, the order of those citizens, institutions, and artifacts with which he has personal contact and which are therefore most familiar to him. Because he knows them best he thinks he knows them well, but this is deceptive. Familiarity may be more misleading than unfamiliarity. Many husbands and wives who unexpectedly encounter critical situations together can attest to this. How much greater the surprise inherent in the relations with others who are familiar yet not so close. In the effort to act for his own interests he is often baffled by novelties of reaction in the members of his immediate community who, he might have predicted, should have behaved otherwise.

These are differences, but political similarities also exist. There are others around him who share his approach and consequently vote the same way. They produce a common pool of sympathies, principles, sentiments and loyalties of which the political "machine" takes advantage. In this way it counts on a certain number of votes at every election because average citizens tend to vote the same way. I am talking chiefly about local primary elections, the lowest political level of democracy. Upon this foundation you find yourself engaged with state and national elections, with political parties, and even with institutions and the collective ideologies making up the culture.

Once he gets past the level of the separate and solitary individual voter, other considerations are introduced thanks to existing similarities and differences. People sort themselves out according to economic class, ethnic group, traditional party affiliation, or election issue. These differences are seized upon by party machines and dealt with in an unofficial way so that they can be counted on to last. The next step is one of coalitions on particular issues at the polls; the rich, for instance, may change sides and vote with Irish Catholics, against the middle class and Negroes, on the choice of a mayor.

The average citizen rarely questions the way things are and tacitly mistakes them for things as they always were. He cannot imagine them differently even as they change under his very eyes. The established morality reaches him in the shape of those few laws which he encounters either through their use to him as guidelines or through infractions which he commits or hears of others committing. Custom and tradition seem imbedded in the material things of the nonhuman world which he rarely encounters and in artifacts of the human world that surround him, lending to the established morality a solidity and a permanence it does not in fact possess. It is this very solidity that politicians in ordinary times can depend on when they weigh the support they will need for actions they propose to take.

For the average voter there is, in addition to politics, his ordinary life. On this base the security and continuity of the existing system chiefly rests. His participation in politics is a sometime thing; it interrupts the usual course of events, gets him all stirred up until elections, then drops him back into his conventional slot with no noticeable change. Over a period, this kind of irritation produces an apathy which leaves him indifferent to what happens. There was already, to be sure, a large group of citizens who, out of ignorance, resentment, indifference, or laziness, never took advantage of their franchise.

The result of combining these two groups is that a very small class of enthusiasts is responsible for all the political differences. I am sure the world would be shocked if it knew how few people make a revolution. The original Christian Church was founded by a handful of believers, and proportionally not many more than that made the communist revolution in Russia. Admittedly, it is always done with the tacit and passive permission of the many who have the power to stop it but do not; those who approve yet do not participate. Without them it could not be done, yet their help is very feeble, indeed, and consists chiefly in their standing aside. A small and highly disciplined group of devoted followers, called "fanatics" by their opponents, can accomplish a great deal.

In short, those who make politics their business have great political advantage over those for whom it is of occasional concern. The result is often tyranny and oppression, all because the average citizen cannot bring himself to recognize that what he does not resist will steadily come to dominate him to his own disadvantage. Perpetual vigilance is the price of good government, though paradoxically it carries a higher price than that. For it is impossible for a man to serve two masters.

In an age when every civilization exacts extreme specialization for every achievement, when every trained citizen is professionally absorbed in his craft, art, or science, it is not possible for him to be equally devoted to anything else—neither to politics nor to anything else. A good business man or good chemist eats and sleeps with his preoccupation of business or chemistry twenty-four hours a day. If he has any time left over, he needs it for his family and recreation. He has no time to turn himself into a fervent politician.

What I have been reporting is not peculiar to any particular time, place, or form of government; it was as true of ancient Greece as it is now in England. The internecine struggle for control of the government on the part of those who ordinarily do not concern themselves with political matters often has results which are disastrous to the state as a whole, often paralyzing, at least crippling. Indecision and vacillation are common. After the unsuccessful revolt against Athens by the citizens of Mitylene during the Second Peloponnesian War of 431 B.C., the Athenian assembly voted to put them all to death and sent a ship with these orders. Only after reconsideration did the moderates prevail and send another ship with orders in time to execute only the ringleaders. In England during the last several decades, the steel industry has been nationalized twice.

Section 3. The Private Involvement of the Public Official

The various dilemmas of politics on which the political principles I have detected rest are echoes of the conflicting, if unexpressed, needs of the voter. He wants good government, now, and he wants better government in the future for his children. But sometimes, as we have noted, spending political capital may mortgage the political future, as when a government accumulates a huge national indebtedness. Conversely, a government may decide to sacrifice the present generation to build a stronger nation for the future, as Stalin did with his Russian contemporaries. The voter cannot have it both ways, and, faced with this choice, he will take the current cash and let the credit go. But it is the virtue of democracy that he has a voice in making the decision. In so many other cases he has not; he has not in a dictatorship of any kind, including a dictatorship of the proletariat which is in the hands of the party that purportedly represents it.

No wonder that, so often when the voter bothers at all, he is confused, and his opinions are as emphatic as the absence of true knowledge or the presence of false knowledge compel them to be. On the whole, he will not bother with politics until he is forced to do so either by the exigencies of his situation, which he feels keenly; or the rhythm of the political system under which he lives, for the most part obliviously. When things go wrong—there is a hurricane and the water supply fails; there is no money to pay the public school teachers; the bus drivers are on strike and there is no public transportation—he blames the politicians. But he does not credit them when things go well and there are no difficulties of any sort.

A citizen ought to be able to ignore government most of the time. Transparent facilitation, which is the role of all service institutions, among which number government can count itself preeminently, should make this possible; for a state which functions efficiently makes for citizens who can function in other than political connections.

Government is impersonal, and the larger the state the more impersonal the government. Therefore the citizen takes no pride in it; he does not feel that it concerns him, and because it does not especially he feels that it does not at all. And this provides the stability of the government which obtains from the prevalence of such an attitude the independence to act without consultations or referenda. It makes, as a matter of fact, an effective breach between the functioning government and its base of authority. The citizen is deceived to the extent to which he does not care to be bothered, and this can be stretched to operate in such a way that he is not informed even of crucial decisions which will intimately and perhaps fatally affect him when it is too late to reverse them.

The relationship between government and the voting citizen is ambivalent and never gets resolved, thus perpetuating difficulties. It makes demands on him when he does not want interference; he makes demands of it under circumstances which make a satisfactory response impossible. The silent but effective and authoritative voter is the ghost that hovers over every government official as he goes about his duties unguided but responsible. The heavy hand of the government always rests upon the shoulders of the citizen and adds nothing to the accomplishment of his private labors, only taking its toll of them in distracting and impeding ways, through regulations, restrictions and taxations.

Government is administration *sui generis*, and administration, no matter how smoothly operated, no matter how unobtrusive and transparent its performance, must still issue permits and refusals, must allow and restrain, though, where it restrains, it is resented. There is no established order that did not to some extent irk those who wandered over its limits. A price of freedom must always be paid for order; yet, without order, anarchy would totally abolish freedom. Therefore it would be well to think of social order as providing the only kind of freedom possible. What gives the citizen pause is that there are orders and orders: some orders provide more freedoms than others, while absolute order is a way of abolishing freedom. Between total anarchy and absolute order there is an optimal pragmatic arrangement which uses a minimal amount of order to provide a maximum amount of freedom. Just how to achieve such an arrangement and, more important, how to hold it once it is achieved, involves decisions of great delicacy and firmness.

Chapter IX

POLITICAL CORRUPTION

Political corruption I define as the practice of bad politics. The latter term does not necessarily mean unsuccessful politics. It means political theory or practice which in the short or long run operates harmfully against more people than it helps. In any existing society there is always a degree of disorganization, the work of apathetic masses or of predatory rulers. It must always be less than a determinable functional degree, otherwise the society breaks down internally or proves unable to defend itself externally. The state ceases to function as a state. The dynamics of disorganization in the state needs to be studied, for the practice of good politics is aided by an understanding of the methods which could be practiced in the avoidance of bad politics.

The whole concept of corruption would be meaningless were there nothing to corrupt. What is corrupted is of course principle. Political action or any action having political effects could not be called corrupt unless it involved a departure from or debasement of accepted principles. Practicality is allowed a certain latitude of freedom in application; after that it becomes corrupt. Principles, in this case, mean the approved universals underlying the preferred practices at every level.

At the center of political corruption is usually found a false evaluation. This can be put positively as well as negatively: the concentration of reality upon some political element to which it does not exclusively belong. Every level of political organization, from the solitary individual to the vast empire, has at some time and place been prized beyond its real value. Today, that unenviable eminence is accorded to the nation. Fascism, communism and, even democracy are all guilty of placing the nation above all other political entities by assuming that it alone carries the kind of reality which justifies sacrifice. No doubt in time this phase will pass, to be replaced by another equally mistaken. For the increase in population, unless it is severely controlled, will do nothing to abate the worship of political organization and the sacrifice of all other values to it. The degree of attention accorded politics is the measure of its corruption, for men have other pursuits, many of which are more worthy of sacrifice, and these are hurt by the interference of what ought to be an invisible and silent facilitation.

Section 1. The Corruption of Leaders: Malversation

Malversation is defined as the use of public office for private ends. It has two forms: one, when the private ends are those of a ruler or ruling group, and, another, when they are those of a dominant class. In either case it represents the replacement of good political behavior by bad. Its seriousness is predicated on the fact that it has the effect of the ultimate betrayal of a people and the defeat of their united efforts to lead a good life. No more heinous or far-reaching crime exists than the selfish use of political power and the manipulation of the sovereignty of the people for the benefit of the holders of public office. No crime is more common.

We have noted in Chapter II that the reduction of all of the needs of the individual would require that he dominate his entire environment, which on the face of it, is impossible. But he tries, and this leads him into inevitable conflict with his fellows. In addition, there are the leftover drives, those drives which continue to exist after the needs have been temporarily reduced. His craving for power is insatiable, and he will stop at nothing to gain it.

There are two kinds of drives: the drive to dominate the entire environment which cannot be reduced, and the leftover drive for needs he can reduce. These are particularly strong in the politician whose professional life lies in somewhat the same direction. He is a holder of power; and the inclination to resort to force, in excess of his authority for his own ends rather than for the legitimate ends of the state he serves, is almost inevitable. It constitutes the most virulent danger in practical politics. The forthrightness of action lends to the behavior of the practical politician a kind of endorsement of absoluteness which the total social situation in which he is involved seldom warrants. The legitimate powers of good government are constantly under the necessity of getting rid of the absolute authority or at least of holding it within bounds.

Governments are called into existence to establish and preserve order. But order requires regulation. Excessive behavior does not allow the politician to stop there but urges him to go on to exercise control. For it is but a short logical distance from regulation to control. To declare what cannot be allowed, to announce what will not be supported while not necessarily involving legal prohibitions or sanctions, inclines citizens toward what can be allowed and what will be supported, and compels the requisite decisions respecting positive actions. Thus the politician who is called in to provide "transparent facilitation" ends by running things dictatorially. From furnishing the means, he shifts to imposing ends.

I have been talking thus far about strong men in politics who are inclined to rule for themselves. But it is just as true of weak men in office. Corruption can issue from weakness as much as from strength, and, bad politics can result from the loss of political power as well as from an excessive use of it. The Aaron Burr conspiracy is an illustration. The corruption in the central government of the United States was greater under the administration of weak Presidents, such as Grant, than under strong ones.

Corrupt politicians have their own methods of working and their own rules of deviation. Very probably, an examination of history in terms of the intrigues and cheating which has been practiced would not differ too much because of time and place. There are usually more ways of doing a thing wrong than of doing it right, but not all are as strategically effective. Therefore, a monotonous pattern emerges even in the case of malversation. Those who wish to circumvent the law appeal to its ambiguities with the same degree of assurance as those who wish to administer it with justice. The dishonest put on the same face as the honest.

So much for the phenomenon of malversation on the part of a ruler or ruling group. We have yet to discuss the same phenomenon when it occurs on the part of a ruling class.

Politically, it is the tendency of some part of the state—in this instance an entire social class—to use the whole of the state power for its own ends, and to justify this action by identifying its interests with the state's and thus to act solely for itself on the assumption that it is acting for the state. Marx and Engels evidently thought there was no other arrangement possible in the state, that the dominant class was always the propertied class, and the state its instrument.

Certainly such a situation has existed at times. It existed in the Western democracies more often before capitalism was modified by the rise of strong labor unions and the politics of the "welfare state." Remnants of it still exist and are still harmful, as for example in the Congress of Industrial Organizations and in the National Association of Manufacturers. A parody occurred recently when the president of a large industrial concern announced solemnly that what was good for his company was good for the country.

But there is no change in the type of corruption when a "dictatorship of the proletariat" takes over. A small class still dominates, for the proletariat does not dictate. "The Party" does, and the Party is after all only a small part of the proletariat. When a limited class or an interest group identifies its interests with those of the state, the result is harmful, and can equally be labelled malversation along with the corruption of the single official or head of state.

The dominant class, Marxists included, do not hesitate to deceive the masses by invoking one kind of principle for another kind of practice. Every dominant class insists that it is acting in the best interests of the country and, beyond the country, in the interests of mankind. This often takes strange forms. In the ritual of politics, it is not too unusual to find that up is down. To argue for world peace but foment revolution abroad is the method currently approved and employed by the Soviet Union.

Malversation is not always the result of deliberate corruption. The use of public office for private ends can occur in other ways, and in some ways inadvertently. One example is what occurs through the growth of Big Government. At local levels it may mean supporting deadheads by giving an increased number of jobs to incompetents. At the state or national level it may occur because conflicts arise in areas which have not yet been defined. When developments occur contrary to public interest, new governmental bureaus must be created and new officials appointed to deal with them. With the spread of drugs, a Food and Drug Act was passed and a new department given existence. The same thing happened with the increase in travel by airplane. And now with the need for safety devices in automobiles and the prevention of air pollution, more departments will be made and more officials appointed.

In modern industrial cultures, where the requisite productivity can be reached with the labor of very few individuals, the governmental machinery can become so large that it constitutes an appreciable segment of the population. The ratio of governmental employees to other citizens may rise to a percentage that indicates a kind of malversation since it means that the state has begun to exist in order to be operated. This has happened in the United States as well as in the Soviet Union.

Malversation is the most monstrous crime it is possible to commit against society because a properly functioning social system is mankind's only hope for attaining the good life. And the good life here means the moral life, the true, the beautiful life. The only remedy possible seems to be to change the aims of an aggressive leadership in order to shift the nature of prestige and gain. Somehow the elegance of leadership must be marked out in a way other than that which is achieved through victory in status rivalry. Leadership must not be indicated so strongly by putting social distance between leader and people. The world could well follow the traditional practices of the Eskimo for whom voluntary agreement requires no organized reinforcement and whose leaders gain nothing from their position.

In cultures with large populations and advanced technologies, all political distinction operates to the disadvantage of the society. The leaders, whether political, military or ecclesiastical, seem to be prestigious in proportion to the extent to which they can seize personal advantage. But men will work as hard for prestige whatever established form it takes, and surely it could take other forms. It could take the form of obligation rather than privilege, of pride in responsibility rather than of concealed irresponsibility based on personal advantage.

Section 2. The Corruption of Individuals: The Nature of Man

In Chapter II the aggressive and ambivalent nature of individual man was set forth. There is inherent political corruption in the competition for need-reductions, in left-over drives, and in demands of the individual for controlling his entire environment. When we stop to consider that the state is an attempt to make a political order out of an aggregate of such individuals, it is easy to understand the difficulties. The political corruption of an individual who stops at nothing to gain his own ends in the state is almost a truism.

In every society there is a subculture of violence; in the most orderly states, it may remain at a minimum of subsidence and so be hardly noticeable. But because it is a natural consequence of the destructive side of aggression it can become organized and express itself through a majority when the state engages in war. However, in the best of times it is always there, and it can be increased quite easily, often to the point of threatening the internal security of the state through a series of episodes involving vandalism, protest, revolt, or civil war. It may merely be an outlet for aggression, or it may contain idealists and revolutionaries, as was the case with the subculture of violence in Czarist Russia prior to the revolution of 1914.

In any case, it is necessary to recognize the character of this subculture and its permanent presence in any concentrated population. There is in larger cities a kind of human detritus made up of poverty-stricken and ignorant individuals whose good fellowship has been eroded by the harshness of their slum environment, leaving them with naked and unfocused aggression.

There is little reason to belabor a point which has already been made and of which it will be necessary to remind ourselves again, especially when we come to consider the prevalence of wars. It is an irrefrangible part of the nature of individual man that he is com-

petitive and destructive as well as cooperative and constructive, and
therefore only half of his nature is able to lend itself to conformity
within the state. The other half can be organized only for un-
harmonized ends, for ends which lead to wars and too often to the
destruction of the state. In periods of peace, the need to reduce aggression sits uneasily on the citizen who is busily engaged in reducing other needs.

Perhaps it would be helpful to view the situation somewhat more
closely, as it appears to the citizen himself when he looks at the
state and at his own position within it. We shall see in at least three
of his relationships to state power that he is led into a morass of
political corruption because of dilemmas which are involved in the
ambivalence of his reactions. The citizen suffers from not being
the state, from legitimate competition with other citizens, and from
the restrictions imposed by the established morality.

First, the needs of the citizen can be reduced only within limits.
Yet he is not the state. Individually and separately, he can see no
cogent reason why he should not be his own supreme political authority, why he cannot impose his own private morality on society,
and why he should not be the prime benefactor of its prosperity.
Individuals tend both to act in terms of expediency and to defend
their actions in terms of ideals. The more limited and selfish the
former, the more detached and lofty the latter. The traits of the old
Pithecanthropus, which he has brought up with him through many
millennia of generations, prevent him from truly acknowledging to
himself that any of his instincts must be curbed in the interest of
living together with his fellows closely packed in villages, towns
and cities. Deep down within his animal nature, he rebels against
any restrictions, knowing that if he himself were the last authority
to which he would have to submit, those restrictions would not
exist.

Politics can be overdone, and there is an area in which the autonomy of the individual prevails over all other considerations. It
has happened many times that the individual has championed lost
causes at the expense of his happiness, his security, and even his life.
Moreover in doing so, he thought he was defending the right, as
indeed he may have been. To save nothing is no disgrace provided
that what he fights for is worth saving, and there are heroes whose

efforts may be considered tragic; so, because tragedy is the victory
of the vanquished, their efforts are not for nothing. There are values
beyond the present, and what recurs may be nonexistent yet may return. So it was with the heroes of the Resistance who offered opposition to Hitler both inside and outside Germany during the
Nazi regime.

At the same time, the individual shrinks in horror from the
responsibility which would be his were he to be delivered to his
own political custody. Decision-making is not for every man, and
indeed few have the initiative, forthrightness, and intelligence to
commit themselves to decisions by which they must abide and for
which they themselves must assume entire resonsibility. So they
need the state for this function. It is true that they need the state
and also that they are irked by its restrictions, a dilemma from which
a certain measure of political corruption is sure to result.

Secondly, it is in the same vein that the citizen chafes under the
necessity of keeping within the limits imposed by the state his competition for those material goods which hold out the promise of need-
reductions. Left to his own devices, he would become so aggressive
that his behavior would tend to end the competition once and for
all. What Hobbes has described as "the war of all against all" is always just under the surface. Legal restrictions limit him to avenues
of legitimate competition when he would earnestly not wish to be
so limited.

At the same time, he seeks the approval of his fellow citizens,
and their approbation is important to him. Every individual wants
social approval; every individual must belong to social groups and
not merely interest groups, but groups based perhaps on himself as a
center. He cannot have both the elimination of competition
through the defeat of his fellows and at the same time their support.
Yet he needs both; he needs victory over others and support from
them; from the former he earns their respect and from the latter
their affection. His dilemma is that in gaining both, political corruption is inevitable.

Third, the need-reductions of individual citizens are often prevented by the state. Where private enterprise is prohibited or where
the emphasis of the state is on other values, even his primary needs
may often go unreduced. In the former case, we have the example

of the Soviet Union and Communist China which do not allow their citizens to engage in private capitalistic enterprises. We have also the example of India where starving millions will not eat beef because of religious prohibitions.

At the same time, the citizen cannot survive without the state and its morality to organize a continuity for his need-reductions. The laws of the state are not all restrictive; many are permissive and facilitative. Thus he must have a morality backed by the state, and yet he objects to it. The dilemma inevitably produces political corruption, since it requires of him that he behave on different occasions in different fashions.

No state could afford a police force of sufficient size and strength to keep the majority of its citizens honest through the exercise of sheer physical coercion. The state rests on a basis of voluntary association and that is what makes honesty possible. It should always be kept in mind that there is no hope for the state unless its citizens defend its established morality as they would their wives and children. No stronger element exists than the established morality which, as we have seen, is the very basis and texture of the state itself.

Section 3. The Corruption of the Masses: "Social Tyranny"

"Social tyranny"—the term is Tocqueville's—may be described as the tyranny of the many over the few. It is usually a matter of accepted ideas, of tastes and preferences, of customs and institutions, but not usually of speculative thought. It may be the few who advance culture, but it is the many who maintain it. Novelty and innovation are correctly interpreted as threats to maintenance. Any change, even improvement, is read as a challenge to the established order, which for that matter it assuredly is. John Stuart Mill, like Tocqueville, saw the dangers to progress in social tyranny. And there is an additional one, and this consists in the cheapening process of mass applications. By the time an elegant or subtle conception spreads to the masses, a lot of excellence has rubbed off, and it is not as good as it was.

Here too is a dilemma. For every productive genius wishes his gains to be shared by the masses. But in their efforts he knows the gains will be somewhat cheapened and spoiled. So basically he rejects both alternatives, for he does not wish the quality of his work to be lost.

By way of illustration, it may be pointed out that the dangers of social tyranny today are greater than ever because of two new factors which have come into the picture: the rise of the great populations and the rise of the mass media. There are vastly more living people and far better methods of reaching them. The masses express themselves most directly through mob action. Such phenomena do not date from the rise of the great populations but have been increased and enlarged by them. Civil disorders and riots represent the masses acting on their own. No better illustration could be had of the material of humanity in its raw state, unshaped by political order. It is in this way that humanity endeavors now and then to shed its acquired cultural properties and to fall to the most basic condition of humanity. Left to themselves and free of all restrictions, the natural expression of people consists in random and unfocused aggression of a destructive nature. Evidently, some sort of political order is an absolute human necessity.

It is a common mistake to suppose that civil disorders are caused by poverty. If this were the case, the poorer countries such as India would be in a continual state of unrest. But the poor and underprivileged are too apathetic to behave in such a dynamic fashion. Considerable energy is required to disrupt a society, to get a riot going, to inspire a mob to action. The subculture of violence is conducted by those who have enjoyed sufficient food and shelter to render them fit for vigorous undertakings. Solving the problem of poverty, however greatly this is desirable for other reasons, will not by itself prevent unfocused aggression.

Unfortunately, the control of the mass media by demagogues is more often than not used to reinforce the prejudices of the masses—those illogical or counterfactual beliefs which are held emotionally and defended by means of fallacies. In this way social tyranny is self-reenforcing and hence becomes more tyrannical. The number of citizens who can be counted among the masses is so vast in proportion that the elite tends to hide in what can best be described as a kind of open underground, and there tends to become overwhelmed. When men exist in great numbers they seem inevitably the victims of tyranny in one way or another, and tyranny surely is a form of political corruption.

We have noted the tyranny of the many over the few. Now I wish to point also to the tyranny of the few over the many. There is a property of the masses which makes them easy victims of demagogues and other self-seeking individuals posing as friends and leaders. The masses demand absolute truth from those who would lead them, and usually they receive it from the government, either as authorized by the state itself or by some other institution. Now inasmuch as many if not all of the "absolute truths" they are given are false, the result is political corruption. So long as this prevails, there will be trouble in the state, for the average citizen is incapable of skepticism, and the craving to believe in absolutes delivers the masses to those unscrupulous persons who claim absolute authority; this situation renders malversation inevitable. Moreover, there are always a number of competing absolutes, a situation which opens the way to those who wish to impose their own chosen absolute but understand that first they must free the masses from the tyranny of those absolutes they know to be false. Under these circumstances, violent conflict and political corruption are again inevitable.

The tyranny of the few over the many—a product of the degree of corruption that the politician can "get by" with—is made possible by the gullibility of the voting public. The average citizen is already prepared to be led, for this is his normal stance. It includes a readiness to idealize his leaders and to resist the suggestion that the corruption involved may far exceed what appears on the surface of social action. He is unwilling to suspect that things are not as his leaders tell him they are. So he is an inadvertent party to the duplicity. The leaders themselves know this and are encouraged to take even greater advantage, since there is clearly to be no penalty.

The only remedy against the perilous use of absolutes and the consequent social tyranny lies in the hope that those who have learned to conduct their personal lives in terms of probabilities will increase in number to a majority and demand the abolition of all absolutes. A government operated in terms of high probabilities rather than in terms of absolutes would have to be an open system. And an open system is one with built-in provisions for its own improvement and for the correction of errors. The state at its best functions as a facilitative extension of each individual; at its worst, the citizen is captive; but an open system would have no captives, for it would not be exploitative.

Section 4. The Corruption of Institutions: Social Organization

Political organizations begin at the lowest level, the level of city machines and governmental bureaus.

Local political organizations often lend themselves to systematic arrangements of bribery. City politics is characterized in this way. The political "boss" is often the channel through which special favors and monetary rewards are exchanged. Political power can often become corrupt in the hands of the lobbyist, and the practice of lobbying generally is a morally tender one. In California in 1949, it was contended that a master lobbyist was the most important political force; he was able to appoint officials, get laws enacted, and otherwise act like the supreme head. In addition and since the Twenty-first Amendment to the Constitution repealed the Eighteenth in 1933, the influence of organized crime has reached upward in politics and proved itself more powerful than some city and state governments.

But bribery can reach all the way to the highest branches of government. The corruption of public officials by industrialists is not uncommon. Lincoln Steffens in his *Autobiography* was at pains to point out that, while business men complained loudly of the nefariousness of politicians, it was the business men themselves who had been responsible for bribing them. Politicians, he explained patiently, could not be "bought" if there was not someone to buy them. Witness the Teapot Dome scandal of 1922-23 when two members of President Harding's cabinet were found by a Senate committee to have accepted substantial sums in return for leasing oil fields secretly to private interests. The adherence to established morality is stronger at national than local levels. It often happens that the national government has to step in to correct local corruption. This occurred just recently in connection with bad meat which is sold within a state and which does not therefore come under federal regulations concerning sanitary slaughtering.

The corruption of government by business is not the only variety of corrupting political institutions. Another variety is the result of the competition between divisions of government. That there is competition between the Army, Navy, and Air Force is now public knowledge. It often happens that the Foreign Office is at odds with the Treasury Department, or local government with the national government. Such internecine conflicts are forms of corruption since they do serious damage to the state.

Even more serious is the domination of the military over civilian sectors of the government. The military may know best how to plan and fight wars—even though all the important technological gains such as the tank, automatic weapon, bombing plane and atomic bomb have come from civilian inventors—but they should not be the ones to decide when and with whom wars are to be fought or what the policy of the government should be in peacetime. They do not have the requisite knowledge and are not specialists in professional politics. General Grant was one of the worst American Presidents, and General Franco has seen to it that Spain lags behind all other countries in western Europe in scientific, industrial, and agricultural development.

The corruption of institutions may result from their excessive or defective functioning.

Excessive functioning is perhaps the more familiar variety. The corruption of bureaucracy generally was observed by Max Weber, and may be described as that corruption of officialdom in which form takes precedence over content; when the institution itself becomes the end it was supposed to serve. The overzealous official who tends to forget that the purpose of his office is not his own self-aggrandizement is a familiar figure.

The defective functioning of bureaucracy can be equally disastrous. When the bureaucrat fails to perform his duties, the defective use of office becomes as obstructive as the excessive variety. Bureaucrats do tend to take advantage of their positions, particularly when they are appointed rather than elected. The occupant of many a political office owes his appointment to the payment of favor on the part of some higher administrator, and as a consequence there seems little incentive to work at the job. The bureaucrat who occupies his office as though there were no obligations attached to it, the benefactor of nepotism, and the incompetent, all enjoy the emoluments of office without seeing it as requiring from them the fulfillment of any duties.

The protection of the citizens against the abuse of government, with its control of the armed forces and the mass media, consists of many devices. The most recent is the office of the ombudsman; another is the proper kind of publicity. No corner of an executive's life should be safe from the press. Abuses are promoted when it is possible for the executive to hide. A simple law would prevent much corruption. If it were necessary for every public official to publish his income tax returns in the years before, during, and after he takes office, the possibility of financial gain from his political position would be diminished. There would be no hampering of efficiency in such a regulation, and corruption would be reduced, especially at lower levels.

Section 5. The Corruption of States: The Tyranny of Governments

The state itself can be the source of political corruption in at least two ways. The structure of the state can be inherently bad, or a good structure can be put to bad uses. Let us glance at each briefly.

The structures of states which do not operate for the good of the majority of citizens, I define as bad states. Whether this criterion is sufficient will be argued in another connection later, but its legitimacy will not be questioned, only its exclusivity. Totalitarian regimes and dictatorships are of this character. Plato wished to substitute reason for violence in human affairs but the competition for need-reductions has made intraspecific aggression a fact of life. The Marxists have gone further, however, for they have not only recognized the existence of violence in politics but endorsed it. Despite whatever progress they make, such endorsement will set the hope of human cooperation back many centuries. It has already appeared in the conflicts between communist countries—Communist China and the Soviet Union, for instance.

The employment of violence, legitimate or illegitimate, is hardly new, and, if it is still going on, that cannot be said to be a gain. Is the use of violence ever legitimate, for that matter? The "divine right of kings" which often justified a solitary individual in running the state for his own private benefit, fascism which claims legitimacy in using the state for the benefit of a party, class or race—these also fall short in this regard and have the additional fatal shortcoming that they are always directed toward war and conquest. Governments which are designed solely for war are not supposed to lose wars; yet no government designed solely for war wins all wars; therefore, governments designed solely for war are self-defeating. They are sources of extreme political corruption.

The ugly facts of social life must be faced, and the ferocity and double-dealing must be recognized if there is to be any ground for improvement. Consider some weaknesses occasioned by the Nazi offensive in the West: the support of Hitler by the German people so long as they thought him victorious, France's rapid and complete collapse before the German armies, and the Pope's unwillingness to take a firm stand against Nazi atrocities.

Fascism illustrates the phenomenon of governments which exceed their proper function. It is the task of the state to make the good life of citizens possible, not in itself to become the aim of that life. The state is intended to serve its citizens, not absorb them. When a state enters obtrusively and forcefully into a citizen's life, then it is exceeding its proper function. Such a structure, even though it had Hegel's approval because of the superior quality of wholes over parts, violates the canon adopted here which recognizes the autonomy of the parts, in this case each of the political integrative levels, including that of the individual citizen, who certainly does have inalienable rights against the state.

Whenever the government of a country becomes so large and important that it outweighs everything else, a variety of corruption occurs. Big government is often bad government, as when a disproportionate part of the population earns a living as government employees. In the United States in 1960 with a population of 179,-

323,175, 8,353,000 worked for the government at some level. Since then the number of citizens employed by the government has risen even more sharply in proportion to population.

Often, the efforts of the various branches of the government are not coordinated and the work of some agencies may be at odds with others. In 1968, the Department of Agriculture was subsidizing tobacco farmers while the Surgeon General's office was conducting a campaign against the smoking of cigarettes and the National Institute of Health was paying for inquiries about lung cancer from smoking.

The multiplicity of political jurisdiction makes some kind of confusion inevitable in the United States, the city, county, state, and federal government have overlapping authority. Very strong governments tend to exploit their citizens, and it is often forgotten that countries do not exist in order to be governed but are governed in order to exist. Yet because, as we noted in Chapter II, the state is the repository of a degree of aggression of which individuals are separately incapable, a certain amount of corruption in the state is inevitable. It cannot be said that a certain amount of corruption in the individual is also inevitable. The argument can be presented quite simply. No countries behave well; some people behave well; therefore no countries behave as well as some people.

A good state can be corrupted into a bad one. An arm of the government brought into existence to perform one function may perform another. Consider the Central Intelligence Agency in the United States, intended solely to deal with external affairs, the charter of which specifically excludes "domestic operations." Yet, the CIA has been charged with actually setting up a Domestic Operations Division. Again, an arm of the government may engage in external affairs other than those intended. Consider in this connection the preoccupation of an espionage system which is supposed to ferret out the military secrets of a potential enemy but which often engages in intense spying on a rival espionage system.

Certainly the worst of all forms of corruption of the state which can result from its functioning, or malfunctioning, is war. Since I propose to treat this topic in a later chapter, I will not discuss it here but merely observe that it constitutes the largest form of the state's corruption.

In the case of a good government, like a democracy, the weakness of popular sovereignty may have a corrupting influence. Popular participation in politics has its bad as well as its good side. Its bad side is that it makes for concentration on an institution which at best is unobtrusive and facilitative. Politics ought to be an institution *by* which, not *for* which, the country is run. Consider some of the methods employed in obtaining the consent of the people, methods which tend to elevate the rabble rouser, showman, spellbinder, opportunist, and propagandist, rather than the gifted and dedicated administrator and lawmaker.

It is important that government established to provide an arena for individual need-reductions not be allowed to interfere with those need-reductions. For politics provides for the activities of cultural elements and is not intended to take over their governance. When it does so it amounts to serious corruption. Governent supplies the means and acts as a facility; it is not the end and should not interpose itself in the culture except as a regulating force. It should make no decisions respecting culture, and indeed none that do not concern strictly regulatory matters.

Such political corruption can of course be brought about by the citizens themselves when they look to the state for other than legitimate political services. Except for the young, elderly and infirm, no one should depend upon the state for economic support.

The state is not a producer but a regulator of goods. Any economic resources it has must of necessity be the result of the labors of citizens, and no more than an absolute minimum of their labors ought to be devoted to such a purpose. The state is a regulative institution, not a constitutive one; and so it should have no goods of its own to divide, no economic favors to grant. The corruption of politics occurs when the institution of the state becomes its own end.

The larger the political unit, the better for mankind. The biological fact that there is only one human species means that a single government should suffice. The species admittedly is not ready for this yet, and we shall have more to say about it toward the end of the book. Meanwhile, we might use it as a rough guide to one kind of political corruption in the state. If the state is a nation and looks to cooperation with other nations, even to uniting with them in a larger political organization, that is good. But if the state as a nation limits its cooperation beyond itself and instead looks down to its own lesser units as parts of an ultimate structure, that is bad.

A good illustration is to be found currently in the emerging nations of Africa. To combine tribes into some semblance of nationhood is certainly a step in the right direction and amounts to good politics; but to exhibit, as a few of them have, some chauvinistic features, then it is bad politics. I cite some of the worst abuses of nationalism: the worship of the political leader; his absolute rule by fiat; warlike attitudes toward neighboring states; the expectation of aid from more advanced industrial countries, such as financial grants and obligatory technical assistance. Jealousy in the demands of the developing state is the rule rather than the exception. They ask for privileges long surrendered by the older and more powerful nations, such as the immunity of diplomatic representatives. In this sense, fervent nationalism can amount to a backward step.

Political corruption occurs when principles are invoked to conceal the true nature of actual practices. This means employing state machinery for ends less than the state as a whole; for ends which indeed may be private and even inimical to the best interest of the state. For a contemporary example we have only to note that those who argue for "states' rights"—certainly a legitimate claim—mean to maintain the superiority of the political position of the whites over that of Negroes. A similar corruption is found in the plea for international justice when a great power wishes to impose its own rule on weaker states. Unfortunately for principles, there is only one recognized virtue in practical politics: success, and only one vice: failure. The venal nature of man is such that there is no system he cannot corrupt.

Established morality is what makes the social organization of the state possible and as such enjoins the state to accept and administer a theory of good. But while there is a clear dominance of ethics over politics in importance, there is also a clear dominance of politics over ethics in importunateness. Morality may, it is true, determine how every man should conduct himself as the citizen of a state, but politics is the structure of the state. The state is the largest form ever taken by an overt social morality and is kept alive by maintaining it. There is no government when there is a breakdown of order, and morality provides that order, but the order must be maintained.

It is essential, then, that the citizens be educated in the part played in their individual lives by the political order. Paradoxically, a good government intrudes less than a bad government on the privacy of citizens. In order to have a private life, some of the effort of citizens must be devoted to public matters. This would present no problem were there proper understanding. An education in political responsibilities could perhaps furnish necessary safeguards.

Section 6. The Corruption of Artifacts: Tools

Material tools have made human life possible. Ever since the species first emerged as a species, tools have played a crucial role. It is not too surprising to discover that artifacts, without which there could be no state, can themselves be a source of political corruption. We may note a few of the ways in which this has happened.

Abuses of the control of property in the state are well known. Concentration of ownership seems to be one of the most familiar ways in which such abuses occur. It often happens under a system of private ownership that there are comparatively few rich and many poor, and the rich get richer while the poor get poorer. This leads to luxury on one hand and privation on the other. Unless there are effective remedies, this may lead to revolution. I should add parenthetically that private ownership does not always have such bad results. It has not had them in the modern "welfare state," as in Sweden, and so it need not have them in well-run democracies.

But gross inequalities in wealth certainly are capable of furnishing prime examples of political corruption. For it can happen that the wealthy few get the political power in their hands and subsequently run the state for their own benefit, with disastrous results to everybody, including themselves or their descendants. Oligarchical dictatorships and revolutions were known to the Greeks, and they have been known ever since.

The very existence of some artifacts is a source of political corruption. Efficiency is often a bad thing. Consider the weapons of war and their uses. I shall have much more to say about war as an intrinsic political corruption in a later chapter. Here it is important only to note that the greater the efficiency in devising and employing the weapons of war, the worse for human beings.

Efficient military hardware concentrates power in the hands of those in charge of the state, and so makes them a greater force for bad politics as well as for good. The more complex the system the more efficient, but also the greater number of opportunities for malversation. The interlocking and complicated systems of modern industrial technology extend many benefits to the people but may do harm to individual autonomy, to citizens who become numbers on a card or punches on a tape—mere items in a statistical survey which computes the resources of the country in terms of manpower or skill. It is appalling to think what a leader who is also commander-in-chief of the armed forces could do when armed with the missile and the rigged hydrogen bomb. A less efficient weapons system might lessen the risk of damage to the state caused by an error in judgment.

Any attempt to suggest a remedy for the corruption of tools must first presuppose the knowledge of their total social involvement. For tools are used only in the service of individuals, interest groups or institutions, ending with the largest of institutions, the state itself. The "gross national product" is divided into goods and services. It has never been planned as a whole and to do so would involve more information than is at present in anyone's possession. For property is involved as well as "goods and services," and they cannot be separated from it. What we are dealing with in the case of tools involves primarily what is now fashionable to call property or goods. Services always involve tools.

The corruption of tools must be considered to be the activity of the society looked at from the perspective of its tools in so far as that society is adversely affected. The only criterion we have to measure the absence of corruption is an old one: due proportionality, or the extent to which things are out of proper order. Pending the accumulation of statistics which could be computerized, judgments will have to depend upon the intuition of leaders—a very tenuous and easily deflected affair. But due proportionality is the ideal on which to set our sights for we have no other.

Section 7. The Corruption of Artifacts: Languages

Political corruption through the misuse of language is a more familiar affair than it is through the misuse of tools, probably because tools have only recently been developed to such a dangerous point, whereas the misuse of language is much older.

The political corruption which is due to the misuse of language occurs chiefly in the form of propaganda. Propaganda may be described as the promulgation of false knowledge in order to bring about certain desired effects. It exerts a kind of psychological pressure in order to win acceptance for a particular viewpoint. A deliberate campaign of propaganda employs verbal weapons which include lies, exaggeration, distortion, threats, and even the promise of rewards, all of which may be false. It may include also the withholding of information by means of the avoidance of communication.

A skillful demagogue can, through the use of the dramatic lie, lead the multitude into choosing his policies even though they go against the public interest. The successful statesman will declare himself in favor of the loftiest ideals while engaging in the most nefarious practices. In the days of Mussolini, Hitler and Franco, Huey Long once observed that he planned to become the fascist dictator of the United States, but, knowing the American bias, he expected to run for office on an antifascist platform.

False knowledge consists of false propositions parading as true ones. The feeling that a proposition is true is often sufficient to gain its general acceptance. False knowledge has a certain political value which makes its use attractive. It is charming because it is simple and therefore readily understood, appealing because emotional and therefore easy to spread, effective because directed and therefore easy to follow in action. It is often more negative than positive, and calls for destruction more often than construction. It is exciting, invigorating, stimulating, vital, and hard to combat.

No reasonable truth can compete with the emotionalism of falsehood. We can only hope that in the long run it will be reversed, for in the long run falsehoods have the opportunity to spread

and stand exposed in all their failure. The only assignment left to
men of good will is to survive the horrors which may and only too
often do occur in the short run.

The role of false knowledge in determining political decisions
and actions can hardly be overestimated. One has only to emphasize
the conception, already held by most citizens, of the glory of their
nation and incidentally of themselves. Political leaders encourage
such concepts even when knowing better; but often leaders, too, are
its victims. Nasser must be aware of the almost total incompetence
and incapacity of the Egyptians in warfare, but de Gaulle probably
believes what he tells the French people about the potential might
of France as a third force on a par with that of the United States
and Soviet Union.

Deceptions in politics are practiced all the time, so much so
that one might describe them as fairly routine. But this does not
make them any different from what they are. President Johnson at
no time informed the American people that he was gradually leading them into a full-scale war against North Viet Nam, with the
use of half a million soldiers. The conflict was escalated so gradually as to constitute a first class deception.

Again, in our own times, there is the constant call for pacifism
on a unilateral basis, as though laying down our arms would prevent wars and end the exploitation and enslavement of our people.
The pleas for international peace from behind the iron curtain are
not matched by pacific practices by the communist countries. It certainly would be an immense help to the promotion of communist
revolutions in non-communist countries if those inclined toward
world peace would decrease their own resistance to it.

The use of truth as a political weapon with recognized power of
its own has hardly been tried except by one man and that in recent times. Gandhi used religion to further politics, and he acknowledged a God of Truth. Besides him, there have been few others, if
any, whereas falsehood has had its adherents, both theoretical and
practical, and the latter have been overwhelming in number. Both
fascism and communism cynically employ strategic falsehoods
to gain their ends, and their adherents even defend this practice.
Marxists define truth as historical and accept no other aspect. But
truth, defined as what can be learned rather than as what we

know, has been the professed ideal of democracies, even though they seldom practice it.

False propositions are more vivid, simple and forceful than corresponding true propositions would be under the same set of circumstances. This makes them appeal to more people and so more useful to working politicians. The citizens of the Soviet Union might not have been willing to undergo the kind of privations they endured while their country was catching up with Western industrialism had they been told the truth about the standard of living of workers in the capitalist nations. Yet there is a calculated risk involved. For truths manufactured to justify any course of action may be successful in the short run but in the end there is always the threat that the facts will prevail.

Could truth as a political ideal not be established in a formal and secular way, its value demonstrated and its function defined? Perhaps it would be best to begin with language and to learn what words mean—what they connote as well as denote. Political words, emotive, factual and general, could be disciplined and their uses supervised, perhaps by a literary academy which would have its political branch operating in an advisory capacity. I would not think that those to whom political words are directed—the electorate—could function as well without the widespread knowledge of the meanings employed in politics. Thus the deliberate cultivation of accurate language in all political matters would inhibit major corruptions in this direction, as Confucius so often pointed out. He gave it perhaps more credit than it was due; but we give it far less.

Political corruption occurs on all political levels and in forms difficult to detect. We have not yet looked at the worst form of political corruption, which is enslavement. This is so grave and widespread that it justifies a separate chapter.

Chapter X

ENSLAVEMENT AND FREEDOM

Section 1. Enslavement

There are many kinds of enslavement, in fact all restrictions can be read that way. One has only to struggle against limitations to feel their constraint. There is, for instance, physical enslavement in the confinement of the human individual to a given time and place, to the living space and time of his brief life span. There is a kind of biological enslavement in the genetic conditions given him by his ancestors and in the responsibilities brought into existence by his progeny. There is a psychological enslavement in the very nature of the individual's own personality which has been imposed upon him by the changes and modifications his experience makes in his inheritance. There is a broad cultural enslavement in the type of ideas and hardware an individual finds already established in his own human and artificial environment. Cultural enslavement can be subdivided into the political, the moral, the economic and the technological varieties.

We shall be concerned in this chapter chiefly with the political variety. In what follows, from the definition on, the political aspects will be uppermost.

I define enslavement as the possession or control of one person by another for selfish purposes. It could be defined also as the condition of being the property of another, but this is an extreme case and, as such, a subclass. The more inclusive version simply means the possession or control of a person for ends not his own. The degree of enslavement varies from the effects of oppressive laws and regulations to the possession of the whole person as chattel. Some trace of enslavement is difficult to avoid. It exists even in the light restrictions which facilitative laws cannot help having as side effects. Any restriction is felt as a form of enslavement since it comes under the heading of control.

Enslavement is something in itself and not merely the opposite of freedom. It has its own characteristics. Enslavement is a condition of non-being, for freedom is a condition of being. It can be said of the man who is not free that to that extent he does not exist in that way. Positive otherness is the consideration here. At least he does not exist as a free and independent person who in virtue of his status as an adult human being has been delivered over to his own responsibility. But such a variety of non-being does exist and is common, and so we shall have to consider it, together with all of its implications.

Everyone who has ever thought about the political range has recognized the prevalence throughout history of some form of slavery. Slaves were chattel among the Greeks, and there is slavery still in the Yemen and a few other, comparatively inaccessible, places. Some of the highest authorities, among them Plato and Aristotle, who devoted themselves to designing ideals, approved of slavery and considered it both natural and necessary.

It is perhaps a question whether one considers the aim of good government to so order the state that there is a hierarchy of subordination, the wealthiest or the best or the most highly authorized being the first and most privileged class, and so on with the others in turn until one comes to the lowest class, which is hardly a class of citizens at all but of slaves who belong to citizens; or to so order the state that all benefit equally from a social order which all equally need.

No doubt the dialectic of human progress, which can be charted as the progress from cannibalism to altruism, takes the human species through strange twistings and turnings, including wholesale abuses such as the official slavery which has been installed as an institution in many societies. Everyone who has taken part in the modern world and who has kept up with the march of history recognizes slavery as wrong. For while slavery has not disappeared altogether, it has diminished, at least in its chattel form, while other considerations, such as altruism, have increased proportionately and have gained as ideals even where not practiced.

Of even greater popularity has been a partial slavery where some social classes are less privileged than others. It consists of prohibiting members of certain social classes from enjoying rights reserved to others. At a period of great scarcity of consumer goods in the Soviet Union, in the early 1930's and 1940's, only members of the Communist Party were allowed to make purchases in stores reserved for them. Economic inequality in capitalist countries imposes a differential with regard to the purchase of such goods. Theoretically anyone anywhere can buy anything that is for sale, while practically only those who have the requisite funds not needed for other purposes can do so.

It may seem odd to include as a form of enslavement varieties of poverty, but poverty sanctioned by law where there is plenty is a form of comparative enslavement, since some human individuals are thereby kept behind a retaining wall of economic preference. Anyone who has ever wished to own something he could not afford will know what I mean. But economic enslavement is the most common modern form and ought to be recognized as such.

It is still a serious theoretical question whether absolute equality in all respects—which is the only condition for the total elimination of enslavement—is justifiable under the rubric of equality.

There is no room here to set forth a complete inventory of the varieties of enslavement. I shall therefore confine myself to mention the most prominent because they are most pertinent. We shall, therefore, consider several varieties of voluntary enslavement. Among them are enslavement due to ignorance and those due to the knowledge of "absolute truth." Voluntary enslavement is not always bad, as we shall presently see.

I should point out that in these considerations the element of recognition is often omitted. In societies, such as that of the ancient Greeks where the institution of slavery was officially established, the slave knew he was a slave. But in other societies where more subtle forms of slavery are found this is not always true. For a slave is no less a slave for not knowing himelf to be one. He suffers as much from his condition but is spared only the painful awareness. The deprivations which ensue remain deprivations, and, if they are serious, he suffers seriously from them.

The voluntary enslavement inherent in ignorance puts a citizen's emotions, and often as a result his person, entirely at the disposal of another. The appeal to violent emotions is among the favored techniques of the demagogue who can at will lead people into almost any precipitate action, often directly against their best interests. Falsehoods, oversimplifications, prejudices, elaborate promises, and threats—all are common to the demagogue. The only remedies are education and the individual's power of reasoning. Admittedly, there are slowly put into effect, and often, by the time they are, damage has been done. The demagogue has the advantage that ordinary man is a believer, and the less demands they make on him, the easier he accepts them.

There is a strong element of truth in the doctrine which has been around since the days of Plato that intelligent men are free and that powers of reasoning are among the greatest individual safeguards. He who is able to think for himself is, at least to that extent, no man's slave. This is on the individual side of course; but there is a social and political side as well, and this consists of the ability to recognize unconventional forms of enslavement. He who knows he is being made a slave is on his way to freedom, but he who does not know is likely to remain a slave and suffer the consequences.

Therefore, "Question the truth of what you have come to believe" is a good maxim, even though the result be to confirm you in your beliefs. Even in the latter case you would then have better reasons for your beliefs and would believe on acceptable and defensible grounds. He who believes for less than good reasons will awaken one day to discover the ground shaking beneath him, and suddenly, and sickeningly, find that he is without a base.

The ally of the demagogue is the absolute truth. The greatest cause of enslavement is the promulgation of the absolute truth as a principle of politics or one from which political consequences follow. The most extreme expression of such a principle is Hegel's when he proclaimed that "The state is the Divine Idea as it exists on earth" and the "march of God through the world." Not many have gone that far, but some who have been influenced by Hegel even at second hand have put his principle into practice, refraining only from his theological justification of it because of an official atheism. The restrictions upon the free flow of ideas which the alleged possession of the absolute truth in any form imposes is a form of thought control and, hence, one kind of enslavement.

As has already been pointed out in many places throughout the early chapters of this book, one problem with absolute truth is the number of contenders for that position that have existed and still make themselves felt today. There is nothing cheaper or more common than the knowledge of the "absolute truth." Almost all theologians have it and many politicians as well. Buddhists are willing to commit suicide by burning themselves to death because of convictions, and communists will readily kill those they cannot succeed in convincing. Both threats have been used in recent years as political weapons. The use of force via religious affiliation is without doubt an indication of the extreme lengths to which adherents of the absolute truth are ready and willing to go. Wars are often the direct result of a conflict between absolute truths. Certainly, the subscription to an absolute truth of any sort is a kind of voluntary enslavement, for it leads the subscriber to behave accordingly even when it is not in his best personal interest to do so.

Once again, free speculation and the awareness of the scarcity of reliable knowledge is the only remedy. The fear of false knowledge is the beginning of wisdom, and an examination of the grounds on which all information rests might reduce the degree to which beliefs are accepted. Only the amateur is sure of what he "knows," while the intelligent man adds to his areas of ignorance. It is not only what is known that we must learn but even what in fact is not yet known; for we must always be in a position to add slowly but solidly to our store of information. Bold speculation, combined with a cautious acceptance of the truth of propositions, is the best equipment with which to approach the possibilities of reliable knowledge; and this is no less true in political matters which may be personally disastrous than in others where the dangers are lessened.

The result of such deliberations brings us to a paradox. For while enslavement is politically bad, a certain amount of it is neces-sary. No social order is possible without laws, and no laws exist which are not to some extent restrictive. To the extent that they are restrictive, there follows a certain measure of enslavement. For example, no government can be conducted without revenues to meet legitimate expenses. There is no source of income except the earnings of the individual citizen and taxation is a form of ap-propriation. But since it is necessary, in a well-run state a modicum of enslavement is unavoidable. Restrictions are the price of freedom.

It is in this connection that some authorities have recognized the voluntary nature of some forms of enslavement. Laws seem less restrictive when citizens accept them gladly and regard them as liberative. Plato described an older time when the laws afforded no controls and when all citizens were voluntary slaves to the law. The agreement to abide by the law must depend upon the recogni-tion by all citizens that the law as framed is just, and that the good life is furthered by a happy adherence to it. Freedom as we shall see is not merely a matter of casting off restraints but in finding the proper course of action.

Section 2. Freedom

There are as many kinds of freedom as there are kinds of en-slavement; but, as with the consideration of enslavement at the out-set of the previous section, we shall deal primarily with the political variety.

I define freedom as the capacity for latitudes of action within prescribed limits. Political freedom, then, would be the capacity for latitudes of moral action within the limits by which a moral or-der is prescribed.

I limit deliberately the definition of freedom to action. For, while the capacities of the individual include feeling and thought, these are not strictly speaking to be held within the political pur-view. The feelings are under neither individual nor political con-trol; an individual feels what he feels and that is that; it is the interpretation which is the variable. But that takes us into the domain of thought.

Freedom of thought is definitely under the control of the individual and there secure from political interference. He can think his own thoughts. The thoughts are indeed the last stronghold of privacy, but, while there is no thought control, there is thought influence. Influences issuing from the state may affect his thinking and usually do, the extreme case being what has recently been labelled brain washing by the Chinese communists but which is as old as socially held beliefs involving philosophical systems. There have been sufficient instances that the individual, armed with confirmed beliefs, has resisted invasions of privacy.

In order to understand political freedom, it is necessary to introduce a distinction between the individual and the citizen. The citizen is the individual in his political connections. The citizen is the politically responsible individual. No equality of individuals exists, only of citizens. Equality is limited to privilege; there is no equality of obligation which has to be measured by unequal contributive capacities. The individual may want freedoms the citizen could not ask for and would not be entitled to, such as the right to enjoy entirely unrestricted liberty. The citizen should only want liberty that will not interfere with the liberty of others. Liberty conceived as the unlimited power to act without interference does not exist in any well-ordered state.

The question of liberty arises in connection with action in the case of the physical invasion of privacy. Does the citizen have the right to be secure in the privacy of his living quarters and his place of business? For instance, does the government have the right to install miniaturized listening devices in his home or office? Does it have the right to tap his telephone?

Here we reach the outer limits where the issue is debatable. It would seem that the decision in such cases should rest upon the degree of threat to the national security which prompts the invasion of privacy by the government. It is a restriction of freedom, no doubt, but how serious? Consider in this connection the loss of freedom which would be involved in a successful attack on his government.

Freedom is actually found in the course of action permissible to the citizen within his society. Freedom is always one integrative level above determinism. Determinism at any given level is freedom at the level above; determinism is what makes freedom possible by providing necessary facilities. The degree of freedom may be defined by the number of courses opened, the choice of determinisms. Admittedly, some societies provide more freedom than others, but then it is true that in some societies more freedom is desired by the citizen than it is in others. Not every society subscribes to a political system which suggests to the citizen that he has or lacks freedom to a degree which might be desirable. Thus, the citizen's attitude toward freedom is a function of his relation to the society and the type of society.

Freedom is the gift of law and order. Outside the regime of law, there is no freedom, only anarchy which makes freedom impossible. It is true of course that laws may be restrictive and inhibit freedom, but the fact that bad laws restrict freedom does not mean that lawfulness as such is opposed to freedom, for it is not. Given legitimate law, permissive law, orderly law, then freedom is possible. Absolute or total freedom is impossible in any case, since it is not the nature of the human animal to be without some restriction. But the kind of limited freedom which makes it possible for the individual to exercise all his powers and to develop all those potentialities from which neither he, his society or his species will suffer harm is not only allowed by law but indeed provided by law. Thus, freedom and lawfulness are inseparable but not inherently opposite.

The history of human liberty discloses that a society seldom starts with it; freedom nearly always must be won. It is usually an account of tyranny followed by rebellion, which as often as not ends with greater tyranny, and so the unhappy cycle must start all over again. Rebellions always come in the name of liberty but their results do not always provide it. There is an asymptotic improvement in the human social condition. It gradually approaches betterment but not without retrogressive periods when economic and political conditions actually worsen.

The endless debate between those who defend individual liberties and those who insist upon the superiority of the state overlooks the autonomy of levels. Clearly both the individual and the state have their own justification and each must be protected against undue encroachments by the other. There is some truth in what

Rousseau's insistence on the inalienable sovereignty of the individual. It cannot be used to injure him without his revoking any delegation of it which he may have previously made. But it is also true that the individual does not have the right to use his power against the state, and this is a truth often forgotten by professional nonconformists.

The measure of the size and strength of a state is the degree to which it is able to contain and provide for nonconformists without damaging itself. How much difference and decentralization, for example, can a modern scientific-industrial society support? The richness of individual differences is a measure of the greatness of a state, for among nonconformists are to be counted the originative geniuses responsible for cultural advances which are made within the state.

Of two things you may be sure: first, that the individual is here to stay with all his stubborn separateness; more important, the state will not wither away. It will be with us until the day men do only what they want to do, and when what they want to do and what they should do are the same. Meanwhile, some measure of constraint is necessary if men are to be allowed liberties consistent with the liberties of others. Freedom is an arrangement which has to be made under the circumstances as they exist. More freedom is possible at some time than at others. In almost every nation the degree of freedom is sharply reduced during war, but in some it is restored when war is over. In other societies the deprivation of freedom in peace resembles that of war.

We shall have to divest ourselves of the false notion that freedom is psychological, that only they who feel free are free. The Stoic and Spinozistic idea that a man can be free in a prison provided that he feels free and can think his own thoughts is false. We now know that thoughts too can be controlled, and that the feeling of freedom corresponds to the freedom of the person. A free man is one who is without constraints other than those imposed equally on all of his fellows and necessary to insure the continuance of the society.

Freedom is not merely psychological because it issues from lower levels of institutions within the society. The arrangements institutions make among themselves provide such freedom of movement for the individual as he can hope to attain. Freedom, in other words, is a function of the structure of cultures and not something arbitrarily written into the conditions. Special liberties provided by the Constitution of the United States were first present in the moral needs of the members of the new community.

Not everyone wishes to be free and not everyone is prepared for it. Freedom is a delicate balance. Those who for reasons of character or intelligence are happier when they are told exactly what to do are quite naturally not candidates for the condition of freedom. They do not understand it and they would not know what to do with it if they had it. The ignorant and the undernourished can think of things they need more than they need political freedom, and this is a truth about which the communists continually remind themselves. The only shortcoming of such a view is that well-fed men might then look around for other values, including freedom. Provided with the necessary means, people always go off in search of ends; and for this search freedom is a necessary precondition.

But for those who are intelligent and well-fed, freedom is a prize for which they would be prepared to sacrifice anything. There is no greater political gift than for individual citizens to make decisions on matters directly affecting themselves. If they are capable of dealing with freedom then they should have freedom. A people capable of a government of freedom will operate it successfully. If they are sufficiently informed and intelligent to think for themselves, they can think also for their country.

As a rule, the condition of men at our stage of evolutionary development does not disclose any widespread talent for independent thought and action. As we have already noted, they are given to readily aroused emotions and are inclined to follow any demogogic leader who preys on them. But men who are ready and easy victims of their emotions cannot be free. Their very irrationality precludes the possibility of the condition of freedom. As Burke pointed out, "their passions forge their fetters."

The prerequisites of freedom are: (a) the possession of a certain amount of information, and (b) a disposition to be rational in making decisions. Emotions may determine the choice of premises, but they are no substitute for deductions or for the habit of thinking rationally about practical consequences. The fact that rational men are capable of choosing premises which are too narrow and of arguing deductively in terms of rational systems which are consistent but incomplete, does not indicate that any other method is preferable. Education of the right kind is the key to good government and to political stability.

Since the decisions of a prisoner are impotent, freedom must somehow be concerned with action. But if so, it must be social rather than individual, since any individual action in a society will have serious social consequences. Civil liberty is a function of the autonomy of the individual conceived on a basis of equality. But property as such is not necessarily involved, for vast inequalities in property have at times all but destroyed the functioning of individual liberty in capitalistic democracies. On the other hand, the remedy of communism removes the obstacle of vast economic inequalities only to take away many of the basic liberties of the individual citizen.

There is no *a priori* reason why the preservation of the political rights of the individual cannot be combined with a concern for the economic welfare of the masses. The Magna Carta looked to the political rights of the individual as early as 1215, and they were still being protected in the American Declaration of Independence of 1776 and in the Constitution of the United States of 1787. The welfare of the masses was the concern of the Soviet Constitution of 1918, but in neither of the subsequent revisions of 1924 and 1936 were individual political rights mentioned. At long last efforts are being made to combine individual political rights with economic well-being in what is called in Great Britain and the United States "the welfare state."

The political device of the ombudsman, who is the citizen's friend against the state and who takes the individual's side against the vast bureaucratic machinery, may furnish a permanent remedy whatever the political structure. There ought to be a court of appeal for any citizen whose rights have been impugned.

But what about interest groups and entire economic classes? Ought they not to have their appropriate channels of appeal, their own ombudsman? It is not always only the little man who has a legitimate case against the state, but groups, institutions, and even classes. At such levels, admittedly, the structure of the state is being called into question. But this might mark the beginning of the proper legal channels for making serious alterations in the constitution of the state. In the open society, a kind of institutional ombudsman is very much needed and can serve as a safety valve for forces which might otherwise seek remedies through violence.

Section 3. The Power Game

The power game can be played within the state or without, as a matter of internal or external tactics. I use the term, "game," here as in "game-theory" in mathematics. In this section I propose to discuss the power game as it is played within the state and, in the second section of Chapter XIV, as it is played on the outside, in such activities as diplomacy.

It is important to recognize that enslavement and freedom are relative terms. There is no absolute freedom possible to the individual, for such freedom would obviously encroach upon the freedom of other individuals. Therefore, as we saw at the outset of this chapter, freedom, while genuine, is always relative and limited. In some societies individuals have more freedom than in others. But in all societies it is restricted within well-defined boundaries. It is only a question of when such restrictions have reached the point where it is legitimate to call their effects enslavement.

There is always a certain measure of enslavement in any society providing freedoms. And since we have noted that the enslavement may be in part either unrecognized or voluntary, it may be carried very far, often with the consent of the citizens. The trick is to see that both enslavement and freedom balance, that the laws which restrict and enslave are there for liberating ends, and that the freedoms obtained are also employed toward such ends. The proper mixture is a delicate affair and a blend, often the result of a balance of forces which left to themselves would destroy the state and everything in it. The established morality provides such freedom and enslavement as exist in the state, whose character makes them vary. The individual's choice is to assent to the morality, or to utilize the channels provided for changing it without wrecking the fabric of the state itself.

Chance is destiny, and this becomes obviously more effective in large populations in which more chances occur. But there are no practical values in the Judeo-Christian tradition that cannot be found to emerge as exigencies from the practical problems of many men living together. Without the principle of inviolable individual integrity, no individual would be safe among others and society itself would become impossible. There do exist absolute individual rights which ought not be abrogated except for the general good. The best way to preserve them is to imbed them in the established morality: to build into the legal-moral structure the individual right to make his own peculiar contribution to the society.

Here then is a new principle which ought to be established. Freedom should consist in the unique approach of the individual to his duties. In short, *the individual should see his personal liberties as his right to fulfill social duties in his own peculiar way.*

We have noted many times thus far that the state represents a third party in every dispute, a party with supreme power interposing itself between any two contending parties. And so it is fair to say also that the state maintains an equilibrium of opposed forces. In this sense the state is merely a device to order the struggle: how shall the various forces contend with each other and in what order? What are the rules of the power game which individuals, interest groups, institutions, and political subdivisions play with each other in the fight for increased power and for increased participation in the state?

The power game is difficult to establish and perhaps even more difficult to support. It relies upon the accepted restrictions and the use of the consequent freedoms, upon how they shall be deployed within the limits of retaining the structure of the state whose function at all times it is to act as a disinterested umpire. For the first interest of the state must be the continuation of the state. The old term, sovereignty, indicates where the residence of state power is to be found, and the newer term, power structure, indicates how that sovereignty is to be used in practice and how it is to be manipulated. The power game is the game played with sovereignty by those who are ceaselessly engaged in maintaining or in acquiring political power, for which the rewards are various degrees of freedom and punishment, various kinds of enslavement.

Chapter XI

PRACTICAL PROBLEMS OF
GOVERNMENT

In this chapter I propose to look at some of the practical problems of government as they present themselves to working politicians. It is one thing to think in terms of principles and policies and quite another to be in the area of operation where the difficulties and shortcomings make themselves felt so strongly. We shall try here to see what the man who makes his living from politics is facing from day to day.

Section 1. Getting the Job Done

The working politician has, above all other assignments, the task of keeping the country going. He must try to juggle opposed interests and supervise the distribution of available material resources. He must at once promote production by encouraging initiative and see that the initiative does not get out of bounds. Nothing promotes order so much as the threat of force should that order be disturbed. An order which cannot be supported overtly by the law courts, police, and jails is not apt to remain effective.

Political events which take place in a state cannot be analyzed entirely in terms of the planned factors and they cannot be guided entirely in terms of known events. There are more variables in any

social context than has yet been ascertained, and, thanks to this ignorance, the dynamism of the state takes a direction of its own. Not
only are political events composed of many variables but very small
actions can constitute the causes of large-scale effects. It follows that
no working politician can foresee the results of applying policies,
and this holds for small incidents as well as for far-reaching programs.

Admittedly, the administration of an established morality, for
that is what politics must be, is in the hands of the government,
which is to say, in the hands of those individuals who have been
elected, appointed, or have otherwise worked themselves into some
corner of the power structure. The art of politics seems to consist of
the skillful use of resources to maintain a power advantage,
whether by means of adopting a policy to employ a particular strategy to gain an end or by means of indulging the prejudice involved
in the emotional attachment to a fallacy.

In order to push toward these goals, the working politicians must
stay in office. The strength of the state, and that for which it earns
the allegiance of its citizens, is the security and protection it affords
them. So long as it does this, the working politician can count on
support; and this is no less true because the support is in most cases
passive. Practical politics is almost entirely in the hands of a vociferous minority of the electorate which acts as spokesman for the majority. The indifference and consequent tacit consent of the majority is the most important factor in practical politics and the one
on which all parties count enormously. Revolutions, like evolu-
tions, are the same. The Russian revolution of 1914, like the French
of 1789, was the work of comparatively few people.

Unless a voting majority of citizens can be persuaded that a
political idea will in practice be to their interests, they will not support it. By the phrase "their interests" is meant primarily their economic interests. It also includes their political interests, such as issues involving liberty; their intellectual interests, such as freedom of
thought and efficient channels of information; and their emotional
interests, such as ultimate survival.

I am discussing here the interests of people at an advanced stage
of culture. Below that level the apathy of those who are kept near
starvation and in ignorance makes what I have said untrue. The hun-

gry and illiterate live from day to day without plan and with only such hope as can be aroused in them momentarily by demagogues whose promises are in direct proportion to their inability to deliver. Nasser's assurances to the Egyptians today strongly resemble Mussolini's to the Italian people in the second decade of the twentieth century.

The final criterion of politics is the measure of what it does in the short and long run for the individual citizen. Political units, such as governments, are not artificial organizations just because they are wholes, and it is not true that they have little reality compared to the reality of individual parts. There is an autonomy at every level, and all are equally real. But for this very reason the evaluation must eventually be brought down to the solitary individual and be based on the help he gets in the reduction of his organic needs and consequent enjoyment of life.

As Bentham correctly saw, obedience as well as resistance can constitute a mischief so far as the individual's own welfare is concerned when the circumstances surrounding his assent are inappropriate to it. Consider tyranny such as Italian fascism or German national socialism, and you see that individual citizens in the long run were harmed by it, and "the long run" in this case did not extend beyond a single generation.

Government is so easy to describe, so difficult to administer. The size and complexity of the tasks that arise in a sovereign state can hardly be enumerated in a short space. I will list a few at random: the protection of the country and the destruction of its enemies; the creation of money; the design of appropriate tariffs; the preservation of natural resources; the protection of citizens against abuse; the detection of fraud; the collection of taxes; the preservation of public order; the apprehension, prosecution and custody of criminals; the abolition of poverty; the provision of welfare services; the passage of laws; the conduct of elections; the supervision of immigration; the regulation of transportation and communication facilities; the avoidance of private monopoly; the conduct of international affairs.

Ideals are necessary but they are foolish if those who set them as goals overlook the actual conditions with which any people who wish to apply them in practice will be confronted. Good government is efficient government, providing its aims are good; and efficient government emerges naturally from the prevailing conditions. The ideals will always be subjected to actual economic and social restrictions. Is it possible to combine the Soviet type of central industrial control with the American type of universal suffrage? Is it possible to combine the European type of cultural advance with the American type of general economic and educational welfare? Is it possible for any one society to do all four things?

Government is a very expensive business, and no inexpensive form has yet been devised. Also there is no form of government which has remained entirely responsive to the needs of its people. In almost every case the government decides what those needs are and arranges their rank order to suit itself. On the basis of both cost effectiveness and of controls it has not yet been learned how to operate an efficient and economic state. All governments are wasteful in choice of leaders, administrative expenses, human losses through war. The chief problem confronting a society is how to reduce the cost of its government and how to make that government an instrument serving society.

Actions are sometimes prompted by ideals, sometimes by exigencies. If the ideals are bad or if they are applied too absolutely, the effects on action can be stultifying. Good expedience is often to be preferred to bad ideals applied without compromise. For it is not true that ideals are always good and expedience always bad. The perfect method of the practicing politician would be the application of a good ideal with compromise and consideration for all extenuating circumstances. But this rarely happens. The working politician is aided by the knowledge that in all matters concerning the state factual truths are hard to come by and general truths difficult to establish.

States have seldom acted against their own interests or entirely in terms of the interests of the species. They are motivated almost exclusively by narrow self-interests. Even when the appearance is the other way, as it was in the middle of the twentieth century when the United States and the Soviet Union vied with each other to see whose giveaway program to underdeveloped countries would be larger, it was still true that both countries were acting selfishly, each to arrest the spreading influence of the other. They were courting allies in a contest between them, and not being altruistic at all. Fortunately, results are what count and not motives, and the results were often good, as when the hungry were fed and the ignorant educated.

The value of efficiency obviously depends upon the end which is sought. Excellence serves efficiency. In war, brutality and ruthlessness are virtues. The exigence of rule demands that both ends and means be chosen in the field of action in short-range terms. It is necessary first to serve immediate survival at whatever cost. But the success and the ultimate survival of a state cannot be best managed in this way. Thus while the state is being maintained as a going concern, those occupied with its long-range interests must be at work on the matter of moral principles and the deduction from them of laws.

Section 2. *Internal Strains*

Governments are subject to strains and stresses. The strains are those produced by internal pressures asymmetrically applied, and the stresses are the corresponding external pressures. I shall discuss them in this and following sections.

Internal strains are produced by the struggle for power of individuals and of various interest groups and institutions. We have already noted that every government is made up of an equilibrium of forces, a balance of pressures under tension. In such a structure, so strong is the balance thus maintained that individual citizens are often able to relax under the security and stability the system affords, almost to forget sometimes that a government exists or that anything connected with it could be an issue.

The equilibrium on which stability depends is a matter of offsetting tensions. They may have been balanced for so long and the equilibrium so well established that a tradition comes into existence which makes any other alternative unthinkable. This is the value of tradition in establishing an uneasy truce between opposed interests: the longer it exists the less uneasy. But there are other times marked by disequilibrium and imbalance, when the very existence of the government is threatened and nothing else in human life seems so critical; then the support of the government becomes an individual concern.

I see no reason to doubt the obvious truth—of which conservative political thinkers like Gaetano Mosca and Vilfredo Pareto make so much—that in most societies a distinction between two principal classes can be made: between a small class of rulers and a large class of those who are ruled. The crucial distinction is between those rulers who rule for the good of the ruled and those who rule for the good of themselves.

It is in the last group that political corruption lies and that all of the damage is done. Admittedly, the crucial distinction is difficult to detect, for all clever rulers want to give the appearance of ruling for the sake of the ruled and all make that claim. But some actually do it, and it is these we wish to exempt from the accusation of corruption. Perhaps I have drawn the distinction too rigidly; for all men are human as well as mortal, and every ruler thinks also of himself. It is then more a matter of degree than of kind; but this does not mean that the distinction cannot be made and recognized. Those who rule more for the sake of the ruled than for themselves will have to be applauded for coming as close as most mortal men are likely to come to doing the right things when in a position of power.

Government justifies itself finally through its ability to maintain law and order. This is the traditional view, but it is necessary to remember that it does not have to be the same law and the same order. The English government maintained both through a period of sharp transition that would in another country have perhaps upset both.

Considering the government as an institution to some extent distinct from the rest of the country, it can be readily seen that there are two kinds of adjustment it has to make. There are adjustments peculiar to government and constituted by the fact that its various branches do not always work harmoniously together. Does the Foreign Office come into conflict with the military? Is the Congress in accord with the actions of the President? Is there the proper kind of cooperation between the various law enforcing agencies or do they clash in the field? Then, too, there are adjustments peculiar to the various branches of government when these come into direct contact with the citizens. To the extent to which elements of the public sector encroach upon the private sector, for the sake of ends

many individuals in the private sector consider unwarranted, there is
sure to be trouble.

In any case a minimal government is always required, though
the greater the population the larger the government. This is true
because relations between the elements—individuals, interest groups
and institutions—increase. Ever since Ortega y Gasset first pointed
it out, we have become distressingly aware that the rapid climb in
population, and hence in the number of the poor, hungry and ignorant degrades civilization as a whole and sharpens political instability. This is most noticeable in the cities where sympathies and
antipathies, amity and enmity are greatly intensified.

There are desirable as well as undesirable internal strains within
the state. The undesirable strains occasioned by the power struggle
are inevitable, those, for instance, which result from great numbers
of poor and ignorant. But we shall also look at one occasion for internal strain which is desirable. This for want of a better term might
be described as the richness of difference. The regional and even
individual right to cultural distinctions is some measure of the
achievement of a society. The richness of difference is to be encouraged rather than discouraged because it means that the culture is
more densely packed with values than it would have been had it had
greatly similar parts. The cultural value of a state is marked by the
extent to which it can tolerate and even promote large individual
and group differences. Uniformity of culture is frustrating and
deadening, while the richness of difference is stimulating and en-
livening. In this sense the state is asked to offer a base for those
efforts which extend beyond the state, to the fine arts, pure sciences, and originative religions.

Section 3. External Stresses

External stresses consist of those pressures which are brought to
bear on the state by its negative relations with other states. There is
always competition between states, and there are various forms of
friction even between those which are for the most part friendly.
In the case of others, the competition can extend to the extreme
instance of war.

In our time an intermediate condition has been invented which goes by the name, "the cold war," a condition which is neither peace nor war but a kind of undeclared war which does not lead to open conflict except in small test areas. In peacetime, the conflict is carried on under the name of diplomacy, and the battles of the negotiation table are fought with words while other battles are conducted by means of international trade. Diplomacy and trade often serve as varieties of conflict.

The cold war can extend the conflict until peripheral wars conducted by satellites or by the main thrust of the enemy operating under self-imposed restrictions are allowed to exist. War, open and total, is the final kind of external stress which a state must undergo and endure if it is to remain a state. For while other conflicts challenge the size and the strength of a state, war challenges its very right to exist as a state, its independence and its sovereignty.

External pressures, like internal strains, are the normal conditions for a state, and both continually present problems to any government which it must meet as a matter almost of routine. That some states exist as long as they do is a source of wonder, and what is not a wonder is that none exist for very long as time is measured in human and evolutionary terms. Civilization appears now to be about 10,000 years old, certainly no more; but there is no state which has lasted much more than 1000 years. Cultures have survived longer than that. The most notable instances are the Chinese and the Indians who have kept their cultures going longer than any others.

The prime question of what determines the length of life of states has yet to be answered. They come into existence, they flourish, and they come to an end, and nobody can say why. Certainly, it must be true that flourishing means having the strength to support internal stresses and external strains without serious damage to the political structure. But what does that mean, and of what does it consist? Societies greatly outlast their political organizations, and the state is not characteristically a long-lived affair.

We can assert here that while internal strains are to a large extent subject to the state's own determination, external stresses are not. The state does not choose how strong or how antagonistic neighboring states shall be or whether they shall constitute themselves enemies. In these terms the world has always been a small one.

No doubt the citizens of Rome and Carthage, of Athens and Sparta, thought of themselves as competing in a very crowded living space too small for both of them; and the citizens of Soviet Russia and the United States now hold the same opinion. The increase in the size of the arena is matched by the increase in the size of the contestants, so that the struggle remains a more or less constant one. The methods of dealing with issues change but not the issues. It may just be that the practical problems of government are not so very different over the comparatively few millennia in which man has been living in civilization.

Section 4. Some Principles of Practice

Ideals stand behind constitutions and laws are framed in terms of them. In working politics the scheme is to apply the constitution and laws to the life of the people. We should recognize, however, that practice has its own principles, *modus operandi* principles not usually found in the pure theory devised by the framers of a constitution. Pure theory is indispensable to practice, but so are the principles of practice even though they are secondary.

One of these may be stated as follows: *in practice the assumption is always made that actions follow from expediency and not from principles.*

In the course of actual practices, if there are any principles involved they are always well hidden. Appeals to principles are reserved to the speeches of candidates for political office, and are as rarely meant as they are seldom believed and even then for no longer than the occasion on which they were proclaimed. It always impresses a man of affairs that principles do not count because he sees chiefly if not exclusively the workings of self-interest and of personal advantage. That the country within which these are enabled to operate successfully possesses a government installed in terms of principles never strikes him as relevant, if, indeed, it occurs to him at all.

Practical minded men deal almost entirely with the actual problems of administration, with concrete situations. Does this bureau have adequate funds? What will the courts do in fact? How does the mind of the chief political officer work? That such practices are based on theories in the first place; that the government which established the bureaus and the legal systems, was based on theories; that a change in the theories would bring about a radical change in the practices, never occurs to those whose lives are filled with the details of practice.

Theories and their respective practices never agree more than approximately, so that it is not always apparent that the practices follow from the theories and were founded by them. This makes it appear that practices lead independent existences, when they do not; for either they follow from some theory which was made explicit or they assume a theory which remains implicit. Every particular is a member of some class, and there are no absolutely unique particulars even though every particular is unique in some regard.

Another principle of practice may be stated in this way: *it is impractical to suppose that there is any system of politics which would not suffer from abuses when put into practice.*

The ideal design from the point of view of political strategy would be that political system which put into practice and subject to usual amounts of corruption would still provide the greatest amount of goods for the greatest number of citizens. When submitted to exigencies, any ideal constitution is going to prove inadequate. The man of action is apt to regard truth as of no moment in the heat of the struggle to get on with the job. But half-truths are exactly those on which he must rely to support political action; he cannot afford to let them seem entirely haphazard and opportunistic. For while half-truths are only half-truths where we would prefer whole truths, still they are also half-true.

A great deal of modification can always be expected whenever ideologies encounter local extenuating circumstances. Consider the distinction between Russian and Chinese communism, or between the American and Spanish Catholic churches. Consider also in a single country the distinction between aims and effects. The effects of ideal legislation are not always ideal. The eighteenth amendment was intended to eliminate drunkenness, but the consumption of alcohol increased and the leviathan of organized crime was born.

Section 5. Leadership

In considering the problems of the working state, we shall have to remember that it can be broken up into three important parts: the leader, the bureaucracy, and the electorate. We may discuss them briefly in that order.

I distinguish carefully between leader and leadership. The former is always an individual or a group, the latter an office. It is the occupant of the office with whom I am chiefly concerned. Deference is a reciprocal relation, of as much use to the dependents as to the leader who lives naturally on the level for which he seems organically equipped and which involves the assumption of responsibilities.

Leadership may be permanent, temporary or functional. A divinely appointed monarch has the office for life and passes it on to his descendants. The president of a democratic state enjoys his position temporarily, either for a stipulated period or until a parliamentary vote of no confidence forces another election. Functional leadership, the most temporary form, is exemplified by the practices of some North American Indian tribes that appointed leaders for the duration of military campaigns.

The capabilities of leadership form a peculiar set. I shall list some of them.

First is the intuitive understanding of what people want. This differs from society to society, and also from time to time in the same society. The leader in this narrow sense is not a leader but a follower. He must race his opponents to popular favor by finding out where the people are going and getting there first.

Given the number of variables that exist in all cultural situations, there are severe limits to the amount of effective planning. The leader has his guidelines furnished by the laws of the state and, more broadly, by that background morality in terms of which the laws were established and amendments made. It often happens that leaders are called on to make decisions, unforeseen when they were elected, concerning immediate practical actions. It is the challenge presented by the necessity for making immediate crucial decisions which determines whether leaders are true leaders. To some extent every elected official is given an open mandate, and how well he executes it determines his size as a politician. The office of political leader is always open-ended, pointing toward success or failure; the larger the position the greater the discrepancy, so that greatness or ignominy is the outcome.

Next is a certain energy and enthusiasm which is both communicable and infectious. This is the quality which Max Weber has named "charisma," or charm. It acts by motivating people to want most in the world to follow the leader who has it, because it both inspires confidence and suggests the hope that the quality will somehow be communicated and transmitted.

Then again a certain amount of ignorance is essential. To understand both sides of an issue, would be to render most leaders immobile and to cancel their ability as leaders. A leader cannot act with emphasis and forthright decision if he understands too well; for justice is never altogether on one side, yet there must be a decision and there must be action, both of which are usually one-sided.

The social developments in scientific-industrial cultures call for decision-making on the part of the chief executive for which he does not and indeed cannot have sufficient information. No man can be an expert in all technical fields. Therefore what is needed is training of a professional nature for the politician. The first level of decisions are to be made by the specialists in various institutions where familiarity with technical details is commonplace. Then these are to be reviewed and checked by a chief executive whose own technical preparation should be in the area of decision-making. He will have the task that no one else has of matching decisions; for instance, given limited funds, which proposals are to be preferred for the short-term benefits of living citizens and which for the long-term benefits of the citizens of the future? The professional politician in the scientific-industrial culture has to have his own kind of specialized and technical competence.

More rare than any other characteristic is origination. An originative genius is one who does not play by the rules but instead plays with the rules. He keeps the state going, sometimes at the cost of upsetting it considerably. His insight may be communicated to his culture, in which it comprises thereafter a distinguishing feature, noticeable as such, for instance, to the foreign visitor. But whether in such a case the origination has been truly imposed *on* the society by the leader or invoked *in* the society by him is a matter of no moment, for both awake echoing relations.

The equipment of the leader, in addition to the value of his training and experience, consists in the ability to assess the forces at work and to balance their relative effects politically in order to make the proper decisions. He is the one ultimately responsible for laying down policies and for adopting courses of action. It is he whose success or failure as a leader depends upon the success or failure of his guidance in practical affairs. A cause may be defined, following the physicist, Bohm, as a statistical trend, and an accident is nothing more than one among a number of causes. The leader moves with design among unpredictable accidents, always somewhat at their mercy. He grasps the plan of the whole, but in terms of the effects of accidents must stand ready to modify anything planned; to shift, to temporize, to amend, and in extreme cases to cancel.

Leadership is a function of the degrees of freedom of a society. If the society be rigidly organized, as in a hereditary monarchy with divine right, then the leader is completely free to do whatever he wishes. It is evident from the careers of Napoleon and Alexander the Great that an unfettered leader can accomplish a great deal. If the society be more loosely organized, as in a democracy, then the leader seems more tightly bound since he must be responsive to the wishes of a majority of the electorate. Therefore: *the freedom of the leader and of the people is inverse; the more freedom the one has the less the other.*

In a democracy, what appears often to be leadership is actually followship. For leadership consists of the leader's ability to foresee correctly what the electorate will want and to be the first to give it to them. He stays one jump ahead of his people by correctly anticipating their wishes.

It would appear that leaders have an immense amount of freedom and initiative at their disposal. But it would equally appear that they have little choice: they do what they have to do at the time, given all the forces then playing upon them. *In the case of political leadership, as in any other instance of action, freedom is one integrative level above determinism and one chronological step before it.*

The elevation of men to a position of power often has a curious effect. Men of lowly stature have been known to rise to meet their responsibilities, and others of great capacity have been known to become corrupt. Malversation is, as we have seen, among the greatest of crimes, for it affects more people adversely than almost any other form of human action. Yet it is not power that corrupts, as Lord Acton declared, but the position of power; and this does not corrupt any more often than it elevates through the burden of responsibility.

Seldom, if ever, has a politician made a move without considering whether it would retain or increase his power. States benefit from leadership when moves made by politicians in the interest of power also benefit the country, and of course a favorite way of increasing power is to do something that will benefit the country. Its citizens are then disposed to reward the politician. So the enterprise of politics is, from the point of view of the state, a game of compromise between the holders of power and the needs of the citizens. The politician gains on the people to the extent that unforeseen problems arise which require ingenuity and initiative for their immediate solution. The people protect themselves and their interests against the politician to the extent to which they can anticipate his moves by imposing a constitution upon him and in this way limiting his field of action.

Always the leader works in the name of the masses, and, to be effective, he must be acepted by the masses. This does not mean that he is necessarily understood by the masses or that, if he is sufficiently cynical, he works for them. He is, for political reasons, in some necessary way connected to them while, as their leader, he stands somewhat apart from them. To accomplish anything, he must represent something in them, and it is often something that neither he nor they understand overtly.

The leader is in a vulnerable position. The higher he is and the more authority he is given or assumes, the more his leadership is challenged. The challenge may come in a number of ways. It may come through legitimate channels, through the criticism of his own party, or, usually with more vehemence, from those of an opposition party. Or it may come through illegitimate channels, through assassination. Both President Kennedy and, in the Dominican Republic, the dictator, Trujillo, were murdered while in office. Republicans insisted that Franklin D. Roosevelt had become a dictator during his four terms in office and that he was destroying the democratic form of government even though he regularly submitted himself to elections and could not be held responsible for the fact that there was no effective opposition. The same charge of destroying the democratic process had been levelled earlier against Andrew Jackson when he introduced the "spoils system."

Section 6. The Politics of the Cultural Elite

Politics, the domain of those who constitute the government of the state, is not confined to what has traditionally passed by that name. For there are many cultural influences at work which eventually issue in political effects. "Politics" is the name for current politics, but there is the politics of the future, and this usually germinates in the present without political recognition of any kind.

There always is, for instance, a cultural aristocracy. It may be represented chiefly by the most effective minority in the state, one associated with and drawing its power from that institution which is accorded the greatest degree of reality. This will be true whether the institution is economic, religious, or scientific. The cultural aristocracy from time to time identifies its interests with different classes depending upon the peculiar makeup of the culture. In Renaissance Italy, it had perforce to identify with the petty princes and church leaders. In the Soviet Union, it identifies with "the toiling masses." Always it operates in terms of the human species as seen through the peculiar perspective provided by local social conditions.

The cultural aristocracy idiosyncratically appears concerned with its own society, for its interests are fundamentally trans-cultural. In its interests, which are those of the arts, science, religion and philosophy, it seeks to move beyond the state to cosmic considerations. Thus the class affiliations of the cultural aristocracy are nominal, and only such as will allow its members to continue to work with as little disturbance as possible. That the cultural aristocracy has nevertheless an effect on the state makes of it a political asset or liability.

We may take it as a fact that the political administrator is the sworn enemy and natural antagonist of the cultural genius. The man whose work may alter the future of the state in which he is a citizen can hardly be a congenial figure to the political leader whose work requires the continuance of the state as presently constituted. There is a legitimate above-board talented minority with whom he finds he can work, but there is also an underground elite whose functions may be illegitimate from the perspective of the current interests of the state.

An important section of the cultural elite, then, may be discovered "underground" in the sense that they are hidden from the scouting of politically astute citizens. The legitimate underground elite consists of that group whose work is not disapproved but neglected. We can pass over it quickly because we are not as concerned with it as we are with the illegitimate underground elite, those whose work would have nothing but disapproval if it were known to exist and would in all likelihood be suppressed. That an underground elite does exist at all presents a practical problem in government for there is always the possibility that it may pose a potential threat to the existing political conditions.

Since the thoughts of the underground elite are often inimical to the existing order, its members may be considered dangerous. Friedrich Engels, running his German father's factory in Manchester, and Karl Marx, quietly reading in the British Museum Library, certainly gave no indication of the effect their writings would have on the politics of the immediate future. If we drop the curtain to denote the lapse of a century and raise it on the political scene in the Soviet Union, we get a different stage setting. The political leaders we find are not those who would tolerate political revolution any more than the Czar's police would have a hundred years before. Today's revolutionaries may be tomorrow's arch conservatives. This can be seen clearly in the fortunes of those who stand to benefit or lose from political shifts and changes.

Although dangerous thoughts are not confined to politics they almost always do exist there. It is perilous to advocate capitalism in

Moscow or communism in New York. The productive intellectual is, as a rule, dissatisfied with things as they are, and he would look to suggested improvements. He is perhaps worse than a political revolutionary: he is a general revolutionary. He would exchange what-is for what-ought-to-be in everything everywhere.

The political potential of the members of the underground elite, in so far as their work is capable of affecting the politics of the future, is best illustrated by the work of the atomic scientists in the period preceding the explosion of the first atomic bomb over Hiroshima. No one knew then that what was being done in the Chicago Stadium and at Los Alamos would heavily affect future political considerations all over the world. The cultural timetable is now a product of the balance of atomic power in the hands of the politicians, and its assessment is very difficult. Just now there may be other developments equally obscure which might prove equally influential.

Section 7. *Bureaucracy*

No way has been discovered for conducting the operations of government other than by means of bureaus, secretariats, and committees. Government is an institution, and institutions work in no other way. There are obvious virtues here: the perpetuation of the structure beyond the lifetime of single citizens, the protection of the government against the vagaries of the random individual.

Whether we are talking about ancient China or modern Britain, the facts remain the same. An effective bureaucracy rests on the selection and promotion of its personnel by impartial and objective criteria of competence. Civil servants selected according to standards of excellence formed both by levels of intelligence and levels of information are apt to give the kind of performance on which the quality of administration can securely rest.

In the best system of bureaucracy, recruitment is conducted by competitive examinations and promotions are made on the same basis, as was the custom of the Chinese during the Han dynasty from the first century B.C. onward. Through this method, capable individuals are selected with the ever present possibility of advancement. However, this process does not encourage decision-making abilities; and if decisions are made they will fall well within the prescribed system by which the bureaucracy is operated. No fresh solutions to old problems and no solutions at all to new problems may be expected, and that is why an efficient bureaucracy must always be quantitatively less than the highest personnel of the state.

No government of any dimensions nowadays can hope to function smoothly without the aid of an effective bureaucracy, though the existence of bureaucracy as an institution remains largely unrecognized. Despite the necessity of bureaucracy to administration, there are limitations and drawbacks. There is an inefficiency built into the system which produces bad effects: it insures uniformity where diversity might be more desirable; it provides stereotypes where new forms and fresh approaches are needed; and it advances the mediocre over the man of originality and genius. Again, institutionalization means entrenchment, and bureaucrats are entrenched careerists. Like all institutional men, they seek to perpetuate their own positions. Bureaucracy was not designed to come first in its own considerations or in any other. To consider it so is a corruption, and bureaucracies are as susceptible to corruption as any other social organization.

Bureaucracy must never be the center of power and authority but only the sector of government responsible for the efficient and impartial execution of adopted policies and decisions. It should not be at the disposal of the executive, either, but function as a semi-independent branch of government not answerable to any other branch but by means of the machinery of the government responsible for its maintenance through a wilderness of changes which tend to render it unstable. Bureaucracy initiates nothing and changes only with reasonable slowness in response to those wider changes with which the people find themselves confronted.

Bureaucracy itself, of course, is capable of becoming corrupt. And the only buffer to a corrupt bureaucracy is an educated electorate capable of taking vigorous action to bring about necessary reforms.

The politician and bureaucrat make a strange contrast. The politician is inventive, the bureaucrat restricted; the politician never has to organize a department or operate one, while the bureaucrat never has to stand for an election. Each in a sense deplores the existence of the other, but it is clear both are necessary.

The daring of leadership is a permanent requirement, but so strong is the need for a bureaucracy that one is usually constituted although it has not officially and formally been provided for. Even when there is the autocratic rule of a single individual, there always are men around him who constitute a bureaucracy for his pleasure. The politician is forever meeting new conditions which confront him with problems that must be settled in ways unprovided for when the constitution of the state was first formulated. This never endears him to the bureaucrats who are often assigned the task of fitting the settlements into the already existing framework of government.

Bureaucracy in the negative sense connotes excessive organization. The closed secret proceedings of the group at the top of a governmental agency may have results beneficial to its members and not necessarily to the whole agency or the whole government. Bureaucracy is designed to increase the power of leadership because it does not have to submit its decisions to the criticism of all those who might be involved in its results.

The methods of the bureaucrat are to work through discussions and agreements. It is they who are responsible for what may be called the fallacy of the conference table. As Bentham said, "Men, let them but once clearly understand one another, will not be long ere they agree." This is a psychological error and very widespread. Material interests may be opposed and may remain in this condition no matter how clearly men understand one another. If Germany and France both want the Ruhr, what difference does it make that each knows what the other wants? They will still both want it, and no amount of clarity will prevent them from taking such steps, not excluding the use of violence, as may promise success.

The bureau exists to implement outstanding agreements, not to bring those agreements into effect. There is a hope that while men are talking they will not fight. But the Japanese were talking to the Americans in Washington while their airplanes were bombing the

American navy in Pearl Harbor. The Russian specialty seems to be to argue one way in political conferences while acting in quite another away from the conference table.

Section 8. The Electorate

The modern concept of sovereignty resides in those citizens entitled to take part in the legal operation of the state. It is their support which the leader must have if he is to function legitimately. It is for their welfare that the state exists in the first place. This is still true even in those systems of politics which are not allowed to share in political decision-making, such as in Marxism. For people do not exist for the state but the state does exist for the people. If their welfare is not served, to that extent the state has failed.

There are, however, two considerations which must give us pause while we contemplate such contentions. First, what is the welfare of the people? This would seem to depend upon the ends chosen, since all bodies of citizens would not choose the same ends. Some would prefer war with a view to the conquest of territory or of other peoples; others would prefer that the entire energies of the state be devoted to furthering the worship of God. No doubt there are many other ends which have been and will be chosen.

The second consideration is: who should decide about the welfare of the people? Surely not the people themselves, for they always wait on decisions from other quarters. They are passive in this sense and prefer to select alternatives from those offered. This leaves such crucial issues to leaders, those appointed or self-selected. And we have already seen that the leaders must choose what they feel the people want. So it is often the case that others know better than the people themselves the nature of their preferences.

A contemporary consideration, one which affects political affairs at every level, is the size of the population. The citizens of the modern state have grown in such number that this fact alone determines many issues. As the population increases, the character of its structure changes. A large middle class serves to bridge the wide gap between a wealthy class of shareholders and a large laboring class; and by siding with the first class helps it to reduce the effect of dissatisfaction of the second. The kind of dominant minority it will tolerate also changes, and so does its relation to that minority. The proportion of government officials to citizens may remain the same, but the result is a large and powerful government which can threaten to become an end in itself. The government of a small town is not in the same relation to its citizens as the government of a large city, and the same is true of countries.

Those for whom the state exists generically constitute themselves followers; they wish not to lead but be led. The arrogance of the holders of power is matched only by the widespread sycophancy of the masses.

Therefore, *it is the primary property of the electorate that they paradoxically insist on being led in ways not consciously known to themselves as the price of their non-resistance.*

The electorate has other properties, chiefly negative, which we will examine briefly.

Citizens generally possess very short memories. Indeed this is something on which the practicing politician heavily relies. When it appears that he is on the losing side of an issue, he has only to wait a little before undertaking to see that he is counted emphatically on the other side. He knows that last year's bad laws or criminal actions are equally forgotten in the heat of the contest over current issues. Few today remember the eighteenth amendment, Hitler, or the "starving Armenians" after World War I. Few can recall the corruptions which occurred in the United States in connection with the building of the early railroads or with perpetuating southern slavery. No one even remembers last year's campaign promises or notices how little they are fulfilled. Leaders are often elected on a platform of peace, only to be enthusiastically supported in the waging of war. The failure of citizens to remember means that politicians can arise at any time and offer competition to others who have become entrenched; it means that policies need not be consistent or pursued for very long; and it means a very high turnover in men and principles and an unsteady state of affairs.

Most citizens are easily led by their emotions. Every demagogue knows that he need not appeal to reason when he can use prejudices to greater effect. It is a characteristic of men en masse that they are easily excited and given to approving of, or of even engaging in, drastic actions. "Mob rule" never means rule in accordance with reason. When emotions are aroused the results often precipitate actions for which the people may soon be sorry and for which they will blame not themselves but their leaders. It is the people themselves who are at fault because their assent was obtained emotionally.

From similar evidence it is clear that most people are fickle. Any decisions they make or approve of today may be as easily cancelled or reversed tomorrow. The Athenians banished an admiral and the next day sent a ship to recall him—after changing their minds about his value to the state. What is true of people is often equally true of their governments. The United States in World War II fought the Germans and the Japanese, but it was not long after the war that these two countries became her chief allies. An isolationist policy in international matters before World War II was changed afterwards in the United States to extreme participation and even interference in world affairs. A leader who is popular may quickly become a liability at the polls.

Most people are selfish. Their decisions are made chiefly on the basis of what will benefit them personally. Every politician knows this and couches his appeal accordingly. If he promises to keep the peace, reduce taxes, increase the public benefits through a welfare program, provide health, increase safety, and abolish all restrictive legislation, he may in fact do the opposite without suffering penalty if he does it quietly. It is enough for citizens to recognize that they would benefit, for, as we have noted, they never remember or check to see if promises were kept.

Most people are stupid. They cannot be trained to analyze appearances, to challenge claims, "facts" and figures, to ask provocative questions, in short, to think for themselves. Granted the genuineness of their political sense of responsibility and willingness to do their political duty, still their ignorance comes with a high price so far as its effects on the state are concerned. The average citizen has a desire to know the truth but a limited capacity for understanding it. This makes him an easy mark for those who offer him a simple concept purported to be the whole of truth, particularly when it appeals more to his emotions than to his difficult and less accessible capacity for reasoning.

Lastly, most people are apathetic in matters political. They have to be elaborately roused before they will express an interest in anything so abstract as government or their own future. They live from moment to moment in the trifling affairs of the day, which seem, from their narrow perspective, unrelated to great public issues or national decisions. They prefer on the whole to be left alone, and they delegate the making of decisions to the professional politicians, and only afterwards blame them if they are guilty of serious mistakes. They never help in crucial political affairs but they do stand ready to retaliate. Leaders, in their unexpressed opinions, exist in order to take the responsibility for divining and executing successfully what they unconsciously want done. Meanwhile they have no wish to become involved, and postpone all tacit approval or overt disapproval until they can see the results.

What was for Bentham a habit of obedience is a necessary ingredient in any settled or orderly government, though we have seen that such obedience can be carried too far. The world can learn a lot from the English tradition of a free people having the habit of obedience yet holding themselves responsible for gradual and orderly change when it is obvious that change has become necessary. A characteristically rebellious population, such as are now to be found in so many Central and South American states, are not the reliable foundations upon which an orderly and democratic government can securely rest.

Leaders and followers need each other more than leaders usually recognize. The masses know this better for they are incontestible followers, whereas the leaders are not so certain of the permanence of their leadership. The masses are for the most part without initiative, and they need to be able to look up to a leader because they depend so completely upon him. This fact can be good or bad depending upon the leader. When abuses grow too heavy, the mute masses arise, but even then only on the basis of a new mass leader, a "man of the people." So it nearly always comes down to a matter of leader against leader, on the basis of divided and opposed followers.

Revolutions are made by tiny minorities in the name of the masses—those who speak for the masses as well as those who speak to the masses in the name of a privileged and entrenched minority. To lead in the name of the masses, however, is not always to lead for the benefit of the masses. This is a lesson the masses seem incapable of learning. The inability or unwillingness of even intelligent people to look behind the scenes and not to take events at their face value is the permanent protection against those who would deceive the masses. For people tend to foist upon all of their leaders a rosy idealism few leaders ever possess. The tendency to think of leaders as demigods rather than as individuals exceptionally equipped to appeal to the masses is all but irresistible.

Chapter XII

POLITICAL CHANGE

Section 1. Stability and Change

Everything in existence changes continually and political organizations are no exception. We tend to consider as changing only those things which are changing rapidly and to consider as not changing those which are changing slowly. People usually do whatever seems expedient; they act from the most practical motives and without regard for long-range causes and effects. Yet, looking back, it is always possible to see a shape to the sequence of social actions in terms of the rise and fall of a social organization, whether it be a nation-state, an empire, or an entire culture.

Also, what looks like stability may be responsible for the most drastic of changes. At the outbreak of World War II there were in the United States some ten million unemployed. The problem had not been solved by the Works Progress Administration nor by any number similar devices. It was solved by putting that many men into uniform and shipping them overseas. After the war, the country was saved from unemployment and the consequent economic collapse by the threat of the Soviet Union and its gigantic war potential. Now the Americans do not dare disarm because the threat of world revolution has never been abandoned by the communists. The result has been an enormous outlay for arms and an unparalleled prosperity based on a steady and rather large inflationary trend which has prevailed since the last world war.

In a sense, then, it can be said that the state is never altogether secure. The prospect of change as a probability is always present in one form or another, either as slow eroding evolution or as rapid and violent revolution, with the former more common than the latter though in its cumulative effect no less drastic.

If we consider a political organization to be an entity and its development a process, then we can say that the continued existence of the entity is a function of the slowness of the process. No political entity remains the same without change of any kind; while, on the other end of the spectrum of change, a fast process allows it to become an entity of a different kind. To exhibit energy of any marked degree means to change appreciably. There are limits to this if the entity is to be preserved.

Perhaps an example will help here. For some years now in the United States, the gross national product has increased sharply. This has led to a different kind of culture and within it to severe political changes which have come near to straining the limits of democracy as it was conceived and established by the Founding Fathers. The survival of the American government in the sense to which it can be read as continuous with its past is a function of a steady rate of increase in manufacture and trade. That such an increase can be counted on is absurd. There have got to be limits to economic expansion, and politically it will mean a serious change when these have been reached.

Any approach to governmental forms which considers only the fact that they *are* forms leads to the impression that they remain static. This is not the case, for there is a continual process of alteration at work. Compare the American democracy of 1868 with that of 1968 and you will see that, although invariants do exist to justify the continuity of naming, the changes are often quite severe.

Two opposed tendencies which are equally responsible for change make themselves felt at various times and under varying conditions. The first is that a tiny minority can accomplish what would have been supposed impossible and intolerable, provided it has the passive support—or silent aloofness from action—of the majority. The systematic murder of millions of Jews and liberals by the German Nazis is an example. The second is that, despite the passive opposition of the majority, there is much that a violent and vociferous minority can accomplish. The destructive riots in the principal American cities in the summer of 1967 are examples. In the 1960's a handful of intellectual dissidents in the Soviet Union managed to demonstrate the absence of and the need for cultural freedoms.

What these two tendencies have in common—what makes them possible in the first place—is the superficial nature of all social establishments no matter how long they have been entrenched and no matter how deeply they seem to have been adopted. Political arrangements are only reluctantly accepted conveniences. The aggressive nature of individual man is older than any civilization, older by hundreds of thousands and perhaps millions of years. It may reassert itself at any time; and, when it does, the social restraints which a state may have imposed are swept aside as though they never existed except as convenient fictions. It takes more time, which is to say more repetition of instances, to instill in the human animal the kind of rational arrangement which is public order and to guarantee to that order any kind of reliable stability. No merit bureaucracy that was ever devised is capable of ensuring that the public order will prevail over any disturbance that might occur to challenge it.

The difficulty is one to which Bergson has called attention. For just as it is demonstrated over and over by events that the reality of existence, its richness of complexity and its constant change, is sure to prove in the end to be more than man's limited schemes can encompass, so it happens also that no political system which has ever been devised is capable of the consistency and completeness which would enable it to anticipate and provide for all possible eventualities.

Conditions resting on any number of unforeseen and perhaps unforeseeable conflicts, shortcomings, and social demands of an excessive nature may arise at any time to threaten public order. It may even be that a sufficiently long period of peace and tranquility proves so monotonous to a bored population that it welcomes any internal or external disturbance. In times of war, men long for the safety and security of peace, and in times of peace they crave the danger and novelty of war. No merit bureaucracy can offer the proper renewal in sufficient quantity under these circumstances, and no military adventure can furnish a sufficient stability. It is of the true order of genius when a political leader senses what of either ingredient is missing in his time and sets out to provide it.

In this chapter I shall consider changes at each of the political levels, for purposes of brevity examining only the cultural, national, institutional and individual levels, and omitting the communal and social. The rate of change will be a function of the structure examined.

Section 2. Cultural Changes

Civilizations are the largest of human organizations. As we should expect, they move slowly, though rapid changes do occur. Changes of entire civilizations usually consist of the exchange of cultures, for instance, the relatively abrupt exchange of the religious culture of the Middle Ages for the scientific culture of the modern world. Such radical revisions bring political alterations with them. Cultures may remain stable while accepting partial changes from within. It is only when these partial changes dominate the whole culture that an exchange at the cultural level results.

The sharp transitions—which take place in civilizations as they come into existence, grow and flourish, decline and fall, and eventually disappear altogether—have been studied intensively by such men as Ibn Khaldûn, Vico, Danilevsky, Oswald Spengler and Arnold Toynbee, though usually without any special attention to politics. To some extent this neglect is justified, for the political is only one segment of the cultural and to a great degree comes under cultural influence. It just happens, however, that in this particular study we are more concerned with politics than we are with culture.

Politics is one institution among many even though it occupies a special place in the culture, and it is possible to find within the confines of a single civilization a number of different political systems operating concurrently. At present, capitalistic democracies and communisms, fascist dictatorships and monarchies, exist side by side in western civilization. Examples, in the order given, are: England, Yugoslavia, Spain and Jordan.

The English segment of western civilization enjoyed a continuous culture while the political transition from monarchy to democracy was more or less peacefully effected. On the other hand the French segment suffered a violent social revolution. Political orders are changed by peaceful evolution or by violent revolution, and often without disturbing the underlying continuity of the culture.

Changes in cultures are seldom if ever planned. They happen usually because they are forced by internal events or imposed from without as a result of contacts between cultures. The changes which take place in a culture often begin and have their most powerful influences before they become effective on the political level. It can happen in a stable country that everyone reaches the point of indifference to the knowledge that the government is there and that its demands must be met. Events taking place at the cultural level are so fundamental and slow that often they are not even noticed until their effects have had time to make themselves felt. A few perceptive geniuses living in a period of cultural revolution may know that they stand at the threshold of a new age, but I doubt if this is the condition of most individuals at the time.

The very existence of cultures as historical units has come to be recognized only recently, and some historians still maintain that they do not exist. It is only when one looks beyond the national level that a cultural configuration can be made out. Surely the countries of western Europe have many things in common, enough in fact for observers to discriminate them from other countries. There is at the present time a western culture, a Moslem culture, a Chinese and an Indian culture, and they are unmistakable. They influence and are influenced by political developments within their national units, yet to a large extent they remain independent of all political considerations.

What is most significant about culture perhaps is the kind of conformity it imposes. We shall encounter this phenomenon later on in the chapter when we come to consider the individual on the lowest political levels. Here it is necessary only to say that there is such an imposition and that it is obviously not deliberate on the part of the culture nor felt as a constraint by the individuals who are its chief recipients. Cultures are wider than nations, and while, as we

have noted, different political structures may exist side by side, there
is still a tendency to uniformity.

Section 3. National Changes

Among the forms of political organization, the nation has been
the most important. Nations are ruled by their governments, and
any change in government is felt openly, significantly, and everywhere. Important changes at the national level either cause or are
caused by political changes.

The modern concept of the nation-state belongs to western culture. It was the invention of western Europe and of North America
and did not always exist. Nation-statehood has been introduced
throughout the world wherever western culture has touched it, and
it has been taken on in such a fashion that people who are just becoming politically aware wish to emulate it to form new nation-
states. In some cases, achieving nationhood has meant to the populations concerned a way of aiding their rulers rather than themselves, and in other cases has been accepted as an agreement which
has to be made in exchange for material aid.

Nations come into existence in many ways. They are formed
out of neighbor states, as Belgium was from France and Holland;
they are formed by colonial secession, as the United States was from
Great Britain; they are formed by conquest, like the city-state of
Athens; they are formed by the consolidation of smaller units from
principalities, like Germany. When by means of a superior force,
provided usually by a superior technology with the added assurance it gives the will, a people decide to govern themselves through
their appointed representatives, a state comes into existence, overcoming the little resistances from within and the major resistance
which is usually brought to bear from without.

Countries can deal with other countries only in terms of a relative autonomy. In all events the world is getting to be a much
smaller place and foreign relations are now practically unavoidable.
Under these circumstances, nationalism appears inevitable. The
pressure for conformity has come from the need for international

law, from trade, and lately from the prospect of membership in the United Nations. It has come, in some countries formerly organized along tribal lines, from the ebbing of the colonial administration of the great European powers, usually with the promise of foreign aid by the United States or the Soviet Union, and always with the price tag of adherence to one or the other of two political systems.

A period of consolidation is usually occasioned by the development of a newly found sense of social solidarity, by the formation of a tradition through the covert and inadvertent establishment of a set of values. Deeply rooted traditionalism discloses the presence of metaphysical beliefs, and these stand in the way of change. The religion of Islam in Turkey and Iran, the caste system in India, the system of totem and lineage in Australia, the ancestor worship and relative autonomy of Ashanti chiefs—all these have stood effectively in the way of transitions to western scientific-industrial cultures.

The assumption underlying many contemporary political studies, that progress necessarily consists only in following the course of development of the modern scientific-industrial culture under the political domination either of capitalistic democracies or of communism, is undemonstrated. There are several reasons which can be adduced to justify this statement.

In the first place, many of the cultural adaptations which underdeveloped countries abandon in order to fall in with the march of technology might have been better preserved. This is essentially true of small groups in rigorous or isolated situations. The Eskimo forgot how to use his bow and arrow when he exchanged it for rifles and bullets not always in supply. The Tahitian native has not gained much from his contact with the white man. He has lost both his country and the freedom to follow his ancient traditional practices.

In the second place, it has yet to be demonstrated that in scientific-industrial nations a way has been found to avoid war. It may well be that on balance, counting the effects of war as well as the techniques of peace, the new alternative does not represent the kind of gain more backward countries would choose to make. The obvious and perhaps fatal limitation of the scientific-industrial culture is that it has failed to keep pace in the social field with gains in the physical and biological. The discovery and control of immense physical forces and organisms has been sudden and enormous in scope. But the corresponding discovery of the nature of social forces and of social controls is wanting.

One form of political change involves the impact of a greater on a lesser civilization. Often the lesser is given no option, as the case with the Japanese when confronted by Europeans. The cross, or death by the sword—the Spanish alternative in South America—hardly left much choice. Currently, thanks to the competition between communist and capitalist blocs, underdeveloped countries are offered tempting gifts of money, goods and services if they will choose one version of western civilization rather than another, a situation which makes them forget the lesson which Gandhi tried to teach India, namely, that the third alternative of rejecting the proffered civilization does exist, a lesson which by the way his ablest political disciple, Nehru, promptly rejected.

Encounters between lesser and greater cultures generally result in the disintegration of the lesser. The newly developing nations of Asia and Africa represent today the cultures which have long ago survived contact with western civilization. They are the amalgam which has resulted from years of colonial occupation and rule; they have learned how to survive, though only under the modifications imposed by the greater powers with whom they have come into contact. Head-hunting and human sacrificing have been eliminated, for instance, and many of the artifacts of the greater powers, including some which are undesirable like whiskey and firearms, have been adopted.

But other and more primitive cultures have declined under the impact of the west to the point where they have lost their political identity. Change came to the Indians of the North American plains by way of defeat and consequent political dissolution. There are said to be as many Indians in the United States today as there were when the Europeans first discovered North America, but in proportion this means a pitiful few considering how the Europeans have prospered and multiplied in the United States during that same period. The original inhabitants of Greece were lost to their conquest by the invading Greeks, and the hairy Ainu of Japan were no match for the Japanese. Political organizations are not always augmented by stimulation from the outside; often it happens that they cannot meet the challenge in any way which will enable them to maintain their existence, and so they disappear even though segments of their population may survive under other rule.

Bentley was right when he called government a process but he was wrong in thinking it only a process. The very business of maintaining a government relies upon stability of structure in the midst of change. When a government is in transition this means that the structure of the government is changing, and in such a case it functions only with difficulty. In so far as a government is engaged in change, it cannot operate; and in so far as it operates, to that extent it does not change. But it can operate and it does change. Government is the generic name for a political organization which includes not only a process but also a structure.

Political changes on the national level at their most violent are called revolutions and are the result usually of internecine conflict. The Civil War in the United States from 1861 to 1865 was fought on one side at least in the interest of preserving the *status quo ante bellum;* it was fought and lost, and so there took place profound changes in the country, such as the freeing of the slaves. But the changes which occurred after the Civil War had more far-reaching effects, as, for instance, in the North the development of industrialism and the rapid acceleration of immigration. The results of peaceful evolution can be more drastic in their effects than those of violent revolution even though the former brings about changes more slowly.

Not all permanence is for the worse. The moves which are made to preserve the identity of a nation may give the appearance of change when in fact they are actions taken to avoid change. The restoration of the status quo is in itself neither good nor bad; it all depends upon effects on the remainder of the culture. That there was no restoration of slavery after the American Civil War was a good thing, but that after World War II there was a restoration in the United States of all those civil rights which had been suspended as a war measure was also good.

Not all change, violent or otherwise, is for the better. The French Revolution of 1789 caused much harm at the time but eventually brought about many improvements, including democracy; but the Nazis in Germany wrecked their democracy and installed an absolute dictatorship under which many Germans were ruined, until the nation itself was defeated in war.

Given the efficiency of destructive aggression as a generic need, it follows that revolution with all its mass violence is not difficult to foment. It might be important to remember, however, that although material constructions are slow and painful methods of need-reduction, they are in the long run the most satisfactory because civilization has been built in this way. It is relatively easy to tear down but difficult and painful to build up. And this is as true of the state as it is of any other construction. Anarchy is a method of getting rid of the old to make way for the new, but it is an interim method only and not a social and political way of life.

It should be remembered that not every change is for the better, and indeed many are for the worse. Progress is not a straight line upward. The Athenians were never again as culturally productive under the Macedonians or the Romans as they had been under their own rule. And the destruction of the Roman Empire by the Goths swept away a level of civilization that was not attained in the same area, not in fact by the Holy Roman Empire of Christianity and not until after the Renaissance and the coming of science to western Europe in the seventeenth century.

Nations rise and flourish through a concomitance of happy accidents. They fall through the failure of a series of deliberate actions designed to maintain or increase their success. In other words, their initial access to power was not planned but occurred fortuitously, and the decline of that power was largely the result of miscalculations. From the American Civil War of 1861-65 to the prosperous decades following World War II, the United States owed its position as the number one world power to the advantages of a new country with enormous natural resources; to the waves of immigration due to religious persecutions, to the potato famine in Ireland, to the effort of many Germans to escape military service; to the inventiveness of practical minded American applied scientists and technologists; and to a host of other unplanned and uncoordinated activities. If the United States declines hereafter, it will be due to the foolish actions of leaders who understood nothing of international politics and not enough about domestic difficulties.

There are other forces at work which can account for political decline, however. It is obvious that change is a continual process. Conditions never remain the same, and so a stabilized organization must also be a flexible one able to engage in give and take with contingent elements in its environment in a way best designed to maintain its integrity. If we look for the causes of failure, we will find them in the loss of this flexibility and the consequent downward adjustment.

The only possible way to run a country with a large population is by means of an efficient and well-established bureaucracy. But the more strongly the bureaucracy is established the less receptive it is to change. It defends the status quo in which it has a vested interest against change from whatever quarter. Changes occur none the less; they come from many sources, from the work of men of genius, from adjustments in the existing order made exigent by its inadequacies, and from changing conditions.

When a people through its government is no longer able to meet the challenge of change, that government declines in efficiency, and either falls as the result or becomes subordinate to the government of another country which exhibits the requisite strengths. The vitality of an organization consists of its adaptive capacity as exhibited in the interchange with its environment. When this is no longer easy, collapse follows. States like individuals die of old age, which is only another way of saying the failure to adapt. Thus in a sense it is the same bureaucratic machinery in a young country which makes its progress possible and which freezes later on into such rigidity that it stands in the way of further progress and even becomes an occasion for national decline.

Generally speaking, it is the idealist who is mindful of principles and permanence, and the materialist of practice and change. The idealist is impatient of expedients and compromises, and the materialist impatient of principles. That both have gotten hold of only half the truth never occurs to either. It is the materialist who notices the prevalence of change because he is looking for opportunities for himself and so is quick to take advantage of any loopholes that transitions so frequently provide.

But even Halifax, that hard-headed contemporary of Locke, insisted that there is a constant in public life which imposes upon any and every ruler the necessity of keeping to the common good. Halifax was aware that despite the power of government it could not do entirely as it liked, and, no matter how despotic it might be temporarily, in the long run it was answerable to an undefined force which eventually restored to the people a government which acted in their interest. Although almost defending expediency and removed from any lofty subscription to immutable principles, Halifax still acknowledged that change was not absolute but took place in terms of more subtle elements that did not change, presumably those basic human values upon which depend the irrefrangible needs of a people to maintain a community.

What human individuals must have from their society is the combination of stability and novelty, that is to say, slow change. Stability provides the background against which a routine can be maintained and existence endured. Novelty insures vitality, not merely life but a chance to make improvements leading to a good life. It so happens that these two elements are contraries: in so far as a nation remains the same it does not change. The compromise is possible only by dividing the elements so that what one furnishes the other does not furnish. Broadly speaking, the ideal of government would be a stable political structure inside of which other institutions could develop novelty.

The firmness of a nation is a function of its established morality and of the articles whereby such a morality is formally adopted, usually by becoming incorporated in a constitution. I have discussed change in connection with moral establishment already in the third section of Chapter IV. Changes in agreement with a charter must be accomplished in terms of revised interpretations of what its articles mean or could be read to mean. That such interpretations are undertaken is evidence of the deep need for stability. That is the only deliberate and recognized side. The need for novelty, which is equally felt, is not always known, though it often appears as efforts toward progress.

The recognition of evolution, of development and progress, probably dates no further back than the middle of the nineteenth century. Before that, progress was considered only as the movement toward perfection. From the Greek city-state to the most primitive forest tribes, improvement was considered in terms of the perfection of an existing order and not as the radical exchange of it for another. However, Darwin has lived and died, and now in all likelihood the notion of evolution, which has spread from biology to all other areas, will never die so long as there are social organizations. The twin demands for permanence and change must be met in some way which does not discontinue the nation as an entity.

Something approaching permanence is introduced through the strength of institutions, in the case of the state chiefly the institution of political bureaucracy. Leadership is apt to provide the novelty and change, and that is basically why leadership and bureaucracy are often opposed. But both furnish an element which is necessary and so both must be maintained. The nation as a whole has somehow to absorb this opposition without being destroyed by it if it is to continue as a cohesive unit. If we wish to understand the nature of permanence and change as these occur in a nation, we had best turn to the level of institutions.

Section 4. Institutional Changes

Institutional changes in so far as they affect politics consist of alterations within the government and in shifts in the struggle for the control of government on the part of other institutions.

Changes in government can be so numerous and varied that it is difficult to know where to begin to describe them. Once again, they can take place either as structural modifications or as departures which do not disturb the structure. A political revolution or an orderly amending of the constitution may equally bring about radical changes. But on the other hand, far-reaching deviations may result from the administration of a strong or weak executive. A strong executive may stretch his office to its extreme limits in order to achieve the effects he desires; a weak executive may exert so little force that others are free to exercise the control that is properly his.

Despite the best efforts of the founders of the state to provide freedoms within the country sufficient to protect and preserve its underlying structure, the mere repetition of routine and all its tiny procedures accumulates subtle changes which, although not recognized at the time, are capable of adding up significantly. When we say that changes occur in time, this is what we mean; for time itself is not causal, only the repetition *in* time. Exact repetition is hardly ever achieved, and if the tiny social differences occur often enough may add up to qualitative changes. The progress in social affairs is akin to the one already noticed in genetic mutations. I doubt whether taxes are ever calculated or laws imposed twice in exactly the same way. For instance, tax provisions are almost always subject to interpretation, and new laws are sometimes introduced while others are either repealed or allowed to become "dead letters."

The various divisions in a government operate in relation to its center. An effective bureaucracy may influence the executive in conservative directions. Then again, the military is often strong enough to dictate policy, at other times not. Sometimes local government is powerful and at other times ineffective. The divisions of government shift and change not only with the changing values which underlie the culture but also with the character of the men who exercise control. There have been no important structural changes in the government of the Soviet Union from Stalin to Kosygin, but everyone outside the country has noticed differences.

Institutional changes occur in the struggle for the control of government on the part of other institutions. Government has its own functions and its strict adherence to them is the method calculated to produce the most efficient political results. But it is always somewhat at the mercy of a shift in the basic value system from which the established morality takes its cues. Other institutions change their positions in the hierarchy, and those that rise to the top always endeavor to reinforce their claims by dictating to government the sort of order they have come to authorize.

We have already noted in another connection that in some states the established religion was so powerful that the chief executive held his authority from it; hence the "divine right of kings." But the influence on government of other institutions is not always so clear and definite as it was during the Christian Middle Ages in Europe or in the Near Eastern Moslem Empire from the ninth to the fourteenth centuries.

Currently, pure and applied science and technology exert strong influences on government in every country where they exist in well-developed forms. Scientific changes can and often do alter the entire face of the country and the lives of its people. But unlike religions, science has its effects in less organized ways. The scientists do not always present to the government the spectacle of an integrated pressure group with specific demands which must be met. Instead, all is informal and piecemeal, and the influence of science must not be thought of as any less effective for that.

Just when it was beginning to be understood that political economy could be fractioned into its political and economic components, Marxists pointed to the dependence of politics upon economics. Communism represents the triumph of the economic over the political. But in practice it has worked out to something quite different from what it was in theory. The dictators of Marxist states—Kosygin, Tito and Mao Tse-tung—are politicians who call the shots for economic development in their respective countries. All one can say is that Marxism represents an attempt on the part of the institution of economics to capture the political citadel, an assault that failed. The political leaders of the state still dominate, and although they consider economics crucial, it is only a secondary effect, not a primary cause.

Although, as we noted much earlier, governments would exist even if there were no conflict of interest, it may still be the varying fortunes of those engaged in the struggle which largely account for changes in government. As interest groups grow stronger or weaker and their influence over government waxes or wanes, revisions in the government appear. The texture of a government is determined to some extent by the arrangements of people in the country: who dominates it and why; the economic ascendancy of one interest or another, the political force of one organized group as opposed to the political weakness of some other which is potentially stronger but does not possess proper organization.

It often happens that cohesive bodies of citizens exercise more political influence than others which are larger and less in accord. The medical profession gets more of its own way in the United States than the academic profession. College and university professors have little in common politically, even though their economic fate is the same. They vote democratic out of conviction when economically they should vote republican out of necessity.

No doubt from the ideal point of view, politics should exist to serve everyone equally: all individuals, all interest-groups, all institutions. This can only happen when the government is free from special pressures which tend to make it partial to one group or other. But this is seldom the case and lobbying of some kind is the rule rather than the exception. The chief hope for a fair administration in any country and under any form of government must rest pragmatically upon a balance of pressure groups and an equilibrium of tensions.

But even when the government is secure enough in its powers to stay in charge and not be subject to the control of other institutions, it sometimes can do this only by overhauling itself, by making such adjustments in its operation, and often in its structure, as the situation demands. Power is not delegated permanently in any case but must be retained at the cost of special effort. This means meeting challenges, but meeting challenges requires in its turn the erection of special defenses requiring alternations; and so the confrontation has an effect even though the power structure remains the same. The realignment of support by a chief executive of the government can often enable him to stand off threats which he could not have done on the basis of an older alignment. Constant vigil is the price of the retention of power and this is true even for those to whom it has been legally delegated.

Section 5. Individual Changes

If the account of the individual given in the fourth chapter of this book is a correct one, then aggression is characteristic of him; such aggression as he is individually unable to express is turned over to the state for that purpose. Thus the greatest power that a single individual could hope to have in his own time is the control of the state itself. The struggles that are waged in every country for the prize of supreme political power, no different in extent for different forms of government, should be all the evidence necessary to support the truth of this statement. Political power is not the only kind, artists, for example, or philosophers, would rather control future generations of men because these constitute a greater population. Yet a political power which can be wielded in the present appeals to most ambitious men.

Broadly speaking, what the individual wants is maximum power for the private sector of the society in which he lives. The least government, provided it functions efficiently, is certainly the best government; and one test of a government is the extent to which in executing its tasks it is able to leave the individual alone. Is there any vigorous man who could truthfully say that he does not want to be his brother's keeper? The negative answer to this question accounts for most of the havoc in the social world.

Men do seek to control each other's destiny, and one familiar form of such control is government: the more complex the culture the more omnipresent the government. An individual living in a culture which offers him a variety of advantages has to pay the rather high price of the enlargement of the public sector. Considering the achievements of ancient Athens, the number of political considerations occupying the average citizen are startling indeed, compared, say, to China under the Sung from the tenth to the thirteenth centuries. Privacy is the condition necessary for many of the greatest human achievements because these are the result of the controlled imagination of solitary individuals, and privacy is a condition which, at the best of times, has to be wrung from publicity.

Individual changes are varied and multiform. The individual citizen is the principal recipient of all the influences that at one time or another pervade the culture. He is the end of the line, and toward him all forces converge, for his name is legion. Thus either a change by the government, or a change in the government forced upon it by a rearrangement of the order of institutions, must find itself reflected in the beliefs which are fundamental to the individual citizen.

The citizen lives according to his most basic beliefs and every effort is made to put them into practice. Not the least of his actions is that which engages him in the political sphere. In times of crisis, a few vociferous and energetic individuals usually carry the day in political matters, but it is the passive permission of the majority which makes ordinary political turns possible. And since what is ordinary may unexpectedly become critical, the part played by the individual citizen may prove collectively decisive.

What the individual citizen wants politically and what he would be willing to fight to get varies greatly. He may seek material benefits, political liberty, aggressive government, all which would enable him to participate in wars of conquest, or do nothing less than exercise his right to rebel. In every instance, however, he tends to see what he wants in the light of two opposed ideals: self-interest and justice. As to the first, no doubt his native instinct for self-preservation operates, and he tends to push hard for political moves which will benefit him personally whatever the cost to the other members of his society.

But it is also true that he tends to see what he wants in the light of justice. Radical changes or mere reforms may enlist his sympathies and support, but always it is in terms for him at least of what ought to be: what ought to be continued, what ought to be changed, what ought to be tried, what ought to be restored. Even his desire to be left alone politically is the demand for a certain kind of government which would be able to preserve his liberties and privileges, his rights and prerogatives.

Every individual, unfortunately, has a distorted and flattering picture of himself. His image is that of an exceedingly stable and upright citizen who is always anxious to do the right thing and be prepared to do it rationally. The image is not always false but it usually is. He tends to be stable only in a stable situation; otherwise, he is easily moved through the appeal to his emotions, quick to change, and unreliable. This may vary from country to country, and in a given population from time to time. But it does mean that those anxious for political stability must look elsewhere for support.

Surely in terms of stable citizenship in European history, England lies at one end of the spectrum and France at the other. The Englishman's talent for self-government has been considerable, the Frenchman's has hardly existed at all. The French citizen, urged this way and that, is not at peace with his society because he is not with himself, being pulled in contrary and conflicting directions because of the ambivalence of his aggression, making of his political participation always to some extent a disturbing and unsettling factor.

Despite the contrast between England and France in political stability, both nations have contributed considerably to western culture, thus showing that the state rests on something besides a mere collection of individuals, or that the individuals themselves are not at all times equally mindful of what binds them indissolubly together.

Chapter XIII

THE INSTITUTIONAL STATE

In this chapter I propose to look at current tendencies in politics as illustrated by what is happening in the United States and the Soviet Union. Leadership in politics emanates from them because they are the most advanced industrial countries in which pure science and its by-products, applied science, and technology, are heavily committed. In terms of this particular development most other countries may be considered either followers of one of these two or regressive and conservative. More importantly, despite their very different origins, the United States and the Soviet Union are drifting closer together in structure and function. Both are products of western civilization and are its inheritors. And so they have more than pure and applied science in common; they have a basically similar established morality to which they wish to conform. It would be instructive to detect the events which lead to this.

I shall explain what I conceive to be the political trend in these larger countries, and then undertake to show how the same structure could work for both of them. But first it will be necessary to outline a theory of institutional classes, for that, I maintain, is the end toward which the structure of both our model countries tend economically and where they may end politically.

Section 1. Theory of Institutional Classes

The state always involves a class structure—so far the Marxists are accurate. There is no state with a classless society. The classes are functional and they cut across institutions. Yet, Marx missed one very crucial distinction, and that is the class division which exists within every institution. For every institution has within it two classes: the subject matter men who are occupied with serving the ends for which the institution was devised, and the institutional men who are occupied with running the institution.

Now it happens that the subject matter men are peculiar to the institution in the sense that they have trained themselves for it and could work in no other, while the institutional men could easily fit into any other. The institutional men are able to unite inter-institutionally. They could if they wished form a league of institutional managers; and they would find, if they did, that they had common problems. The subject matter men could unite only intra-institutionally, which would hardly give them the same amount of political leverage. Thus the subject matter men are divided, as divided as the institutions in which they work; while the institutional men are united, and so could make common cause against the subject matter men. It is native to the institutional men to "play politics," and when subject matter men wish to advance themselves too they have to "play politics," only in their case it means seeking favors from the institutional men.

Given this situation, if adequate representation is sought for the state as a whole, it must be carefully organized. There would have to be politicians elected by the subject matter men, in a kind of upper House or Senate, and others elected by the institutional men in a sort of lower House of Representatives. There ought to be as many men in the upper House as there are types of institutions, and as many men in the lower House as there are percentages of men in the upper House, say of the order of one in the lower House for every ten in the upper House. Both Houses would have the power to initiate legislation, but only the upper House would have the final veto power. And the kind of legislation they initiated would obviously be the kind which suited their representation. Substantive ideas would originate in the upper House, while regulative ideas would come from the lower.

This would obviously not be the only kind of representation. For I would want again to divide the upper House into two branches: the representatives of the service institutions, in one, and those of higher institutions in the other. Men from the service institutions, from communication and transportation systems, for example, could hardly be expected to bring the same representation to bear as men from the higher institutions, from the sciences and arts. But both groups would be representing genuine interests vital to the society as a whole. This then would make three Houses in the Congress: two upper houses and one lower. In addition, there would be men with cabinet rank who were selected in the same fashion, the usual ones plus a minister of technology, for reasons already given in Chapter VI.

The theory of institutional classes is at the center of the theory of the institutional state. However, it is not enough. For, to operate institutional classes, an entire political framework is required. And where is this framework to come from and how is it to be provided? The most radical suggestion would be one made by a backward country which wished to catch up quickly with the developments of western civilization. But there are other and more gradual possibilities. I propose to examine two of these in the following two sections.

The structure of political changes which must take place in time are of a curious nature, for they consist in alterations in political systems which were designed to withstand changes in time and, in this sense, to be atemporal. A state can provide for its own changes, as the Constitution of the United States in fact does, but it can do so only within well-defined limits. In the last analysis, a state, like an individual, looks to its own continuance first and to all other considerations afterwards, so that the very incorporation within it providing for changes goes against its own inherent nature.

Section 2. The Extended Theory of Democracy

Democracy has grown up with capitalism and has benefitted from it.

Capitalism has been responsible for the development of modern industrial society, for experimental science, and for the social benefits which have come through applied science and technology. It has been responsible for individual freedoms and for the rights of the individual against the state. These are on the good side.

But capitalism has been responsible also for cartels, for the separation of ownership from management, for business big enough to threaten government, for the disparity between political freedom and economic dependence. The institutions within a democracy are not necessarily democratic nor need they be. Business is almost never democratic, while labor unions often are.

The politics of democracy has carried with it both a distrust of absolutes and a set of subordinate institutions in which rival absolutes hold sway. It came into prominence and power with the religion of the Protestant Christian sects. Calvin rejected the infallibility of the Catholic Church only to substitute that of the Bible. It was the separation of Church and State which rendered the religious absolutes politically harmless and so protected democracy.

In any developing society the vigor of its efforts always strains against formal political restrictions and calls for a reexamination of structure. In the United States at the present time, it may be that the only political organizations which are genuine and necessary under modern conditions of communication and transportation are: the local community (village, town, city, megalopolis) and the nation-state. Of the intermediate units in the United States, for instance, at least fifty of the separate and to some extent sovereign states have no longer any genuine function. Their lines were artificially and in many cases arbitrarily drawn, and they represent no properly separate interests. A wheat growing community has interests which must be considered apart from the nearest manufacturing community, but together do not form a viable unit merely because they exist in Kansas or Iowa.

Democracy is a word with many meanings. Primarily it has been understood as the retention of sovereignty in the hands of the people who had delegated their power to designated representatives, but actually it has relied more upon political pluralism: the alternation of parties in power, with the maintenance of the rights of the minority on a par with those of the majority in such a way that their roles can be exchanged by due electoral process. This last is the essence of democracy as we have it, even though it is not stipulated anywhere in the documents establishing our government.

However, many changes have occurred in the actual practice of democracy to modify it. Originally it made no provision for the vast expansion of the disparity between capital and labor. The extended theory of democracy includes a graded tax structure with the burden on the rich. It includes also the politically unofficial but officially endorsed labor unions whose demands have done so much to ameliorate the deprivations of the working class and to provide for them.

Democracy in ancient Athens was direct democracy. With the rise of the large populations this was no longer possible and representative democracy took its place. But the size of the populations continued to increase and the maintenance of democracy of the kind presently operating is no longer possible in countries with still larger populations. In order to maintain the democratic form of government in a country with a population in the hundreds of millions, there must again be a revision. It is necessary at this point to split the elite into sectors having diverse power bases. This is in fact what prevails today in the United States.

The original elite, whose power base was in property is having its power curtailed by the addition of another elite of scientific provenience. The political sector already existed but will have to be shifted from its dependence on the property based elite to one resting on the broader base of the masses. Also, it will be necessary to strengthen the academic sector as one contributing more than its proportional share in directing the culture. The sciences together with technology ought to have taught us that economic determination is not enough. Economics furnishes the means but we shall have to look elsewhere for the ends. Society does not exist in order to do what it does well, but it does what it does well in order to reach a goal previously set.

In the United States, for the lowest economic class of the disadvantaged, welfare provisions have been introduced to provide food, education, health, housing, and similar services at the expense of the government. These three steps have been taken in the direction of socialism without abandoning the political elements of democracy which had been established in the first place.

The present tendencies in the United States are as follows: a powerful central government, becoming every day more powerful; the military encroaching more and more upon political power; popular sovereignty; many features of the welfare state, such as medicare, unemployment insurance and old age benefits—in short, what Germany became for a while under Bismarck; but combining with these custodial management and in general greater regulation of popular ownership. The democratic "welfare state" is still democratic in form and socialistic in intent. It represents democracy drifting in the direction of socialism by taking care of economic inequalities which threatened to overthrow the democracy.

There are other changes of which we must also take note.

The rising importance of the armed forces is a threat to democracy which it must somehow manage to absorb and control. Most advances in military techniques are the result of civilian effort. The tank, the war plane, the atom bomb were all civilian discoveries. But the great states have been those in which civilian authorities remain superior to the military. Diplomacy is not a military game, and the military should take over only when diplomacy fails. In effect, the military as a political force, though in this connection only, represents a threat to the democracy it was otherwise devised to defend.

The extended theory of democracy calls for yet another separation of powers to be added to the executive, legislative, judicial and technological: the administrative, whose task it will be to coordinate the various branches of government and of federal agencies at all levels, in order to avoid duplication and conflict. In view of the immense growth of both populations and governments, five separate powers do not seem excessive.

Part of the administrative function would be the new office of ombudsman earlier mentioned, the official appointed by the legislature to receive, investigate, and correct complaints of injustices against individual citizens brought about by administrative action. This is certainly a step in the direction of extended democracy. The system was first instituted in Sweden in 1809, spread to Finland in 1919, and more recently to Denmark, Norway and New Zealand, and has begun to be adopted in the United States. It is strongly democratic in character and gives the individual a sense of security against a vast bureaucracy with which he would otherwise be unable to cope. The idea could be extended to interest groups and even to institutions.

The new understanding of democracy will have to include a better concept of the human predicament. If democracy is to be defended as the best available form of government, it will have to include the recognition of its limitations, itself a very democratic attitude. For we must be aware that the universe in not a democracy and neither is the science of physics. Truth is not a democratic affair. The difficulty arises chiefly from the misunderstanding of just what political democracy means. Democracy never did mean keeping people equal, for they are not. They are not born equal, but have different potentials in every respect. Democratic equality is equality of opportunity which allows those with native ability to rise no matter what their starting point in life, and so renders justice through economic and cultural mobility, that is, to each as much as he is capable of doing.

The justification of democracy as a form of government is clearly based on ignorance with respect to the true course to be followed in politics. If people really knew what was best for them, democratic governments would be better than they are. It is difficult to escape from the grave consequences of this fact, but it is also and more importantly the case that its recognition will mean that many evils could in this way be avoided. In the fourteenth century, Marsilio of Padua admitted that he was not always sure and that a position he was defending might well have been wrong.

A political rule emerges from the dilemma of politics: *It is necessary to accept some doctrines firmly enough to justify admin-*

*istering them by force (an enacted law, for instance,) and yet to
hold them so tentatively that their replacement is not inconceiva-
ble.*

To the extent to which this is true, the society is open. The less
individual citizens are regulated the greater the opportunity for
original and productive work in science, art, and philosophy. The
sense of freedom imparted to the individual citizen has to be
matched against the benefits of the social security he derives from
the welfare state. In the end, also, other generations have to be remembered, not only those that went before but also those to come.
The ideal democracy includes all those citizens who have passed
through it, who currently are passing through it, and who are yet
to pass through it—a tightly related community of generations.

Thus human individuals can assert their claims as individuals
apart from any rights they may enjoy through institutional affiliation. What is called for here is the encounter with the sovereign individual as an inviolable constituent of the polity. Given the
structure of the state as defined by the theory of institutional
classes, what is called for is a balance between a professional institutional bureaucracy and a local electorate. In the United States
the local community—the town, village, city—has more and more
to be counted among the essential political entities. After that there
is nothing until we come to the government of the country. The
two extremes, the smallest and largest unit, come together for political harmony, matched only by an intermediate division into institutional representations.

States do not stand still; they either grow or decline. The
United States is still growing, though signs of consolidation are beginning to appear here and there as the country approaches the
zenith of its curve. Political activity and stability or instability
might have different meanings in periods of growth and in those
of retrenchment. What a country is doing in this regard affects its
use of economic and social power. But that the democratic processes are becoming more flexible and more accommodating still points
to growth. One of the great discoveries of civilization is that a society can be so organized that the competition between individuals
benefits the group and the competition between groups benefits
the society. Here, then, is another political rule: *to assure that*

competition at all levels is constructive, rather than destructive, this is the essence of extended democracy.

Political freedom is needed by the individual in order to preserve the richness of cultural differences. Political similarity with preservation of cultural differences is the goal of democracy properly conceived. Politics is part of culture, too, but it must maintain the similarity at sublevels, otherwise there could be no cultural differences. We shall see in the discussion of extended communism how the preservation of political differences could also be preserved.

Section 3. *The Extended Theory of Communism*

In order to get communism established in Russia, it had to be narrowly conceived and, so to speak, driven home. In its initial stages no compromises were permitted. More than a political doctrine was involved. With communism came the cultural structure necessary for it: that of industrialism.

Schemes invented for one purpose may often serve another. Marxism was intended to serve as the spearhead of the most advanced industrial countries, but instead it proved to be the rallying cry of a self-conscious proletariat leadership engaged in the fast development of the scientific-industrial culture in backward countries at the sacrifice of a couple of generations. In addition to the politics of communism, an agricultural economy had to be turned into a western type of technological industrialism, with applied science in the foreground. This the Russians managed to install in the short span of twenty years.

The Russians of Stalin's era did not fare so well personally. They had to go largely without consumer goods, and they had also to conduct a war with Hitler's Germany. But the result was the solid establishment of socialism in a single country strong enough to withstand almost any attack, and the development of heavy industry to a point where the western democracies could be challenged.

Communism in the twentieth century has come to compete with nationalism left from the nineteenth century. But is not the com-

munism of the Soviet Union and Communist China merely a phil-
osophic-political disguise for the nationalism of lately industrialized
nations which are thereby equipped to compete militarily as well
as economically and politically with the capitalist nations on the
international scene? Does it not bring to the surface what always
lay unacknowledged, that the crusading spirit has always to be
backed up by the kind of justification which can be furnished only
by a political philosophy that is strong because it rests on a metaphysics that is deeper still?

In the communist countries it is possible to see how political
philosophies get changed in both their character and influence in
ways which nobody anticipated. This comes about not merely
through guile—always a factor—but also through the stress of
events. Every actual social situation is a Procrustes' bed for every
theory applied to it; and when we add to this the inverse fact that
every social situation was brought about by the application of a
theory of some kind since theory alone is capable of producing
order, then we see how complex the state really is and how little
even the most powerful is able to predict precisely in what direction it will go.

As these developments took place securely, there began to be a
relaxation of the rigors of communist doctrine, not to any large extent, it is true, but at least a beginning. What was described in the
1950's as a "thaw" permitted more exchange with the western
democracies, the exchange not only of goods but of the performing
arts. In the productive fine arts there also was relaxation, so that
now, for the first time, it is beginning to be possible for poets to
criticize censorship when at home and abroad without serious
penalty.   .

In the Soviet Union enough difficulties still remain, however.
Marx correctly understood the association of property with political
power: the owner of property has the power to exercise control over
the masses who depend upon it for survival. Marx wanted all property to be in the possession of the state. But he seems not to have
foreseen that ownership is not the only form of power; control
will do just as well, and he who controls property without owning
it may behave in just as tyrannical a fashion. Marx seems to have
been oblivious to the tyranny of the communist state. The com-

munists concentrated the control of property in the hands of a few leading politicians when they turned it over to the state, and, as a consequence, politics became everybody's business because the making of a livelihood became the monopoly of politicians.

But the state, properly speaking, should function as a regulative rather than a constitutive institution, a social means and not an end. It should serve the society in a way that enables it to remain as unobtrusive as possible and not itself become the end to which all the efforts of the society are directed. That this is not the usual case distorts the society and defeats its best efforts. The society is in the awkward predicament of having the state preempt the position which rightfully belongs to the higher institutions. In the long run, no permanent good can come of that, no freedom, certainly, and no full cultural development. For similarities are provided for but not differences.

Tocqueville was very aware that equality effects a kind of tyranny that holds everyone on the same level, exercising a dominion by the majority in every domain, so that liberty with respect to differences is not possible. In the underdeveloped countries in which communism has been established, the decision to give up the plan to bring individual liberties to the people was made on the ground that what they first needed was bread, and that this could most quickly be provided for by a state sufficiently powerful to push through industrialization, develop science, and devise an elaborate technology. Thus, true socialism which looks first to political liberties was set aside in order to build the industrial structure which promised to provide economic liberties. The situation would be improved now if some of the political liberties similar to those which have been maintained in western democracies could be added.

It is easy to see how they were lost. We have now had in European history two broadly based revolutions: Christianity and communism. These should have served as a warning that there could be others if we were ever again to forget that government of whatever sort chiefly centers on the masses and is made possible by their passive if not by their active permission—by their sufferance.

Communism began in a manner strikingly similar to Christianity, as so many observers have noted. A mass movement possessing a spirit essentially inimical to organization is to be applied in practice, and for this an organization is found necessary. One is provided, but its effect is to subvert the spirit of the movement, so that what goes by the same name is in effect actually something quite different. There is little in the quotations from Jesus that justifies the strictures imposed by St. Paul, but this was the price of establishing a church. Quite the same things can be said of communism: there is little in the writings of Marx and Engels to justify the strictures imposed by Lenin, but this was the price of establishing a state.

Pauline Christianity is as far from the spirit of Jesus as Leninist communism is from the spirit of Marx and Engels. It has often been noted that the spirit of Christianity is not well represented in a church which has many provisions for which no authorization can be found in the sayings of Jesus. The establishment of a princely hierarchy among the clergy was certainly not provided for and can even be said to be foreign to the spirit of Jesus' intent so far as we can discern it in the Four Gospels. As for Marx, he saw that socialism would be developed and the working man's condition improved in advanced industrial countries, such as the United States and Great Britain, without the necessity of resorting to violent revolution. But the Soviet Russian communists, and the Chinese communists too for that matter, are far from believing any such thing.

Never before in history have people existed in such numbers. It is not possible to exercise rule over so many without their consent because of their power, and this, too, is something new in the world. Henceforth all governments in countries with large populations must be maintained with the consent of the many or at least in their name. The rise of the large populations in western Europe together with the rise of individualism was responsible for representative democracy. The rise of industrialism in the democracies of western Europe was responsible for communism in the underdeveloped countries of Asia with large populations. However, other west European ideas became also popular in Asia, such as nationalism.

The price paid for securing communism firmly in a single country, as has been done in Russia and China, is the retention of a fervid

nationalism of the variety found in noncommunist countries and
very much denounced by Marx and Engels as indicating the control of the capitalists in whose hands the state itself was merely an
instrument for the exploitation of the masses. Such nationalism
is part and parcel of the change that was effected by Lenin in the
original Marxist doctrine.

In order to bring communist countries into line with other
countries in a way designed to promote peace and true cultural
progress, which includes the economic and political as well as the
scientific and artistic, further modifications will have to be effected.
The duplicity of the communists who pretend to be peace-loving
while they promote violent political revolution in capitalist countries will have to be abandoned in favor of a more evolutionary encouragement of change in a socialist direction. The longer communism is established, the more its leaders and, indeed, their followers seem inclined to drift in the direction of an accommodation
with capitalism, for it becomes clear to everyone that more can
be accomplished by it. Soviet Russia has done more of this than
Soviet China, which maintains the attitudes of a state of belligerency
while denouncing as militarist and imperialist any response in kind
made by the western democracies.

The signs of change are slow but they are present. A second
generation of communists is not as prone to war as the first, and we
can hope that a third and a fourth will see even more clearly the
folly of undertaking to settle even basic differences with capitalist
democracies by using military methods, like the hydrogen bomb
or chemical warfare which threaten to destroy the human species
if used on a wide scale. For the west, it is in fact a race between the
death of the older generation of revolutionaries in China and the
development by the Chinese of a stockpile of nuclear weapons.
For the older leaders would not hesitate to use them while the
new leaders might.

There is one more sign that offers encouragement. The opposition which has developed between Soviet Russia and China is
sufficient to demonstrate that Marxist doctrine is not the universal
panacea it had been proclaimed. Communism may cross national
divisions and unite the working class, as Marx and Engels insisted
it does, but surely not in this case. Or at least if it unites the work-

ing classes of Russia and China it has not done so for their leaders. Other grounds of agreement—and hopefully those in which they can be joined by countries with whose political doctrines they have no sympathy—must be found in order to prevent the kind of disastrous conflict of which the industrial countries have been held capable.

The iron curtain erected by Stalin promoted an ignorance which has now to be dissipated. The cultural exchange programs which have been cautiously begun may hopefully be increased to a point where they will do much to replace the falsehoods promulgated by propaganda. Even more importantly these programs may spread a sense of familiarity which insures a certain measure of sympathy.

Section 4. The Party Dialectic

The opposition of the communist countries of Asia to the capitalist democracies of Europe and the United States may well lead to the kind of disastrous war which will effectively destroy them both. This is by no means certain, and they may in time reach sufficient agreement to save them and to give them the common cause of transforming the earth into a place where all people are able to lead enjoyable and useful lives. The key to the entire situation is that advanced industrial countries are developing a tendency to grow in the same direction through modifications in doctrines which are different. The United States and Soviet Russia are developing in similar directions because they contain many of the same elements. In a word, socialist tendencies are appearing in the United States, while democratic tendencies are beginning to be evident in Soviet Russia, though not yet in China.

As I write, the invasion of Czechoslovakia by the armies of Soviet Russia and its Balkan satellites has set back most of the democratic tendencies, though, if I am correct, this reaction will only be temporary. Suffice it to say that the gains the people make against absolute rule are sure to win out in the end and to transform the government into something more acceptable by making it flexible enough to include a political mechanism which would provide for legitimate dissent.

Judging by recent trends in the Russian economy, it would appear that Marxism has served as a speedy political device to bring underdeveloped countries up fast enough to make it possible for industrial production to keep pace with population increase. Both Soviet Russia and the United States may well end at more or less the same stage: a variety of modified and controlled capitalism working on industrial production based on applied science and advanced technology. There will be in both countries, as indeed there is now in the United States, a very large middle-income group, a technological society, and large populations. Life will be lived for its comforts while society builds toward the future, a combination made possible by a mass-responsible electorate and by a powerful central government which is more concerned with caretaking and regulating than with controlling or directing.

Both countries are inclined in the same direction because they represent varieties of the same movement to an extent unknown to themselves. The very democratic process which consists, as we have noted, in the alternation of parties in power is a movement which can only be adequately described in terms of a variation of the Hegelian dialectic. The party dialectic, as we may call it in amalgamated terms, is not one made any longer along class lines but is a division concerning the rate of advance which is to be adopted. It is always hoped that the party dialectic however designed can accommodate an adjustment of this rate without allowing it to disrupt the smooth and continuous functioning of the government.

Conservatism is the name for the way in which the world preserves the advances that have been made; liberalism is the name for the way in which the world seeks to make further advances. Both are susceptible to abuse. The abuse of conservatism is its opposition to progress; the abuse of liberalism is its revolutionary attack upon values currently maintained. The conservatives, anxious to consolidate gains, are aware that a certain amount of traditional observances is necessary for the maintenance of order through a period of transition; the evolutionists, or liberals, anxious to introduce novelty as a way of improving the existing order, are impatient of any traditional observances which threaten to stand in their way. The tensions and the balances between them, best arranged as an alternation of parties in power, constitutes what I have called the party dialectic.

This is how affairs are currently conducted in the United States where the continuing dialogue between political partisans allows for development in policies, for shifts and changes to be made in such a way that law can provide for them. Less than two political parties, incidentally, cannot sufficiently conduct a party dialectic. Too many parties, as in France, split the political organization into so many small fractions of power as to become unworkable.

In the Soviet Union, on the other hand, the maintenance of a single party means that within the party there are factions, usually two: two factions means, in effect, two unofficial subparties. This is a workable arrangement, but it has its own limitations. The situation is so fluid and unorganized as to threaten the political structure itself. Then again, and more seriously, there is no provision for the willing adherence of the losing faction or their toleration by the winning group. Often differences are settled by quiet and unofficial murder, as was the case with those who dared to differ with Stalin, and after him with his immediate successors. Another illustration of the limitations of the one-party system is the struggle that has been in progress for and against Chairman Mao.

Conservatism has a steadying influence and tradition is the name it often goes by, though, as an essential ingredient of the maintenance of a continuing government, it can have also a crippling effect. If national histories, like family trees, can be shown to have been more illustrious in the past than corresponding nations and families are in the present, it only goes to show how steep has been the decline. For states of affairs are altered by the course of events, and change is inevitable. There is almost always a migration of power, sometimes slowly, sometimes rapidly. Planned evolution must take its chances, though it too may occur; for people would be ill-advised to drift, and reason is their only recourse when facing the future.

Given the number of variables in any society, most of which are unknown, then any social situation which is deliberately brought about may be a cause that is sure to have unpredictable and in many cases undesired effects. This is true especially of revolutions. For violent actions may get rid of evils at which they are aimed, but they do away at the same time with many goods at which they are not aimed and usher in other unforeseen evils. No doubt the current struggle for freedom in the arts which is taking place in the Soviet Union will be won in the end, but not before many great works of art—and many artists—have been sacrificed.

What is foreshadowed, finally, by extrapolating the best of the present tendencies at work in the United States and the Soviet Union is an institutional state in which representation will be functional and in which the social enrichment of individual life will be moving toward its maximum. That such an outcome is inevitable is surely more than anyone can predict and no one can even say that it is likely; but given the current state of affairs and the set of ingredients involved—everything from the great mass populations which are awakening to the pursuit of pure science and a rapidly developing and widespread technology—what can be said is that such an outcome is at least potential, and this alone represents a great advance in human progress.

Section 5. The Combined Theory

Simmel pointed out that conflicting groups come to resemble one another. The most famous example is the similarity in customs and dress of the Goths and the Roman soldiers at the frontier toward the end of the fourth century A.D. That the same thing is happening in the United States and the Soviet Union is not immediately evident to either of them.

The concept of a social democracy which will not be entirely democratic or entirely communistic is beginning to develop in both countries. For instance, in the Soviet Union a system of financial rewards for superior abilities in the manufacturing and distribution of goods, which already exists in the arts and sciences, is in the making, while in the United States the line of demarcation between public and private ownership is beginning to be erased. In both countries limited controls over ownership not intended to eradicate it are being constructed; the Russians by relaxing some of their strictest prohibitions, the Americans by increasing theirs. In both countries it will result in federally regulated and widely owned monopolies, similar to the present situation in the American Telephone and Telegraph Company but with the number of shares one person is allowed to have arbitrarily limited.

Functional wealth will come to replace static ownership, by combining the best features of both older systems. As Wall Street moves closer to Washington, this tendency becomes stronger and stronger; and it becomes increasingly the case that control constitutes some variety of ownership and that economics cannot be altogether divorced from politics, in fact less and less so as manufacturing and distribution take nation-wide forms.

While the government of the United States shifts more toward the Soviet Union's kind of economic controls, the Soviet Union must shift politically in the direction of rule by consensus. Consensus is the result of the attempt to discover what social relations people want and to enact legislation in conformity with it in an attempt to give it to them; in effect, to remind them of what they said they wanted, with penalties for those errant exceptions which constitute fallible deviations from the existing and established norms.

One part of the machinery might be the sample periodic referendum, whereby decisions, actions, and enacted laws are referred to the electorate for ratification. It would not be necessary to stop work for this purpose, as in a national election where a holiday is declared to allow voters to get to the voting booths. A good substitute might be a federally operated Gallup Poll, which would take continuous samples of political and economic opinion. The result would be not a party majority but a social concord. For in addition, institutional voting would be on a more significant basis so that expert functioning could be provided.

Thus, two sorts of sampling would be conducted without interruption during the life of the state: the federally operated sample opinion poll and consultating with professional experts within relevant institutions. The second could be weighed more heavily than the first, but the two could be brought into line by the officials of government whose specific task this concord might be.

What I am suggesting is the concept of an industrial timocracy, where honor would be based on the extent of obligation rather than of privilege. An aristocracy based on generosity of contribution would function in such a way that the more distinction accrued to a citizen the better off the state and its people. Honor could be based on positive contributions of any sort, with the highest award reserved for those whose discoveries have been of greatest value, tardiness of recognition notwithstanding.

More often than not, the importance of the productive individual is in direct proportion to his inability to make common cause with his contemporaries. Plato ruled out the genius from his Republic and so prevented the occurrence of another Plato. That this can happen ought to be made more evident than it has been, so that before condemning an original thinker the possibilities that just might result from his work would be remembered. In short, what we need is a genius conscious public whose members are well aware that the social significance of the original contributor is not in proportion to number.

The combination of improvement with stability is the problem for every progressive society. How much change can be endured without a disturbance of equilibrium so great that it threatens survival of the body politic? It should be the task of the Supreme Court to determine the answer to such a question whenever a case arises for which it is relevant. The Supreme Court has the task of saying what is and what is not in the spirit of the Constitution. Perhaps a Constitutional Court should be added to determine what of the Constitution is in need of amendment to keep it consistent with the changing nature of artifacts and the consequent changes in the needs of the citizens. For the last appeal is not to the established morality but to ethics itself in so far as this can be determined by those entrusted with the task.

Part Three

A HAZARD OF DESTINY

Chapter XIV

DIPLOMACY AS GAME AND SPORT

Section 1. Politics as a Power Contest

Politics as a process of government is a generic term with an internal and an external species. We have in this book thus far confined the discussion to internal politics, but now we must turn our attention to the external variety.

For this purpose politics will have to be redefined. It is the theory of social control involved in the settlement of conflicts, a contest in aggression with possibly destructive consequences: either naked aggression, as with Cesar Borgia and his apologist, Machiavelli, or channeled aggression, as with established government under the rule of law.

External politics has three main subdivisions; these are listed in the order of increased intensity of involvement of a nation with others: diplomacy, international relations, and war. We shall deal with diplomacy in this chapter, and with international relations and war in the following two.

I define diplomacy as official contacts between governments conducted by applying principles of rhetoric to negotiations of international relations, usually through the offices of ambassadors and envoys. Diplomacy deals with all the formal external relations of the state, short of war. Delegates emerge from chancellories intent upon exercising the art of persuasion through patient conciliation and compromise or through cajolery, threats, and open intimidation.

In the last sense, diplomacy in its turn is found in two main forms: it is a game or a sport. Before we can consider diplomacy in this way, we shall have to understand our terms.

I define game as a formal contest involving symbolic aggression guided by established ground rules. To play a game is to make a selection of moves from among those which are permitted by the rules, where such rules have the peculiarity that they both limit the moves and make them possible; tennis or chess, for example. I define sport as a game involving actual physical aggression; tiger hunting, say, or professional football. War has sometimes been a sport but more often it has involved total aggression. Diplomacy when properly conducted behaves like a game, but may deteriorate into a sport or even into a war.

When diplomacy leads from strength, it is based on the usable power structure of a state. The power structure contains two elements. For want of better terms these may be labelled "ideas" and "hardware," more formally, propaganda and weaponry. The former may be a philosophy, as is the case with Marxism, and the latter may be a formidable arsenal, as is the case with a stockpile of intercontinental ballistic missiles. Diplomacy might mention neither but it relies upon the existence of both.

The more polite nineteenth century version of diplomacy in western Europe assumed a common politics and therefore never considered philosophy; it was devoted to the niceties of verbal exchanges without reference to fundamentals. But the asymmetrical possession of political philosophies has existed before; it existed in Moslem diplomacy from the seventh to the fourteenth centuries, and it existed prior to that in Asian diplomatic dealings. Thus diplomacy may concern itself with any part of a spectrum running from the polite settlement of trivial differences between nations which are largely in agreement, on the one hand, to the use of political philosophies to engage in thinly veiled threats of the use of weapons in an aggressive and ruthless war, on the other.

Games are competitive contests which depend upon a mixture of chance and skill or strength. Some games require more skill than others; some rely more upon chance. But in either case the outcome is unknown in advance and there is a certain measure of enjoyment in the play. Every culture, every civilization, has its games, and much can be learned from their nature. But all have the elements of the power structure I have mentioned.

No doubt games are symbolic. Life itself is a kind of game which we play through necessity and even enjoy to some extent, though we cannot foresee the outcome. In games, we gamble with anticipation: who will win? All of us wish to foresee the future, if only a little, and we do so to the extent to which we can predict a winner.

Section 2. *The Game of Diplomacy*

Games are either accidental or necessary. Those that are accidental *may* be played, like cards; those that are necessary *must* be played, like diplomacy. In either case, those who play must submit themselves to the rules of the game, for it is in the very nature of a game that, once chosen, everything becomes necessary. Now diplomacy falls into the area of international law, for, in international law, there is no external coercive force able to insure that the rules will be followed by imposing penalties for their infraction. Thus the form of the game must be substituted. Diplomacy, then, becomes a game that must be played well for its own sake if there is to be any semblance of international order.

In calling diplomacy a game I have had in mind several features. It has its own ground rules and its own type of interest, and therefore can be engaged in as though it were a valid social isolate. The fact that its results may determine the fate of nations can be neglected temporarily, indeed ought to be if they are to have the effects intended, just as a surgeon may have to forget the interests of the patient upon whom he is operating in order to concentrate on the technical details that immediately concern him.

It is difficult, I recognize, to understand that games in which nothing imminent is involved—those properly called games—have much in common with games in which everything is at stake. In calling politics a game, more is suggested than a similarity to chess. The common element is strategy.

In the world of between-nations where there are no established rules strategy itself prevails. But strategy practiced long enough develops its own rules. Among the rules so established were those customs defining outward consideration, mutual regard, the honoring of verbal commitments, and agreements about concealing all pending negotiations. The diplomatic niceties conducted in public have had the effect of increasing the probabilities of arriving at international harmonies.

Political ceremonies among diplomats amounted to a kind of ritual, and ritual is a dramatized illustration in concrete materials of an accept belief respecting general objects. Doing is a reinforcer of knowing and so a kind of guarantee of being. Diplomacy conceived in these terms operates against a background of maneuvering to find the elements in common between established systems of morality.

The triumphs of diplomacy are amply illustrated by the achievements of some of Europe's most able diplomats, notably Germany's Bismarck, France's Talleyrand, Italy's Cavour, America's Franklin. Such successes depend in part upon the diplomat's own personal qualities, his charm and intelligence, which often substitute for national power. They would not have been possible without a national power base, but this in its turn requires gifted men if it is to be properly exercised. We see its failure equally in men like Britain's Sir Anthony Eden, America's John Foster Dulles, and Communist China's Chen Yi. Of course, success or failure in such cases can be judged only in terms of international programs in general and national programs in particular.

Diplomacy was once a matter of state representation. The diplomat acted for his sovereign in dealing with foreign governments. He made all decisions for his own government, including crucial ones, and on the spot because there was no other way, communications being as slow as they were; he assumed all the responsibility this entailed. Today the situation is changed. Thanks to the enormous increase in the speed of communication, the diplomat has become a kind of dignified and formal messenger. He still often bargains in the name of principals, but they must be consulted at each stage and it is they who make the final decisions.

With the passing of the need for diplomats to make commitments deeply involving their respective countries, there has arisen a new concept of diplomacy. One new concept has been introduced by the older democracies which have had to conduct negotiations more and more in the open as they were trusted less and less by their electorate. Another new concept has been introduced by the communist nations and has had to be countered by the older democracies who deal with them. The communists have been clever at using diplomacy as a cover for spying and subversion, thus setting international relations back many decades, if not centuries. Trust is so difficult to build up, so easy to destroy. But more of this when we come to discuss diplomacy as a sport.

Many diplomats regret the passing of the old style diplomacy based on secret negotiations in favor of the democratic variety based on open covenants and sensitivity to public opinion at home, and of the communist variety based on deceptions and bluntness. But there is no evidence that any one of the three methods has been more successful than any other in preventing war. The error lies perhaps in supposing that mere diplomacy can settle substantive disputes or that material interests can somehow be abated through personal contact and discussion.

Section 3. The Sport of Diplomacy

When the game becomes a sport, it has grown more serious. For sport is a game with the added risk of actual physical injury or destruction. Sport is a contest in aggression involving violent activity but without destructive consequences, and usually employing symbolic substitutes; usually though not always, for there are the dangerous sports of bullfighting and boxing, which may be fatal. The bullfighter may be gored but more often than not lives to fight another bull. The boxer is knocked down but gets up again after the bout. Like games, which it resembles in all but violence, sport is engaged in for its own sake. While tragedy is contained in the victory of the vanquished, sport endorses the victor of the contest. Short of the most dangerous variety, sport is a form of vicarious aggression capable of drawing off the harmful effects of other kinds of competition.

There are two forms of sublimation for vicarious aggression: sport and art. In sport there is the spectator's emotional role in physical competition. In art there is emotional participation, again with two forms: comedy, in which the violence is accepted as funny, and tragedy, in which it is accepted as inevitable. Sport resembles art to the extent that in both there is emotional spectator participation; but in sport there is actual physical participation, where there is not in art.

We are now in a position to turn back to diplomacy and to consider it as the sporting side of politics. The aims of diplomacy are many. The diplomat is authorized to represent his country and to speak for it. He is charged with obtaining information concerning the country to which he is posted; information including not only facts but feelings, tendencies, dispositions. He should also furnish information about his own country, and give with it a sense of its own dispositions, particularly with respect to contemplated joint projects, such as the making of treaties, the undertaking of alliances, and the attitudes toward third and less friendly countries.

He is, in short, not only a sensitive recording mechanism passing on to superiors the drifts and tendencies characterizing the country of his assignment from day to day, but also an advance agent of that country, able through his authority aided by the force of his personality to convey the power and direction to which his own country is apt to give its full weight. Diplomacy is a delicate business of political fencing, of discussions, of enticement and threats calculated to influence without using force but often, if not always, with the inherent threat of force. The element of threat is proportional to the strength of the state practicing diplomacy; often its very existence is enough to wring concessions from diplomats.

In the last analysis, national power is what counts, and no amount of pretending by the diplomat or reliance upon past eminence will be an adequate substitute. As Stalin is said to have asked when the force of the Roman Catholic Church was mentioned: "The Pope? How many divisions does he have?" Nevertheless, it is sometimes true that personal prestige makes up for national power, as, for instance, when Nehru represented an internationally powerless India at the United Nations.

The efficiency of the new communist methods in diplomacy,

which employ naked threats and deliberate lies, depends upon opponents not using the same tactics. A game cannot be played if one of the players upsets the table when he is losing. It has often been pointed out that the dishonesty of the few relies upon the honesty of the many, otherwise it would not prove workable. If John were to rob Tom's house while Tom was robbing John's, the result would be self-defeating.

In the end, diplomacy will not work unless all governments involved instruct their diplomats to behave like diplomats, or, more important still, unless there is some intent on both sides to reach an agreement and avoid aggression. It is not enough to preach peace while preparing for war. Beating on the table with a shoe as Khrushchev did is not the way to support the common interests and aims of the United Nations.

The picture of diplomacy as exercised among European and American nations was changed with the rise of the communist bloc. The communists did not acknowledge the strategy-made rules, so they proceeded to devise their own set which was much more blunt and included new deceptions. By means of these they were able to take strong advantage of the surprise of the diplomats of older nations to whom it did not occur that anyone would not adhere to the rules.

Communist diplomacy is intended to gain concessions, not always to reach compromises. It is often carried on to advertise positions and not necessarily to effect settlements; it can be a delaying tactic or a diversion from the main engagement of political negotiation. It is a sport undertaken by new rules under which there is no recognition of the permanence of the encounter. Communist diplomacy is self-liquidating and looks forward to the triumph over an adversary, with the surrender of that adversary's sovereignty. There is therefore no trust, no faith, no confidence involved, and, in a sense, none wanted.

The existence of pacific international relations lies outside the requirements of a militant nation on the march. Indeed it often even lies outside their philosophies. The Islamic theology regards everyone outside Islam as an enemy, fit only for conversion, taxation, or death. Similarly the Marxist-Leninist philosophy of the Soviet Union and Communist China considers noncommunist nations backward or imperialist, in any case enemies to be converted or disposed of. The domain of Islam had difficulty in reconciling itself to living with the West after a series of disastrous defeats provided the evidence that such a compromise was necessary. The power of the United States contained in its nuclear weaponry, and the unexpected opposition of Communist China, are slowly convincing the leaders of the Soviet Union that a peaceful *modus vivendi* with the "western imperialists" is advisable.

The kind of diplomacy which the eighteenth and nineteenth century Europeans had developed to the stage of an art was savagely destroyed by the brutal and deceitful dealings of the Soviet Union in the years immediately after the revolution of 1914. It has not been replaced by anything except a kind of defensive and hopeful wariness. The diplomats meet and exchange views, but there is little that could be called good faith on either side. The communists never did trust the democracies, and they have taught the democracies not to trust them; and so the matter stands at a stalemate, in which armed conflict is continually threatened but, given the common knowledge of the devastating nature of nuclear weaponry, not desired on either side.

The only effective countermeasures that can be undertaken involve, what is called in poker playing, table stakes. The communist countries can only be dealt with through diplomacy if their opposite numbers are prepared not only to threaten the use of force but to use it. Since they threaten with force, they are responsive only to counterforce. Wherever this technique has been employed, it has been successful. Consider for example the Berlin air lift, and, better still, the Cuban missile crisis. The second generation of communists who are presently entrusted with the destinies of the Soviet Union do not want war with an equally strong United States, and, when such a war is threatened as the price of a concession, they back down.

The type of diplomacy practiced by the Soviet Union and Communist China can hardly be a longlasting affair. Deceptions, lies and propaganda—under the guise of seeking agreements through negotiation together with thinly veiled threats of force—can work in the communist bloc's favor only so long as western democracies continue to practice the opposite method of relying on truth and mutual respect and the seeking of agreements through legitimate compromise. Once the period of uncertainty and confusion, in which diplomacy as a force disguised as a game has passed, the diplomatic strategy of the communist bloc will break down externally, as it has internally between the Soviet Union and Communist China.

Diplomacy is true diplomacy when it resembles a game that is necessary, that is to say, when the moves are made as though in a contest where the game is its own reason for being. Then, and only then, is there some hope for its success. For the aim of diplomacy is obviously to gain a political end short of the use of violence—short of war. It has sometimes happened that two nations have engaged in diplomatic maneuvres to their common advantage. Disagreements on an international scale have been settled by extended discussions. The United Nations has succeeded in settling some disputes and in preventing armed conflict in some instances. This is not to be belittled for in this direction lies all the hope in the future of the human species. More on this point later.

Diplomacy does not necessarily serve good international relations but national interests and intentions. The function of diplomacy is to further the aims and ambitions of the country represented by the diplomat. If peaceful relations are intended, these usually depend upon a continuation of the status quo. But if aggression is the policy then all representation must implement that intention, in such a case lies, false information and misleading directives.

There are precedents for the present subversion of diplomacy. In the nineteenth century, diplomacy was sometimes conducted with considerable duplicity in order to improve a nation's international position or even to gather allies in preparation for war. The communists have seen to it that diplomacy now includes espionage, subversion, and open threats of violence. In the case of Communist China, there has even been the sudden, deliberate and unannounced unilateral violation of diplomatic immunity. The old concept that opposition and the desire for conquest exist under cover of peaceful relations is perpetuated by the communist notion of the "liberation" of the proletariat in other countries; in this way, the communists justify any action that will contribute toward this end. But national domination is actually the end in sight. A new kind of imperialism cloaked as the international unity of the laboring class clearly reveals intent, even though the strength of nationalism is borne out by the intense antagonism between the Soviet Union and Communist China in their struggle for the control of the communist movement.

Readers will remember from an earlier chapter on the origins of the state in human needs that the total aggression of the individual cannot be continued for him while he remains a citizen because it has been turned over to the state for execution. Diplomacy, if kept within bounds and not allowed to spill over into violent action such as war, might be a device for engaging in political sport by means of which the discharge of aggression is made possible. It is the human version of those sham fights reported by Konrad Lorenz in which large animals capable of killing each other refrain from doing so in a symbolic and physically harmless intra-specific aggression.

Violent sports have always been popular: the Olympic games, Roman gladiatorial contests, the medieval jousts. A violent encounter is for the spectators a purgation of aggression. That is why open diplomacy has become such a popular spectator sport. It makes it possible for the individual citizen to watch a contest in which perhaps his own life as well as the lives of those around him are at stake, and therefore the most exciting of all spectator sports.

It might be asked why the ambivalence of individual motivation drops out of political international relations and becomes replaced with naked aggression—if not in action, at least in the preparation for action and its attendant attitudes. Is it because our adversaries are "not like us?" Is it the threat of difference, the fear of strangeness? Or, is it simply the aberrant and arbitrary strength of nationalism which has proved to be the colossus of our time? The analogue of individual motivation would mean at least on one side a bid for pacific relations between nations to further the constructive efforts of societies in a world at peace. At the present time the threat of another world war equals in size and strength the new weaponry which the scientific-industrial nations are able to call on. Diplomacy may be powerless to stave off the eventual conflict. Whether or not it can will depend upon the state of international relations at that time.

Chapter XV

INTERNATIONAL RELATIONS

Section 1. Foreign Policy

Foreign policy may be defined as international relations treated from the point of view of national interest. Behind the concept of national interest lies the assumption of absolute sovereignty. "State sovereignty," for example, recognizes that there is no power beyond the state to which the state is answerable, that the state power is in effect supreme. But the fact is that no state has ever enjoyed supreme power over its subjects permanently though some practice it for a while and most claim it. The status of sovereignty is internal; its external expression is made "in the national interest." And the assumption of the national interest is equally one of supremacy. But such supremacy could only be the possession of that state which does not have an equal or superior to challenge it, and there is no such state. Nevertheless, the national interest is always paramount; nothing primes it and everything follows it, including participation in international law. This primacy of national interest is always true even if not always admitted.

What exactly is national interest? It is surely not the same for a religion dominated state and for another whose primary motivation is economic; not the same for a people, like the ancient Egyptians, whose sole concern was afterlife, and for the Greeks, whose sole concern was the enjoyment of this life. At great distances of time and space, it is possible to see what the national interest was in such well-defined cases, even if not in all.

What is it today? The answers conflict even in the central government of highly organized modern states. In the United States, the President often differs with his Cabinet and with one of the political parties in Congress, and they with each other, over what international steps should be taken on particular occasions. In the Kremlin councils, the similar differences often appear even though they are less publicized.

The answer to the question of what the foreign policy of a nation state is may be as vague as the answer to the second question of how it was formed.

Government officials in the appropriate office, such as the American Department of State or the British Foreign Office, have two masters. They are: the officials from whom they receive their formal instructions and the people they endeavor to represent in part. I say in part because a strong official might suppose that his own informed views should take precedence over an uninformed electorate. In the near-term, therefore, the head of the government makes foreign policy, and in the long-term the people do. Despite the currently elaborate mechanisms by which the heads of government are able to influence the electorate and sway popular opinion, there is always a stubborn element they do not and cannot control, owing perhaps to the corresponding ignorance on the part of officials of the forces which are brought to play from other quarters on the opinions of the electorate. For the electorate is subject to all kinds of pressures and influences, many that are not perceived, more that are subtle, in a situation which is social and therefore multiply caused.

Over a long period there is no such thing for a nation as a consistent foreign policy. Consistency is possible under the rule of a single leader, as was the case with Germany under Bismarck or of the Soviet Union under Stalin. It is possible, though not usual, in a small country at peace with its neighbors, as in Norway or in Canada recently. But vacillation is more common as more influences are brought to bear on policy.

Even where a policy is clear, its applications may be confused. The United States since World War II has been opposed to the imperialism of the Soviet Union and Communist China, yet while fighting communism in Vietnam only a half-hearted attempt was made to stop it in Cuba. Half a million men and billions of dollars in equipment have been devoted to defending South Vietnam against North Vietnam, when only a fraction of that army and munitions would have been sufficient to save Cuba from the revolution. The inconsistencies of foreign policies certainly contribute to the insecurity of international arrangements; they make military preparedness a necessity and armed conflict a probability.

Foreign policy is often determined by the net result of the interplay of conflicting social forces within a country. Thus, the oil interests in the United States have thrown their weight currently in favor of the Arab countries in the Middle East, while Jews and liberals have preferred to support Israel. The result has been vacillation in effective action. The Soviet Union in the same area is probably more consistent in its policy, being motivated both by a traditional Russian anti-Semitism and by a sympathy with the preponderant masses in the Arab and Moslem countries. Justice is seldom the deciding factor in international politics, not at any rate the kind of justice which is practiced within each country as determined by its laws and enforcing agencies.

Out of the welter of unsorted elements, a kind of foreign policy emerges. But then again there are new difficulties, for the policy itself is rarely stated and is, in fact, imperfectly understood by those who administer it. They know in vague and general terms that they must finally decide issues by the welfare of the state they represent and by the national interest; but just what these are they would be in most cases hard put to say.

Plato's old expression still goes as far as it is possible to go in this direction: be gentle to friends and fierce to enemies, with the addition that it is sometimes necessary to be gentle to enemies if there is any advantage to be gained in this way, and fierce to friends should they pose any serious objections to a course of action which has been decided upon. A foreign policy when administered effectively is intended to acquire an asset without losing an ally, to promote a nation's material interests without setting other nations against it, while leaving the details to be worked out in the course of the execution of the policy.

A more difficult question still remains: what should the national interest be? This question can be answered only in the larger context of a global society in which the national units could prosper in semi-independence, just as the various states within the United States or the various republics within the Soviet Union do now. The fact is, however, that nations are not as a rule goal oriented. Day-to-day survival, on a national scale as well as on an individual one, seems more the determinant of actions. Even the practiced expediency is of a negative variety: activities are undertaken to solve crucial problems as they arise, and little of a positive and far-ranging nature is ever contemplated.

In international relations there is a tacit and sometimes explicit assumption of equality between nations, but there is no such equality. A distinction has to be made between the smaller and weaker nations and the larger and more powerful. The fiction of equality is often maintained even when everyone knows that it is meaningless. Malawi has a vote in the General Assembly of the United Nations equal to the vote of the United States. Such a recognition of the rights of all nations, small as well as great, did not exist in the days of the flourishing of the Roman Empire and does not in fact exist today in the Soviet Union. The distinction is taken into account in the Security Council of the United Nations, though even there not fully.

The national interest of each of the great powers is always read as a *pax* imposed upon the rest of the world. So once with the Roman Empire and Great Britain, so now with Soviet Russia, Communist China and the United States—all of whom are competing on a world scale, for humanitarian reasons, they would insist. But here the line between what constitutes national security and world conquest is tenuous.

State power is no longer merely a matter of mobilizing natural resources, industrial capacity and military potential, however important these may be. It consists also in the ideas which prevail and the dynamism they produce in the force of an applied political philosophy. Contrast the impotence of Russia and India in the nineteenth century with the power of the Soviet Union and the continued impotence of India today.

When a nation reaches a certain critical size and power, as yet unmeasured and undetermined, it turns imperialistic. That is to say, it endeavors through one method or other to gain world domination. The activities of imperialism are effective in many ways. A power does not have to gain territory, as the United States did for instance when it acquired the Virgin Islands from Denmark in 1917, since gifts of money, food and military equipment will accomplish the same end, as the Soviet Union learned when in the 1960's it gave such aid to Egypt. A favorable balance of payments is a form of international conquest at the economic level.

Any spread of influence is in a sense imperialistic; territorial acquisition is simply the most complete and final form. It was the form taken by Communist China in Tibet in 1950. The permanent presence in the Mediterranean of a sizeable number of units of the Russian and American navies, which present the possibility of active confrontation, is certainly imperialism on both sides.

At the present time, the United States, the Soviet Union, and Communist China are engaged in a three-way struggle for world power. No one has ever politically dominated the earth, but that is not to say that no one ever will. The enormous increase in communication and transportation facilities together with the corresponding increase in military technology makes such a possibility a genuine eventuality.

The only question, as yet unsolved, is, what would be the nature of such a world-wide imperialism? Would it be a hegemony, as many fear, or would it be a consortium, as men of good will prefer? I define a man of good will as one who does not wish to exercise his will on his own behalf in any direction in which it would bring harm to others. In the last analysis, a global superstate of any degree of stability could rest only on the shoulders of men of good will, and there would have to be enough of them for such a structure to exist. A way must be found to extend individual good will to the formulation of national policies. Then, and only then, would there be an international morality capable of supporting a global superstate.

What Morgenthau calls cultural imperialism can hardly be avoided and perhaps ought not to be from any ideal point of view.

All productive countries are engaged in a rivalry of cultural exchange which ought to be encouraged rather than discouraged. To
the extent to which the world drinks Brazilian coffee, it is falling under Brazilian cultural influence, and the same can be said for American cigarettes, English poetry, French painting, Russian music. We
do not want an end to such influences. In this direction it is possible
to see some hope of weaving nations together into an economic interdependence whose legitimacy could only be recognized finally
by the construction of a global superstate.

A government can expect to succeed completely only when it
comes into existence as a matter of necessity, when, in other words,
the conditions which could support it have been prepared in advance, and as a result a people and their country are ready to receive
it. This or something like it was the condition of the thirteen colonies in the years before the American Declaration of Independence
in 1776.

International power is not the same as international control.
Hence the military strength of a nation is not a reliable index to its
national power. The military might of ancient Athens was demonstrated against the Persians but went down before the Spartans and
permanently before the Macedonians. By the time of the Roman
conquest, Athens had become a relatively unimportant city state in
the Empire. But its cultural power increased as its military power
declined. The influence of Athenian culture—its architecture,
sculpture, philosophy, drama, poetry, and even its political theory—
conquered the world to such an extent that it remains strong even
today. Roman civilization, and indeed every subsequent one including the medieval and modern European, shows the influence of
Athenian culture.

It has become fashionable to have a justification for conquest
which can be framed in terms of the welfare of the entire human
species, but this new justification itself represents conquest. But
there *is* progress, even though to a pathetically small degree; it consists in the very fact that conquering nations seem to feel that they
have to justify themselves before the world. World opinion has become a factor in international politics.

An explicit international morality does not exist, yet one is sometimes assumed. When, for moral reasons, certain actions are not

taken by nation's though it would be strategically important to take them, an international morality is being invoked. But then there are actions, such as the genocide practiced by the Nazis, which belie this. The fact is that an international morality of an implicit nature does lie below the surface and, while sometimes invoked, is also sometimes abrogated. It flickers like a defective electric light bulb.

Often, when international morality is referred to as a reason for action or inaction, this only means that the national interest is seeking to justify itself on moral grounds. It was for the moral reason— that treaties should be observed—that Great Britain declared war on Germany in August 1914 after the violation of Belgian neutrality. Because of a moral judgment—that communist China did not observe the standards of nations in its own behavior—that the United States withheld recognition from that government. The very fact that nations undertake to defend their actions in terms of an international morality points to the need for one in international politics, and no less so since one does not exist. Impotence leads a nation to concentrate on domestic affairs, for, what a nation cannot influence, it it does not concern itself with. The more power it has, the more international it becomes up to the level of supreme power in world affairs.

Nations bent on consolidating their power through stability are inimical to change. Every international organization works in that direction. But the freezing of the status quo is never effective very long, and those nations which are ambitious in world terms find that they cannot operate within such a framework. It was for this reason that Japan left the League of Nations in 1932, Germany in 1933, and Italy in 1937.

The communist states have evinced none of that respect for sovereignty which has so characterized the western democracies since World War II. Thus the Soviet Union annexed Latvia, Esthonia and Lithuania without a qualm, and China annexed Tibet, while the European states have carefully preserved the identity and independence of Luxembourg and Lichtenstein, and the United States still recognizes the integrity of Nassau and Panama. No doubt the older nations still lean on the principle of legitimacy—or at least a much revised version in which not the claims of a dynasty but rather of a traditionally sovereign state is respected.

Examples of states which are independent in various degrees abound, but it would be fair to question the meaning of the word in certain contexts. The United States allows small countries near its borders to breed communist opposition, but to what extent is Finland independent of the Soviet Union? And is Andorra truly independent of France and Spain? Presumably, Finnish and Andorran policies which became hostile to larger neighboring states would provoke immediate interference by force. In this connection also should be mentioned the pacific intentions of the Benelux countries and Monaco.

The same ambivalence between ideologies and exigencies which prevail within states are also to be found between them. There the theoretical coating is thin while the practical considerations come thick and fast; less adherence to principles and a greater exertion of force is the rule. Within a state it may be at times a case of ideals triumphing over advantage, but externally it is almost always a question of advantage taking precedence over ideals.

Nowhere is the sharp contrast between ideology and expediency more evident than in international relations. The League of Nations and its successor, the United Nations, give clear evidence that while nations can be gotten to agree about vaguely worded humanitarian ideals, they behave more on the basis of brute force which characterizes the law of the jungle. There is no national objective on the international scene which goes beyond survival first and conquest second. Treaties, coalitions, and international organizations are chiefly employed to serve these and seldom anything beyond these. The welfare of humanity, the extension of the good to the human species as a whole, has never yet been the intention of any single nation.

Section 2. International Trade

Consumer needs do not respect political boundaries. While customs and institutions vary widely and with them the needs of the individual, it is yet true that there are very few cultures in which flour, cigarettes, cotton cloth, leather, and whiskey would not be welcome and appreciated. To a lesser extent but still important is the world market for such products as canned foods, pharmaceuticals, motor cars, guns, candy, and building materials. Where consumer goods are sold, political influence is bound to follow, if only because people tend to look with favor on the sources of their need-reductions. Industrial plants are thus the initiating factors in the spread of politics. The state can hardly afford not to approve of such industrial imperialism and not be tempted to follow it up in at least some semi-official recognition.

The more international trade arrangements become established, the greater the interdependence of nations, until a decline in the elasticity of supply and demand indicates an international order which is no less significant politically for being largely economic. For the economic will drag the political with it. Thus the dependence of economics on politics which holds nationally is reversed for a time when the relationship is international. Politics undertakes to maintain its controls internationally, and this leads to economic imperialism through instruments involved in the effort to maintain a favorable balance of payments and exchange control.

As against such efforts, there are the etsablished international relations of economics which have been worked around considerations of nationalism, the complex and informal but nonetheless stable practices, such as the foreign exchange market, national moneys—the dollar and pound sterling which have served in that capacity—international moneys—the Eurodollar, for example—arbitrage, credits, clearing and hedging, and other elements of structures which have developed in the course of doing business. The subterranean flow of capital which crosses frontiers undetected is hard to regulate. It is possible for many such relations to get out of hand and to turn into organizations which are against the best interests of all nationals—cartels, for instance. The advantageous functioning of trade from an international point of view depends upon free trade and unrestricted competition. In their own way, cartels are just as damaging as tariff barriers to free multilateral trade which rests on the price system—buying in the cheapest market and selling in the highest, regardless of frontiers.

International trade bears with it its own kind of conflict. There are many instruments which exist only in order to keep international trade under political restraints: import quotas, export licenses, special commodity surtaxes, blocked currencies, retaliatory tariffs, quarantine restrictions—all used by nations at one time or another to protect themselves against the damaging incursion of foreign influences. The inequalities of international economic developments, which are sharp, militate against any kind of serious commitment that could be based upon equalities of trading privileges. The giant industrial corporations might have become a force for equalization did they not insist on higher returns on foreign investments as an inducement to engage in such activities at all.

International trade is not the same as world free trade. The economic exchanges between capitalist and communist countries are rigidly regulated by the communist countries, and are not intended to be standard and continuing efforts. For communist countries, at the present time at least, international trade is not hooked up to consumer demand at home. It is a function of temporary maintenance and of the construction of an industrial potential which will enable communist countries to compete on world markets in the not too distant future. Hence the import by the Soviet Union chiefly of wheat and machine tools. The international movement of labor has not been allowed to cross bloc boundaries. In the communist countries, economics is entirely subordinate to politics, and therefore international trade is permitted and encouraged only to the extent to which it can be shown to further domestic political considerations.

Within the capitalist and communist blocs there are smaller blocs; on the capitalist side the European Economic Community, excluding England and Spain and on the communist side a consortium of countries centered around the Soviet Union excluding China and Albania. Evidently, the world is learning slowly and painfully the advantages of international cooperation, at least at the level of voluntary international trade associations where mutual advantage is most clearly visible. If it is possible in economic affairs, perhaps it is also in other ways of more far-reaching nature.

The interdependence of politics and economics has been further intensified by the increase since World War II of governmental participation in international business transactions. Consideration of national sovereignty is sometimes brushed aside by the unilateral exigencies of economic assistance when it is furnished by one government to another. In this respect, the two great world blocs have much in common. Both capitalist and communist countries—and notably though not exclusively the United States and the Soviet Union—have extended economic aid in the form of loans, grants or technical assistance to underdeveloped countries. Within limits, the reasons for this have not been altogether good. Competition and rivalry between the blocs has been chiefly responsible. Fortunately, the effects of actions are independent of the motives that occasioned them. Improving crops and installing medical schools can hardly be criticized under any circumstances.

The economic development of underdeveloped countries lies in the direction of uniformity of production, as though every country could be a scientific-industrial country, and every scientific-industrial country could well be like every other. The proper aim ought to be derived from natural conditions. At the present time, raw materials are collected and refined in one place and turned into manufactured products in another. The reasons are usually national. But economically it would make more sense to locate factories at the site of raw materials—they no longer need to be near power sources now that power is to be produced by nuclear plants.

Another criticism of the present program is that growth is the common factor in both developed and underdeveloped countries. The economy of Great Britain, Germany, Japan, the Soviet Union, and the United States has one thing in common with that of Ghana, Indonesia, and Venezuela—an increase in the capacity of the industrial complex. Obviously, although growth is needed, we ought now to be able to look forward to a time when the ability to produce all that the contemporary population can consume is not far away. It is at the moment asymmetrically arranged, so that, while wants are unfilled in one place on the globe, production is cut back in another. When production can be matched against consumption regardless of geographical location, then economic demands will be met, but growth will have to be supplanted by stability as an aim. And so stability in international trade ought to be the ideal on the horizon for which all economies aim.

It has not been sufficiently recognized that international trade, like the communist political philosophy, is a product of a given mode of production. As technology hands over to man the rapidly increasing mastering of materials, this leads to the inevitable emphasis on his common humanity. Geography, race, and previous cultural considerations must give way to advantages to be gained from global cooperation. National systems of income-sharing, while limited, do exist whereby some inequalities are erased by provision for a basic minimum standard of living.

But the application of the principle of equity to global humanity is recognized as a distant ideal even by those who most enthusiastically advocate it. The social techniques for achieving this kind of unlimited community have yet to be invented. Meanwhile we badly need faith that they will come in time.

Thus international trade is a stage on the way to the global society. It can never be more than that, but it ought to be carefully protected and encouraged as the start of something much larger and necessary. In the last analysis, the domination of politics over economics remains, and therefore economic trends toward world cooperation will never have sufficient force until a global government exists. I will have more to say about this in the last chapter.

Section 3. The Direction of Political Organization

International politics ought to be conducted in an orderly way on the international level as much as on the national; as a matter of fact, neither is the case in most of the history of which we have any record. All political change, progressive as well as regressive, usually even if not always, has been marked by extreme violence.

Here, then is another political rule: *there is a conflict inherent in the fact that (a) the state exists for the welfare of its citizens, and (b) the state is directed upward toward larger and larger political organizations.*

These two aims are irreconcilable; what would be good temporarily for the first might be bad in the long run for the second, and so on.

We have noted a political rule earlier in Chapter VI to the effect that since the power of the state must be stronger than any other power within it, politics in the state extends over the economic. Outside the state, however, this rule does not hold. For when we consider international relations it becomes clear that economic organization is larger than political organization; blocs of states covered by economic agreements or by factors of trade and exchange are wider than corresponding political treaties or pacts. Internationally, the economic extends beyond the political.

Despite important periods of retrogression, which may last a long time, the drift of mankind is toward larger populations and also, independently, toward larger political consolidations. Social events in this direction have moved slowly until the recent vast increase in world population. But now the situation has taken a sharp turn. An adequate political organization will have to follow quickly if it is to avert enormous disaster, such as a war fought with thermonuclear weapons. If the probabilities based on the past are to be a guide, such an eventuality will not be easily avoided.

Moral establishment lies at the basis of the state, but this does not mean that all established moralities are alike. They are not, and they could not be. Different environments and populations with different inheritances, both genetic and environmental, bring about different exigencies and can be satisfied only by different moralities. A morality is established by a people deliberately or, more often, inadvertently as the model of what they want to achieve and happily what will work best for them. This differs from country to country. It has never happened that a particular form of government will work equally well for different populations in widely differing environments, and, even when the attempt is made, the local revisions often amount to a change in government despite the retention of the name. Consider the current British monarchy or a Central American democracy, where the former is actually a democracy and the latter an absolute dictatorship.

In moving from the internal affairs of a nation based on its established morality to its international relations based on a quite different and in many ways more primitive morality which is as yet not established, there is a break unwarranted by the hard fact that its internal affairs are influenced by its external circumstances. Despite this, however, the trend in Europe has been from constitutionalism and free city-states to absolute monarchies which were larger, to nations larger still, and finally to the beginnings, at least, of an internationalism as represented by established bodies such as the League of Nations and the United Nations. The political order should extend as far as the reach of human contacts, as far as the extent of terrestrial human society.

As we have noted in an earlier and different context, there are good grounds for this contention in the rapid recent growth of international economic relations. The flourishing of an international money market in which there is an effort to maintain, at best, a superiority or, at worst, a parity with other currencies; the existence of a quasi-international unit of exchange, such as the "Eurodollar"; the effort to attain a favorable balance of trade, which is only another victory in the struggle for power; and the use of inflation or of deflation as a weapon in international politics; all this points to the formation of a larger arena than the domestic.

There is only one human species, and now that it is possible for its members to be in touch with all others, there should be one overall government. The direction is from a sort of loosely organized internationalism to a global superstate and, as we shall see before this book is finished, to a government which reaches even beyond that. The future in all its fine detail is impossible to predict, but not the broad outlines. More than a century ago, two men were able to anticipate a powerful United States and an awakening Russia: Tocqueville in 1805-1859 and Danilevsky in 1822-1887. Considering the paucity of data at their disposal, this was remarkable foresight. But there are other guides, such as the cycle of the existence of civilizations, and the way in which nations rise and fall.

Section 4. The International Jungle

The direction of politics may be toward greater and greater organization until it finally achieves the establishment of a sovereign global superstate. From present indications that goal is some distance off. For we are dealing with an international scene which is far more chaotic and primitive than the national scene. International relations are still where "frontier justice" once was; there are blood feuds conducted by principals without third party judicature or law enforcement machinery of any kind. Wars may break out at any time and often do; imperialism assumes all sorts of ideological disguises; the interference of one country with another's internal affairs is quite common, especially when the internal affairs are those of a smaller country; and there is no international order that every nation recognizes.

In the international jungle, encounters are usually hostile, promises rarely kept, bullies arrogant of their superior strength. In general the sort of behavior which is regarded as deplorable in an individual is undertaken ruthlessly by nations without even the merest hint of apology. When Germany invaded Belgium in the first world war, there was no thought of Belgian belligerence; but that did not stop the Germans. Coalitions and alliances, which ought to be the start of more universal and binding agreements, are often effective but always temporary. Only a couple of decades elapsed between the first and second world wars, but that was enough time for Japan and Italy to engage themselves on one side in the first world war and on the other side in the second.

All large countries and many small ones spy on the military establishments of other countries in order to prepare themselves for an offensive war or to protect themselves against one. No one is altogether safe, and the practice of maintaining secret information-seeking agencies has grown. Where formerly such operations were confined to neighboring countries, they are now world-wide, on the basis that, given modern methods of communication and transportation, all countries may be said to be neighbors. And now that some countries have nuclear weapons and the aircraft and rockets to deliver them anywhere on the surface of the earth, they may be said to be uneasy neighbors.

Spying—the old word being as good as any other though no longer fashionable—has developed into a large enterprise, with rules, practices and customs of its own. Intelligence agencies feeding information concerning the military capability of potential enemy countries to the leaders of their own countries to aid them in the making of decisions concerning international politics is now an established undertaking. Since everyone does pretty much the same thing and receives the same alarming reports, the efforts pretty well cancel out, but no one dares to take the initiative in dispensing with such services. Thus there is yet one more activity added to the arms race and calculated to add distrust to an already hostile situation.

Since all information concerning the military potential of foreign countries comes to the leaders of governments chiefly through their intelligence agencies, the continuing dialogue between governments is bound to be conducted in an air of suspicion and intrigue. Since intelligence agencies are the bureaucracies they are and use the methods they use, it is bound to be true that a large degree of unintentional misrepresentation and factual distortion will inevitably compose a substantial portion of their reports. Information extracted by extortion, bribery, and deception can hardly be entirely accurate though it has upon many occasions no doubt proved strategically useful.

A world-wide humanism consisting of a generalized and an unconditional deference to international altruism can hardly be erected upon the use of miniaturized weapons and listening devices, upon murder and torture, and the many brutal and aggressive techniques routinely employed by intelligence agencies in nearly all civilized countries. It is well known that the intelligence agency of one country is marked down to be the natural prey of another, and a continual armed conflict goes on *sub rosa* between them, made possible by the fact of an unwritten agreement that neither country would take official cognizance of such a conflict.

There is nothing new in all this, except that thanks to the rapid increase in technology, efficient communication, transportation, and the effectiveness of weapons of war, the existence of a disorderly situation has been made more untenable. All thoughtful people have now recognized that to live in a condition of international instability is not as easy as it once was. For, where formerly only another war was threatened, it is now possible to envisage the extermination of the human species. The new situation has been brought about chiefly through the discovery and invention of thermonuclear weapons.

The foreign policy of the United States has not yet taken full cognizance of this fact. Naked power still has a way of overriding principles. Since it became known that the Soviet Union had the atomic bomb and supported the Cuban revolution of Castro, not much has been heard about the Monroe Doctrine. The very possession of power exerts a certain pressure, as the atomic reserves of both the United States and the Soviet Union attest.

The logic of cultural events lies in the direction of strong central government, but the ones now under construction will have to be modified by new checks and balances designed to restore or preserve individual rights and differences. Without individual freedoms, the gains made by governments will be set aside, for there is now in the world an awakened citizen who, whatever his degree of education or economic welfare, is aware that there are human dignities, freedoms, and individual differences which must be preserved if he is not to have to fight for them. In the international jungle, it is not only states which struggle for survival but the solitary individual as well.

Section 5. The Ambivalence of International Organizations

There is seldom a close resemblance between a state's internal politics and its external policy. Inside it is chiefly law, outside it is mostly force; inside order prevails; outside disorder struggles with order. No two societies are identical and every society has a political system. Here we see at work the play of limited law, for regularities abound in a sporting sort of way. Only local conditions can provide the setting, and what prevails cannot be extended to other existing societies. Given a specific situation, the conditions are fixed and the laws, absolute. Thus the play of limited law is no less rigorous for being different from state to state, while the differences cannot be held altogether responsible for the difficulties between states.

Therefore, *the two characteristics of the international behavior of nations are: (a) The high moral demands which always exceed anything that could be hoped for at home, and (b) the law of the jungle, the naked appeal to force, and the unrestricted use of violence abroad.*

These are of course contradictions, and they lend an ambivalence to foreign policy. It is worthy of note that in the formal documents instituting many international alliances, there is a stated adherence to moral principles, and yet the alliance itself would not exist in most cases if it were not as much against certain nonparticipating nations as it was in favor of those participating. So it was with the Treaty of the Holy Alliance which Napoleon's enemies signed in 1815, and so, too, with the Atlantic Charter of 1941 intended to protect the free nations of western Europe and America against communism.

It is true of course that cultural conditioning and its marked differences cut across any attempt to unify states. Thus in some states murder is punishable by death or life imprisonment, while in other states it is permitted, approved, and even required. The first-born among the ancient Jews, the aging parents among Eskimo, and widows in India were once required to be put to death. From the point of view of any coherent system of culture, such as might be the possession of a well-knit and homogeneous population, the rest of the world constitutes a frontier, an unexplored territory of danger and difference, awaiting civilization. This kind of culture does not call for admission to the comity of humanity, which is identified with the laws of all nations, but for conquest and modification.

The same ambivalence which is noted in the leading countries is to be found also in those underdeveloped countries which are the objects of conversion by the large industrial powers. The underdeveloped countries would like to have the technological advantages extended to them by competing communist and capitalist nations, but they reject the propaganda which are part and parcel of such advantages. In short, they are sympathetic to the reception of gifts of goods but unsympathetic to the gifts of those political ideas which are an inevitable accompaniment. For the wisest among them are quick to see that every great technological advance makes colonies of those states who do not have it, and colonial powers of those who do.

Nothing could better illustrate the attitude of the underdeveloped countries in this regard than the widespread appearance in the South Pacific islands of what has come to be known as the "cargo cult." In World War II, American airmen suddenly appeared on these islands and laid down runways. Then the cargo planes came in, bringing with them supplies, some of which were given as presents to the natives to gain their good will—small items like field rations, razor blades, and chocolate bars. Since the airplanes suddenly came from nowhere, the natives thought them visitors with gifts from heaven.

When the war was over, the air force men rolled up their portable airstrips and departed. The natives supposed that they themselves ought to be able to do the same thing, so they levelled crude landing strips, built wooden airplanes to serve as decoys, and at night lit torches for landing lights, then waited for the goods to be brought in again from the sky.

Thus a new native religion was created and with it a new kind of unrest. The cargo cult is symbolic of the attitude of every underdeveloped country toward the industrial products of scientific countries. It has produced the kind of demand and dissatisfaction which the impatient and more technologically advanced countries have come to think of as "progress."

Worse perhaps and more damaging than not wanting an international order is wanting one's own. The communist bloc, whose aim is world domination through world revolution, finds nothing to gain from the maintenance of order and everything to gain through promotion of disorder. The Soviet Union is in the United Nations to prevent any increase in the existing order. Until very recently, peace in the Middle East, which the Soviet Union could easily have promoted between Israel and the Arab nations, was not to its liking. At the same time it presents itself as a peaceloving bulwark against oppression, even though, while attacking the old colonialism of the European powers, it endeavors to impose its own brand.

How then is it possible to establish a permanent peace when those who proclaim themselves pacifists are actually engaged in promoting war? How is it possible to do business with those for whom "business as usual" means a threat to the masses everywhere? How is it possible to agree upon certain political truths with those whose concept of truth itself is only historical correctness? Nationalism was a force for good when it operated against division into lesser political units, such as city-states and principalities, as in the feudal period; but not when it is a force which operates against a combination into larger units and against the effective establishment of a world government. And it may be fatal that the newly constituted communist nations, such as the Soviet Union and Communist China, have encased themselves in the old nationalism they had ostensibly been brought into existence to replace.

Section 6. The Balance of Power

The direction of international relations is toward a single world government, but that is a long way off and there are many steps to be taken meanwhile. One such step is the practical application of the balance of power concept.

The theory that international peace can best be maintained under the existence of sovereign national powers by a balance between the leading powers offers at best only a temporary security. For the balance between nations is by no means permanent, and the reason is that what may be called the power weight of a single nation often is altered with marked rapidity, bringing with it a change in all other international power relations. When the ideology of Russia was shifted from Greek Orthodox Christianity to dialectical materialism, the activation of the inert masses by the new dynamic philosophy became inevitable; and when a large population in a country rich in potential natural resources was involved, then a radical change in the balance of power was bound to occur internationally.

The achievement and the maintenance of international stability can be accomplished temporarily by balancing one bloc of nations against another. The balance of power is the establishment of equilibrium through the opposition of groups of equal powers. In international relations it is managed through powers which balance themselves by means of hegemonies into two opposed and fairly equal forces within a larger environment of international anarchy.

The ancient Chinese had the idea of a *Pax Sinica,* a world-wide hegemony under peaceful Chinese domination. But no one then had entertained the prospect of a world government in which there was no leading national power. We can trace the balance of power concept better from its inception in Europe, more particularly in Renaissance Italy, where it was practiced by the city-states of Rome, Florence, Venice, and Milan, until wrecked by the French invasion of Italy in 1494. We have seen it also in eighteenth century Europe where it was practiced by France, England, Prussia and Austria, until wrecked by two world wars and the emergence of two greater powers, the United States and Soviet Union. We can see it now in the balance between these two superpowers, and we can see how this too will be wrecked by the emergence of Communist China as a world power.

In the relation between states it is safe to say that there is no such thing as peace without the knowledge of where the balance of power resides. The border between Canada and the United States is not guarded because it is unnecessary to do so; the two countries have the most amicable relations; but compare this with the border between Russian Kazakh and Chinese Sinkiang. That is not to say that there is no senior and junior partner in such relationships. It is well known that for a long time in North America, it has been the way the United States wanted it, and, that in Asia, Russian power is temporarily superior to Chinese.

The balance of power does not always have the effect intended. Great Britain attempted to hold the balance between France and Germany but the result was a series of disastrous wars. The United States intervened in the Vietnamese civil war in the 1960's on the side of South Vietnam after Communist China and the Soviet Union had intervened on the side of North Vietnam, but the unexpected and unwanted result was the intensification of the conflict to such an extent that both sides only succeeded in the inadvertently joint effort to destroy South Vietnam—the country as well as the people.

Beyond the horizon of the balance of power it is possible to discern the dim outlines of a broader and more inclusive concept. Collective security, an arrangement of states prepared to combine against aggression in the interest of preserving or restoring world peace, is slowly rising. It lies behind the formation of such international organizations as the United Nations and has, as yet, no firmly founded existence; but it certainly must be the next step toward world government. Its details remain to be worked out, for it is at once more complex, more committed and more comprehensive than the limited concept of the balance of power; and in it lies the hope of the immediate future for the establishment of international peace.

Collective security has thus far been a failure. If the United Nations offered the only hope for world peace, it could be used as evidence that at the present time there is no hope. Yet why do the various nations wish to adhere to the appearance of an international order when in fact they do not behave as though it were binding? This must mean something in terms of world public opinion, which is generally feared and respected even though, in times of critical action, pretty much ignored, counting on the obvious fact that the people en masse have short memories and forget what they cannot forgive.

It is a fact of course that national interest is still the ultimate criterion, and so long as this is true there will be no multistate system of any degree of effectiveness; but at the same time the principal states in their international relations can be observed probing for such a structure. We are in that stage of development where fully formed nations, as a result of improved communication and transportation, are under some constraint to erect the next higher and more inclusive organization, one having world-wide sovereignty.

Consider, for example, just one problem which has taken on fresh urgency in the heat of enormously progressive technological developments. How far in space does national jurisdiction extend? Bynkershoek's rule (1702) that territorial jurisdiction ends where armed power ends—into the ocean for example as far as a cannon can shoot, which was responsible for the three-mile limit—was altered by the invention of the intercontinental ballistics missile. Now that the power of any nation possessing a developed scientific-industrial technology is capable of being extended around the whole earth, the preservation of peaceful international relations is possible only on the basis of a single superstate.

The entire host of thorny international problems, such as the extradition of fugitive criminals, jurisdictional procedures, and the sanctity of contracts, the special status of ambassadorial missions or of diplomatic representations, and the protection of foreigners, press hard for the establishment of a uniform procedure, with standardized penalties for infractions and an all-encompassing authority to administer it.

Section 7. International Law

The aggressive nature of man, which was assigned by him to the state, exists in the state; and that is why the state will be bound by no rules with which it does not agree, not even by those to which it may have subscribed earlier. For the state as custodian of force, there is nothing to which it need respond except superior force. And this, short of instituting an international army, is lacking. All international organizations leave an escape hatch available to separate states. For instance, the provisions for law enforcement provided by the relevant chapters of the United Nations Charter are cancelled by the veto.

Nothing is currently binding on man except his own organically based aggression. But in so far as he has been able to develop his capacity for reasoning and the ability to enter into contractual arrangements with his fellow men which affects their mutual future, there is some hope that the rule of law will replace brute force. It has already done so to some extent on the local level. To suppose that it will do so also on the international level is at the moment only a hope and a feeble effort. Meanwhile, the weapons with which aggression can be equipped have outstripped all other international relations and indeed threaten the continuance of the terrestrial human species itself.

International conventions, whether covenants, charters, alliances, statutes, protocol, agreements, pacts, acts, declarations or treaties, are intended to have the status of law. So long as sanctions do not exist to reinforce such conventions, their unilateral denunciations will continue, and they will have no more force than can be expressed by a temporary good intention.

Everything has some place in the order of nature, and this is no less true for the nation-state than it is for any nonhuman entity. A nation-state is a society with its material artifacts; it does not exist in a vacuum but relies upon the immediate environment for support. It can be considered, therefore, only against a background of wider social organization. This wider organization is foreshadowed by international relations.

We must distinguish between international laws and international relations. International relations do exist and there are all kinds. It is necessary to consider war as a species of negative international relations, but, despite the prevalence of war, there are many species of peaceful relations as well: treaties, trade agreements, exchanges of diplomatic representatives, alliances.

International law, in a certain sense, does exist: it just so happens that, when international law conflicts with the national interest, the national interest prevails. There is no international law with any binding force; there are only international relations. International law is a form and a hope, nothing more. It is agreed that there should be international law governing international relations, but, lacking penalties, the form of international law exists without substance. International law is not binding so long as nations recognize it as an obligation having no sanctions.

Although states have different laws, that would not prevent them from subscribing in addition to an international law which they could hold in common. For internationally their problems are the same while they remain locally and internally quite different.

There cannot be even the possibility of a genuine international law until the separate states adopt an identical social morality; that is to say, until the established morality of the separate states is the same and so gives rise to an identity of the laws of the state. An absolute identity may not be necessary; a partial identity may serve as a starting point. So it may be possible to say that, when the laws of the separate states bear sufficient resemblance, it will be time to begin the establishment of international law.

What is now called international law is no more than a *pro tem* arrangement pending the political organization of a global society. Are there international trade arrangements? Is world travel possible? Must diplomatic representations be exchanged in order to negotiate for peace and war? International relations exist, and international conventions must be established, and requisite international laws discovered. Laws without penalties can still provide many, if not all, of the functions of laws.

That there is a striving toward the establishment of an acceptable international law can hardly be doubted. The historic continuity of the world court under some jurisdiction or other and with

a change of names but not of function is evidence for this statement. The Permanent Court of Arbitration was established at The
Hague in 1900 but it did not have much success. It dealt with one
important case in 1910 and with only one case of any kind since
1932. However, the Permanent Court of International Justice was
established in 1920. In 1946 a supreme court for the United Nations called The International Court of Justice was formed, and succeeded it in such a way that the two courts amounted to the same so
far as statutes, quarters, and staff were concerned.

International law is a halfway stage between the laws of nation-
states and the laws of a projected global superstate. It should be apparent that international law is not the law of any particular state
but of the relations between states. As such it lacks nothing except
legitimacy, and it could achieve this by being incorporated internally as the laws of the superstate. Meanwhile its justification is the
prospect of substituting peaceful legal means of settling disputes for
the outright use of appeal to force in war.

Section 8. International Peace

Nations no more than peoples ought to be expected to share a
uniform culture. It would be a great loss to the world if they did.
We have noted before and will refer again to the fact that there is
a great cultural richness to difference. Even politics may have to vary
if governments are to differ in their structure in accordance with
regional differences. Perhaps a state in the mountains would not require the same kind of government as one in the valley, and such
states as Ecuador and Egypt need different rules. But there is one
political ingredient which does have to be the same if there is to be
international peace, and that is foreign policy. Internationalism requires as its base line an identical foreign policy on the part of all
constituent nations. Short of that, there will be the recurrence of
war.

So long as there is international anarchy, there will be war. The
voluntary surrender of sovereignty to a global superstate is the only
hope. We do not seem ready for it yet, and, if this is truly the case,
the sporadic outbreak of violence is inevitable. If, as I have said

earlier, the function of society is to provide an organization
whereby the competition between individuals can be rendered constructive to the state, then the mechanism of social engineering has
reached the national but not the international level; for we have not
yet devised the means whereby the competition between states can
be rendered internationally constructive.

For several centuries now there has been, and probably in the
indefinite future, there will be, global peace imposed by one or more
nations, at least so long as a global superstate has not been formed.
In the eighteenth and nineteenth centuries, British imperialism in
general and the British navy in particular imposed a *Pax Britannica*
upon the world. It lived under an arrangement with American tacit
support until the invention of the airplane. Two disastrous world
wars so weakened the British that they could no longer sustain their
empire, and the ebb was as significant in the twentieth century as
the flow had been several centuries earlier.

In South Africa, where the Boers took over power from a mildly
protesting English population, that same English population incidentally which in the Boer War had put down the Dutch; in India
where the British voluntarily abdicated a power once wrested from
the French but which had suddenly become more trouble than it
was worth; in the Middle East where a half-vacillating British-
French-Israeli alliance allowed itself to be talked out of continuing
a war against Egypt; the signs were all the same: a diminished
British world power contracting back to the economic interests of
the inhabitants of the British islands with an effort of sufficient size
only to maintain those inhabitants in domestic peace.

The withdrawal of the British from world power left a vacuum
which was bound to be filled by someone. But by whom? The
only two countries capable of struggling for its possession were the
United States and the Soviet Union. Communist China had the
size and will to join in the competition but not the scientific-industrial strength to enable it to compete.

Of the former two, the United States, the logical successor,
was handicapped in several ways. Diplomatically, it had been weakened by several centuries of subordination to the British which
had left it with no authentic duties. The State Department in this
period furnished the foreign service with well-connected men

whose chief ambition was the appearance of European urbanity and suavity on those social occasions which were necessary to the practice of diplomacy. American representatives rarely knew the language of the country to which they were accredited nor were they equipped with the politics of power and the use of veiled threats of possible aggression. It would be unfair to have expected more of them. The United States during this period had no foreign ambitions and was occupied with a prosperity of its own, leaving to the British the management of "natives" for the purposes of British commercial advantage. So when the British Foreign Office declined in influence, it left a vacuum which the State Department was not prepared to fill.

The Russians, on the other hand, had no tradition of niceties with which to disguise their true intent. They moved into the empty places around the world with all the force their domestic requirements could leave unused. They have not yet moved into India and South Africa. China is the deterrent in the case of India and distance in the case of South Africa. In the Middle East, however, they have supplied the Arab countries, Egypt in particular, with immense numbers of arms, and they have done so not once but twice. In addition, there is now a Russian presence in the Mediterranean in the form of a naval force of a size intended to impress bordering countries with the fact that they ought not to count exclusively on the American fleet which had been based there so much longer.

It is too early to say whether the military confrontations of the Americans and Russians in areas left behind by retreating British will result in the triumph of one or the other without exploding into war. It is dangerous to play such power games if they are not meant and fatal if they are. The airplane has been succeeded by the nuclear arsenal, with its delivery systems: the intercontinental ballistics missile and the orbiting satellite. Perhaps all of humanity will perish in the effort to decide who will have the right to rule it.

International peace will never result from the procedures by which states are now conducted. For the only trends which can be detected are either long-range expansion, economic planning, or day-to-day expediency. There has never yet been such a thing as a "department of defense" or an army entirely dedicated to it. Soldiers are professional all-purpose killers, and, by token of their trade, they await the day when their orders will be to go out and shoot.

As we have noted earlier, the needs of individuals are excessive, and so we can see that any collective policy must be inherently expansive. The short period when the United States was not bent on enlarging its foreign influence was when it had the advantage of a frontier of unexplored and unoccupied western states. From that dream it was awakened by two events: its pioneers reached the Pacific Ocean, and it was confronted after two world wars with an ebbing British Empire and an oncoming Soviet Union to whom it wished to deny occupancy of the vacuum.

Even world movements can be the result of day-to-day expediency. Today it seems necessary that the United States send food to India and military advisers to Viet Nam. Today it seems necessary for the Soviet Union to quiet the anticommunist uprising in Hungary. Today it seems necessary for Communist China to maintain bad relations with the Soviet Union. The result of all this unrest is a series of little wars. For conflicts of various sorts, including world wars, will always be the result of the drift of events. If we wish to have international peace, there will have to be international planning for it. At this writing, international peace is what is generally said to be wanted, but I doubt if it is genuinely wanted. What is wanted is "our" sort of peace whoever "we" are, a surrender to "our" sovereignty and an ascendancy of "our" people over all others.

If we would like to see peace, then first we will have to want it truly, and we will have to plan for it. In time of peace prepare for peace. But peace is the opposite of war, and the search for peace lies through an understanding of war. To this topic, then, we next give our attention.

Chapter XVI

WAR AND PEACE

Section 1. Humanism and Rationality

War is the extension of conflict into extreme violence between peoples organized into political units. It involves the utmost use by the state of all the powers of forceful action which were turned over to it initially by individuals. War is not the sole kind of extreme conflict, as anyone who has engaged in economic competition must know, but it does employ more violence. War is fought only when victory by other means seems unobtainable.

Wars are as common as peace and in some form or other perhaps more common. They are, in fact, so common that even in this day of high publicity through mass media, many wars can be waged and yet go almost unnoticed. How many citizens of the United States, I wonder, know about the persistent conflict between the royalists and the Egyptians in the Yemen? How many are aware that a civil war is in progress between Nigeria and the secessionist province of Biafra? "Peace," Richard Burton once said, quoting an ancient Oriental proverb, "is the dream of the wise, war is the history of man."

It is fashionable both to condemn war as inhuman and to wage it in the national interest. For there exists not only actual war but also what Hobbes called a disposition to war which prevails in time

257

of peace, occasioned by disvalues: by fraud, falsehood, and fear, fed by competition, diffidence and glory. I want to add to these the desire for economic gain and power, force illegally used, lies deliberately perpetrated, and fear purposely inculcated.

People often do the same things though they profess to do them for different reasons depending on what is acceptable at the time. They often fight wars even though the justification changes. Thus there have been holy wars, wars of conquest, wars to make the world safe for democracy, to liberate workers, and, indeed, for almost every possible reason.

Evidently, there is always a moral justification for war and never is one hard to find. The base for it exists in the deep-rooted belief in the inherent superiority of the militant nation. Every people, every nation, seeks to impose its morality upon others on the well-intentioned ground that its morality is the universal morality. In this way it seeks to justify its acquisitive aggression.

The moral justification for war is usually contained in the assumption of the conquerors that conquest will be good for all the conquered or for some chosen sector. The Romans took it for granted that any country which came under the domination of the Empire would be better off because of the stable government from which it would benefit and the prosperity which would ensue. It was the firm belief of the leaders of the Ottoman Empire that to force a defeated peoples to accept Islam or the sword was to do what was best for them. And today the Russian communists suppose that they are liberating an oppressed proletariat, and this remains their faith even when that proletariat enjoys a standard of living greater than that which prevails in the Soviet Union.

It is difficult to take seriously the reasons which are given for wars when we see how readily the sides can be changed. In 1512, Henry VIII allied England with the Hapsburgs against France. Three years later he allied England with France against the Hapsburgs. Seven years after that he allied England with the Hapsburgs against France. Yet no one seemed to think his behavior in this respect extraordinary. In point of fact it was not.

More recent examples are not hard to come by. In 1914 Italy and Japan joined with France and Great Britain against Germany. In 1939 Italy and Japan joined with Germany against France and

Great Britain. In 1914 Turkey was with Germany, in 1939 with France and Great Britain. Shifts in foreign policy, up to such complete reversals, are not necessarily the result of whim or perfidy. There are more variables in social affairs than anyone has yet reckoned, and the man of action is forced by his ignorance both to make continual reassessments of the forces involved and to feel his way, and this uncertain process requires him in all honesty sometimes to reverse himself or his country's historic commitments.

This disposition, together with the inherently destructive side of human nature, had been known for many centuries. Yet somehow in the nineteenth century the ameliorative version of humanism spread rapidly and took strong hold in the western countries. War is not a strange and unaccountable phenomenon that suddenly flares up between nations, yet that is exactly the way in which men have come to think of it. It is difficult to understand how such a conception ever got started, for there is little truth in it.

In 1910 there appeared a book entitled *The Great Illusion*. In it Norman Angell explained that another war was impossible because it had come to be regarded as unprofitable to both sides, and that no nation would be so foolish as to start one. The book was translated into many languages and had an immense sale; it said probably what everyone wanted to believe. A mere four years later saw the outbreak of World War I. There were 8,000,000 combat losses before it was over, and, twenty years after that, 10,000,000 combat losses in World War II, to say nothing of the losses in innumerable smaller wars which have succeeded each other since then.

Perhaps the reason for such a misconception is that few have ever understood the nature of peace. What we have grown accustomed to describing as peace is a confusion of conflicts at many levels which does not break out into armed violence. Then too there have been many intermediate varieties of ritualized behavior which could not be described clearly as peace or war; witness the wars between feudal states under the Chou dynasty roughly from the eighth to the third centuries in ancient China when battle was a formal procedure involving the winning or losing of prestige in which few if any on either side were killed. But much goes on that does not deserve the name of peace. I have endeavored to describe some of these events in an earlier chapter on political corruption—Chapter IX. The protest against an existing order is usually made on individual and social grounds in a sporadic and often politically unimportant way. It is the seed for what can be, in a later and more organized fashion, the political phenomenon of war. The elements of war are present in peace, and we shall have to make an effort to understand both if we are to learn how to abolish the former and promote the latter.

Humanism as it was understood in the nineteenth century was a description of the good side of human nature. Man was identified with the man of good will, the reasonable man who meant his fellow men well. Anyone who quarreled with this description of humanism, according to humanism itself, was obviously against it; and what was perfect stood in no need of improvement. Therefore, not negative criticism but satisfied complacency was exacted, and as a result things went from bad to worse.

Because the half-truth of this description of humanism allowed a half-falsity to survive unexamined, its results went unchecked. The favorable image of human nature is so popular that it has blocked the way of progress. No doubt the good side of human nature does exist, but it is not the entire story. For there is, as we have noted in an earlier chapter, a bad and a negative side also, a side in which the destructive emotions come to represent all the emotions, in which prejudices take the place of reason, and in which fallacies are assumed to be the equivalent of rationality.

In particular the rationality which humanism both described and endorsed was misleading. Reason in the nineteenth century suffered from its identification with the humanistic doctrine that man is essentially good. He was good, therefore at bottom he was also rational; it was only necessary in time of threat to appeal to his reason. There are several errors here which we shall want to examine in order to get at the truths they conceal.

Ever since the Greeks it has been supposed that the rational is that which we approve. We do not approve of the use of force, therefore force is not rational. We do not approve of the emotions, therefore emotions are not rational. And of course we do not approve of war, therefore war is not rational.

The politics of rationalism of the older vintage would banish violence and conflict as irrational. But these things exist in human social life and are not exceptional; therefore reason is not reason if it refuses to reckon with them. Reason has been tested for its consistency, not for its completeness. Reason has to reckon with the facts—with what exists—and not merely with what men of good will approve. A good reason would be one that succeeded in accounting for or explaining all of the relevant facts. Too narrowly conceived, reason itself proves irrational. We have identified reason with a particular set of reasons, and the result is that some of the behavior of men has seemed entirely unreasonable. But the recognition of the ugly facts does not imply their approval. To say "Most men enjoy war" is not the same as saying "I approve of war."

Nothing, perhaps, is more conducive to war than not providing in peace for all the elements which threaten it. For it is in time of peace that the forces conducive to war quietly build up. Wars are, indeed, assured when violence is left alone, and I do not think we want violence. We must begin, then, by undertaking to explain it.

Section 2. The Human Nature of War

We have already taken note in Chapter II of how the state takes over that portion of the aggressiveness of individual man that he cannot hope to reduce by means of the use of his own limited powers. The drive to dominate his entire environment in order to reduce his need for eternal survival was handed to the state. War, then, would be simply the attempt on the part of the state to fulfill this undertaking. By means of the political instrument of the state, man endeavors to conquer his environment, and there is some satisfaction in the domination of neighboring and weaker states.

There is another organ-specific need, however, which will have to be reintroduced here if we are to understand war. Hunger has been a primary motivation ever since animals evolved, and must have been inherited by man from his prehumanoid ancestors. Hunger is a primary need, and early man was a hunter.

Out of hundreds of thousands of years of the nomadic state several factors emerge. The first of these is that until recently man was a cannibal. He was from the beginning of the species a hunter of wild animals, and man himself was one of the animals he hunted. The evidence for cannibalism in prehistoric man seems overwhelmingly convincing. Moreover, cannibalism survived as an institution right down to the middle of the nineteenth century when the tribes of Central Africa, and the Fijians and other primitive tribes not in touch with the great civilizations of Asia and Europe, still practiced it.

The second factor is that hunting is fun. All need-reductions are enjoyable, and because of his early hunger man like all hunters enjoyed killing. There is nothing new or startling in the statement that even civilized man loves to hunt. What we forget is that all sports are pursued for their enjoyment, and hunting has long been listed as a sport. But contrary to the fact that hunting other men is also a sport, it has not been so regarded. To understand it better, one has only to have recourse to dangerous sports. The more dangerous the sport, the greater the enjoyment. The most enjoyable kind of hunting is dangerous hunting: hunting animals that present some kind of threat to the hunter, like lions, tigers, wild boar. The most dangerous kind is hunting animals which at the same time are hunting the hunter. In this sense, war is a kind of hunting, the most dangerous and also the most enjoyable form of sport. It legalizes the aggression which is otherwise illegal, and sanctions the killing of men as a contribution to patriotism.

The one thing that becomes clear from all this is that there has been no progress in motivation since Neanderthal days. The same lust for killing other members of the same species that characterized our most remote ancestors still characterizes us. Wars are by no means "a thing of the past," as the recent wars in the Yemen, Viet Nam, and Egypt testify. And their ferocity has been by no means abated if the massacres in Indonesia in suppressing the communist coup of 1965 or the slaughter accompanying the civil war in Nigeria in 1967 are taken as evidence. On March 8, 1968 according to *The New York Times*, the International Commission of

Jurists said from Geneva that if the "escalation of brutality" in Viet Nam were not stopped the world might soon be submerged in a "cataclysm of horror."

The only possible mark of progress that can be noted is the ritualization of killing. It is no longer as random as it probably once was. Sport is now an aspect of the fine arts. War is a form of drama in which physical aggression is often given prescribed limits and operates under strictly accepted ground rules. There are formal declarations of hostility, even though they now occur more often after the hostilities have begun.

A good example of the ritual aspect is to be noted in the account of medieval Europe when armies settled in the field for the single combat of favorite champions witnessed by all. Man still wants to help and hurt his fellows, and in both directions his methods are more refined than they were. He started perhaps with the shaman and the bow and arrow. But he has progressed greatly since then. We now have hospitals and charitable funds, and we have atomic bombs and chemical warfare. But the motivation remains exactly where it was when the species first evolved.

What conclusions are we to draw from this so far as politics is concerned? Primarily that aggression may be expected to continue until there is a mutation of the species. For the species, as it is at present constituted, has retained the traits it has supported these many thousands and perhaps millions of years. But could a page be taken from medieval jousting? Would modern populations be able to work off their aggressiveness by witnessing the mortal combat of champions in the field?

It will be recalled that in the chapter on human motivation the distinction was made between constructive and destructive aggression, the constructive being that which accounts for capital cities and the destructive for burning them down. It so happens that destructive aggression is a more rapid and efficient form of need-reduction than the constructive variety; and since wars offer open opportunities for raw, unlimited aggression, we should expect them to be popular, as they indeed have been.

Thus the reasons usually given for wars only describe the outer coating and not the essence. Wars are fought primarily because they are need-reducing and only secondarily for other reasons. In wars,

nations exercise the authority to exert destructive aggression which
had been handed them by the human individuals to whom in the
state it is otherwise expressly denied. Thus by participating in
wars, they get their own back.

If any corroboration of these facts is needed, it can be found
in the inclination toward war that exists in all countries which
consider themselves powerful enough to wage it, and this means
generally all countries. Imperialism is the name given to this tendency, and it is occasioned by so many kinds of events that it must
be regarded as inevitable under the present condition of man.
Morgenthau has pointed out that both victory and defeat in war
give rise to the same imperialistic policies.

Certainly the aggression is there, and, if no acceptable substitutes are found for it, the effects will continue to be felt, for
there will continue to be wars. The only new element in the picture is that weapons have become so destructive that another
world war could mean the end of the species. But there is no guarantee that one will not occur, not at all. For men are not so constituted that they act only for their own good.

Section 3. The Condition of War

War, understood as the planned and organized collective aggression of one people against another, has been around a long time, so
long that it should be familiar. Despite this fact, it is treated
by men of good will as though it were an intruder and usurper.

Rules respecting the conduct of war, intended to ameliorate
the harshness and ferocity of its conditions and to humanize it—as
though peace were human and war not—were suggested by Francis
Lieber as early as 1863 but were not established until the turn of
the century. The Articles of the Geneva Convention of 1906,
which resulted from the Geneva Conference of 1864, were revived
at the Hague Peace Conference of 1907 as Convention X. The intentions may have been of the best but the assumptions behind
such agreements have never been made plain, and what they indicate is not so favorable as might at first glance appear. The adoption of guidelines for fair play in war regularizes and legitimatizes

it in a way which is hardly consistent with good international relations. The Geneva Conventions assumed that war is here to stay
and might as well be moderated. There was no thought that war
could be or even should be abolished, and that is one serious objection to any agreement concerning how it should be fought.

The attempt to tame war and to reduce its conduct to a set of
rules upon which there can be general agreement among nations
was never more binding than any other international agreement
which depended entirely upon the good will of the participants.
The Articles of the Geneva Convention were not obeyed by the
fascists and the communists. War as an appeal to physical force cannot by its very nature admit of any limitations upon its exercise;
force has its own logic and, by definition, is confined to no rules.
What is wrong from the point of view of the welfare of the human species is not how wars are fought but war itself.

Unfortunately, the traditional posture of the state has been
and still is warlike. Peace is only a war that nobody wins, and, before war can be eliminated altogether, peace will have to be otherwise constituted. Peace has been at once the product of a common
set of positive beliefs and an attitude of vigilance against a common
enemy. It is easy to see how the first could be world-wide but not
the second. If peace is only an organization of security, an extraterrestrial enemy is clearly needed. If one did not exist, he would
have to be invented. Any positive set of beliefs must include an established morality, but that is an internal affair. There are also
external positions and actions required to protect it, and these count
on the need for the continuance of vigilance.

Political unities exist as much for negative as for positive reasons, and people make common cause as often because they fear
a common enemy as because they see positive gains in working together. It can be argued, for instance, that the range of weapons
determines the size of the state. Artillery destroyed the antiquated
castle of the feudal lord and replaced it with the nation-state on a
small scale. The emergence of an economy based on money made
possible the existence of a professional army which could be
based permanently on the frontiers, thus making possible a peace
within its geographical borders. When the first military airplanes
flew over national boundaries in Europe in World War I, the fate

of the modern nation was determined. Only large international coalitions could hope to survive. And with the development of the nuclear arsenal, a global government became not only imperative but inevitable.

Section 4. War as Self-Determined

It is against human interest to venerate human destruction. Yet the politicians who are best remembered and most highly regarded are the war lords, those leaders who succeeded in getting the greatest number of people killed: Alexander, Caesar, Napoleon, Lincoln, Roosevelt. The leaders do not lead in such cases, they only follow deep instincts which are imbedded in the genetics of every human individual. The more power the politicians have, the more such instincts find their logical social outlet. The need for war arises in the individual as part of his inherited nature and finds its expression in leaders who are leaders because of their usefulness to this expression. In this sense, then, wars are largely self-determined.

So long as decisions concerning war and peace are in the hands of politicians, it is only necessary to remember that the use of thermonuclear weapons and the control of the mass media give the contemporary political leader the power to preserve life or deal death to millions and perhaps to the entire human species. It is more power than he ever had before and more than he should have now. Technological advances drive social developments further and faster but always in the direction in which they were heading. Through this mechanism once again war shows itself to be self-determining.

Since war may cause either destruction or the spread of cultural influence by violent social means, it is in a certain sense a neutral term. Its immediate effects are always bad but its long-range effects may be bad or good. War is always bad in itself, but it may lay the ground for constructions. Yet in doing this it may destroy much that is good, including, of course, many members of the younger generation. Wars may spread order or disorder. Alexander's conquest spread Greek culture and so preserved it. Napoleon destroyed the French monarchy but made way for a democracy. That such effects were not intended does not seem to matter in the end.

There are social reservoirs of power of which we have, for the most part, remained unaware and for which we must find an outlet at regular, almost stipulated, periods. The effect of abolishing wars might have more disastrous consequences because of the energy which is in this way released. With our lack of requisite knowledge of social psychology it is difficult at this stage to be sure. Although war fills with horror those who have any hope for humanity on its constructive side, the evidence is not all clear that everyone shares this view. World sympathy is extended to the victims of aggression only when the aggression is long and protracted. No one seems to have evinced much interest in the Baltic states when the Soviet Union absorbed them and so ended their independence. There was nowhere as much sympathy for North Korea as there is currently for North Viet Nam. Sympathy needs time to develop and quick conquest does not allow for it.

Things that are not good politics are worse for humanity the more efficiently they are done. Were it not for the inept military mind, mankind would long ago have vanished. But the military mind is a human mind. It may be taken as axiomatic that the human condition is arduous enough: life is short and filled with pain and difficulties, to say nothing of natural human enemies which always abound: predatory animals, diseases or hostile climates, without adding the woes of torturing, fighting, wounding, and killing. Intra-specific aggression does seem to be peculiar to humanity.

It is only necessary to recall that politicians do not make conflicts, they only make wars, and wars are the logical outcome of the intensification of conflicts. Conflicts exist in the nature of human needs and competition. It could as well be said that—to reverse Clausewitz' dictum—competition for political office through duly established and regulated procedures is merely war pursued by other means. The social effects of large-scale social actions are sometimes not those which have been sought. Often bad effects are intended and good ones achieved. The Crusades were conducted to free the Christian holy places from the Moslem infidel, but what they accomplished was the importation of the knowledge of Greek experimental science into western Europe.

Hegel argued that Kant's "perpetual peace" would be stagnating and that war is healthy. Also, he pointed out, war abroad insures peace at home. As to the point that peace is stagnating, we do not have the experience and so cannot tell, for we have never had peace long enough to be able to watch its prolonged effects. As to the point that war is healthy, well, Hegel always predicated his political theories upon the certainty of German victory. I am not sure that even Hegel would have been able to regard the destruction of Dresden and Hamburg and the defeat of Germany and its consequent reduction to a second class power in World War II as healthy. The difficulty with the appeal to war is that no one can tell who will be the victor. Also, it often happens that the so-called victor proves to be the loser and the loser, the victor. Japan, the loser, has done better since World War II than England, the victor. The outcome of a war is almost never the same as the predictions about it.

Hegel's final point, that war abroad insures peace at home, is a telling one and has frequently been resorted to by dictators who felt their hold slipping or who encountered problems they knew could not be solved. Nothing brings the people of a country so close together and rallies them under the flag, no matter how serious their other difficulties, as a common enemy. The French Resistance of World War II contained communists, Roman Catholic priests, and politicians of all stripes who could make common cause because they were all Frenchmen and wanted the Germans driven out. The difficulty with Hegel's argument is that wars abroad are easy to start and sometimes difficult to stop. Then, too, sometimes they are lost, and the war abroad suddenly appears in the form of invading troops which makes things even more uncomfortable and less than peaceful at home. The Germans who invaded Russia found this out before they were done.

The inevitability of war is a characterization that has seldom been made. I have tried to show that it is inherent in the aggressive human animal who turns his unfulfilled need over to the more powerful state. But I submit that the causes of war, in addition, remain largely unknown.

One of the causes we do know, and one of the most common, surely, is the pretension to the possession of the absolute truth. If a state thinks it has it, there is no choice left but to seek to impose it on others—always, of course, for their own good. Given two or more such states, war is inevitable; even with one, there could be organized military resistance. For the absolute truth may be one of political economy—the Soviet Union—or one of religion—Islam— but it does not matter since the result will be the same. According to Muslim law, for example, the world is divided into a domain of Islam and a domain of war. Had the entire world embraced Islam, we are told, this second domain would not have been necessary, but under the circumstance of resistance to conversion it is.

Any war conducted in the interest of an absolute truth is regarded by those waging it as a just war. The remedy is to attack the absoluteness of the absolute truth, or the truthfulness for that matter. No factual truths are absolute, only logical truths can be; but eventually they make their appeal to facts also. On the basis of evidence no force should be employed since there is never a degree of certainty necessary to justify it.

The absolute truth is not the only cause of war however prevalent it may be. Too many different reasons have been given traditionally for us to see any cause they could have in common. War is certainly a familiar kind of human behavior, a traditional phenomenon of the species. We are not in possession of a sufficient amount of information at this level to know whether war is a form of human self-destruction, like that of the lemmings, or whether it is a natural process for keeping the population on a subsistence level. No countries which engage in periodic wars are in danger of outbreeding their food supply. This has been true for so long that even now, when we can provide the necessary food for any given population by means of industrial agriculture, the practice of war is preserved.

If there is any element in the world which it would be desirable on all sides to reduce, it is that of pain. The world religions for the most part have advanced different methods for the elimination or at least the endurance of pain. But war is responsible for the addition of a great deal of pain. So the elimination of war is a pressing human need.

It is a curious arrangement when in return for the privilege of participating in civil order, the state can exact the life of its citizens. This remains true, certainly, so long as there is a military draft; and it is true for the citizens whether all of them like it or not. Death is a high price to pay for an orderly life, and that is what it comes down to, at least for those who die for their country, and this remains true whether they have chosen to do so or not. In any case, the outcome lies in the social domain. For just as the stability of the individual rests on an equilibrium between competing needs and drives, so peace within the state as well as internationally is a matter of balance between conflicting interests and opposed coalitions. All such arrangements—individual, federal, international—are uneasy affairs, but then so are all other material systems.

The nature of existence is that it contains as much energy as matter and is as much dynamic as static. As we noted in the previous chapter, since no state has proved sufficiently strong to overcome all its rivals and establish a permanent global government, the only method for achieving such a desirable state, even temporarily, would have to lie through a balance of power. The only way in which a coalition could hope to escape the hegemony of its rivals would be to settle for compromise, however much it would have to surrender in this way and however uneasy such an arrangement might be.

Behind the balance of power concept in the minds of those who guide the politics of nations, there must stand a consensus which reflects what all citizens everywhere earnestly want. Such a consensus could become the kind of global morality under which terrestrial man could live at peace with his fellows.

A state of affairs of this kind is not actual, but it is possible, and it lies within the reach of present methods of education and cooperation. On the positive side of expediency, it seems the only short-range hope for the peaceful coexistence for men having fundamental differences of interest and outlook.

Meanwhile, the balance of power, though a basically unstable arrangement, has been infused with ultimate desperation by the nature of advancing applied science and technology. The only known deterrent to the use of nuclear weapons by one side is the possession of those same weapons by the other, as is presently the case with the United States and Soviet Union. The leaders of both

countries recognize that neither side has anything to gain from mutual destruction. Will this be true of Communist China in the future? Will it be true of those small nations who get the atomic bomb
but over whose destinies less practical considerations may prevail;
for instance, among leaders whose security of hold on positions of
political power may be more tenuous? As we have also noted in the
previous chapter, no balance of power can be anything but temporary because the power of nations rises and falls suddenly and de-
cisively. And so it is not particularly wise to look for any permanent
solution in that direction.

There is one long-range remedy, but we will postpone its examination until the next chapter.

The argument often made now, that with the discovery of thermonuclear bombs and global delivery systems there are weapons
so powerful that they are practically useless for any conventional aims, does not reckon with the natural ferocity of man. Those
who insist that self-preservation is "the first law of nature" may
be wrong, for hatred and enmity seem to take precedence more
often than not. If men loved themselves more than they hated their
enemies, they would not be willing to give their lives in war. There
is more self-sacrifice involved in killing than there is in living. Evidently, a man is more willing to lay down his life that his fellows
may die than that they may live.

The argument that no nation could win a thermonuclear war
is insufficient to justify the prediction that none will wage it. Not
everything nations do is in their own interest. It was not in the interest of Communist China to quarrel with Soviet Russia or to send
home the Russian scientists and technicians who were helping the
Chinese to build a scientific-industrial culture.

The humanitarian pleas that it would be inhuman to employ
nuclear weapons comes only from those who do not miss the tradition of humanism, but they are in the paralyzing position of having
been responsible for both the humanist tradition and the bomb.
Poison gas was rarely used, not because it was inhuman, but because it was impractical. But, according to *The New York Times* of
July 21, 1967, the International Red Cross again confirmed the
story that Egyptian planes had been dropping poison gas on Yemeni
villages. Any effective weapon which seems to offer an advantage

is sure to be used when the occasion arises. The ruthlessness and
the brutality of recent small wars around the world do not give much
comfort to those who looked to the Geneva Conventions of 1864,
1906, 1929 and 1949—behind which lay the terrifying assumption
that wars had to be regulated because they could not be stopped—
and only serve to make these repeated declarations of humane treatment appear more like vain hopes than facts.

Section 5. The Hope of Mutation

It would be difficult for anyone who knows about the dark side
of human life—its cruelty, violence, and recurrent wars—not to
hope for a favorable mutation of the human species. The best we
can want now is the evolution of a more admirable animal—what
else? For the human species as now constituted contains too much
aggression in its intra-specific relations, too much ferocity inherent
in its very nature, to dream the dream of the ameliorative liberals
that man will come to live in accordance with the rational side of
his nature and express only his essential goodness. The individual
Rousseau saw does not exist. Wars are inevitable so long as man has
his old ambitions to dominate his environment by himself and, failing that, collectively through the instrument of the state.

It would not be difficult to show that political programs have
had genetic effect. By killing off the healthiest and most able of the
young men and those who carry the best combination of genes
which they are thereby prevented from passing on to successive
generations, a nation can lose its leadership and subside into
the position of a second-class power.

But now the tables are turned and genetic programs are going to
have political effects. If molecular biologists can discover how to design the kind of human beings it would be best to have, then of
course everything in human life, including social and political organizations, will be drastically affected. Let us hope there will be no
parallel with the discoveries of the physicists, for it is the politicians
who now have their fingers on the button. If the politicians were to
be put in possession of the discoveries of molecular biology, the results might be even worse. Thus far, the effect of every scientific

advance has been to make the politicians more powerful, but this latest advance would be too much.

There is still another possibility. A nuclear war might result in a mutation favorable to the species. This could be an unintended result, but a happy one all the same. Animals undergo mutations when the necessity arises of adapting to a new environment. The artifactual environment man has constructed out of the industrial culture of applied science and technology is a new one. We have noted already that almost nothing in his immediate surroundings, not even the earth he walks on or the air he breathes, is as it was before. He has altered all of it; either deliberately, as with cultivated and tilled soil or paved streets, or inadvertently, as with the polluted air of the cities. From man's effort to adapt to this new environment a mutation in his species may be expected, although certainly not immediately. The process will take thousands of years, but if the industrial culture survives that long it will provide the requisite selection pressures.

The adaptation to an artifactual environment involves the exercise of the power of self-determination. The next step in the mutation cycle will occur when man is aware that he has this power, for then he can plan its use. We have already noted that the molecular biologists are working on the problem and can at least envisage its accomplishment. But they are working internally with genetic material. The kind of control we are talking about now is somewhat different. For there is another technique possible, one which would mean working externally. It would consist of two steps: (a) determining the kind of human being that is wanted, and (b) planning the artifactual environment that would produce him through the process of adaptation.

For instance, let us say that we know we want to abolish war. The problem then has two approaches: first, that of genetic control, or the kind of genetic inheritance it is necessary to build into the human individual to reenforce his fellow feeling; second, that of environmental control, or the kind of environment it is necessary to build around the human individual in order that he may adapt to it and become more pacific. At the moment we do not have the answer to either question. But there is hope in both directions that eventually we may be able to eliminate war and promote peace.

However, one difficulty still remains. For war is a product of extreme destructive aggression. There is also such a thing as constructive aggression, for all building—whether it is works of art, books or capital cities—represents alterations of the material environment. If we learn how to eliminate all aggression, there will be no progress, no ambition, no construction—even perhaps no human life. What we want to eliminate, therefore, is to be decided by selection. We want to preserve constructive aggression and do away only with destructive aggression. This presents to the molecular biologists and the environmental planners so specific a task that it may negate the entire program.

Chapter XVII

THE GLOBAL SUPERSTATE

Section 1. The Global Superstate as a Practical Necessity

The state as such, like the fine arts and pure sciences, represents man on his way to something better. But the unsatisfactory condition of international relations suggests that there is a remedy urgently needed. None has been suggested other than a world government. Surely there are no permanently satisfactory solutions on the national level, for, in terms of the existing technology, the nation-state as an autonomous unit is not workable.

Examples are not difficult to find. The United States has never solved the unemployment problem which first made itself felt in the 1929 depression. At the outbreak of World War II there were still ten million unemployed, and since that war the military preparedness against the Soviet Union and Communist China, together with a series of small wars in Korea and Viet Nam, have staved off the economic depression which any prolonged period of peace and disarmament would be bound to produce.

But the difficulty is not a capitalist one only. I will offer two instances from the other side. How much of a nation's resources, for example, should be spent on armaments and how much on consumer goods? The problem exists for nations of every size and strength. Again, the possibility of open conflict between the Soviet Union and Communist China for the control of the communist bloc is a genuine one.

The international organizations which have been tentatively formed, such as the League of Nations and the United Nations, are feeble enough, but they are all we have; and in and through them lies what seems to be our only hope, not only of leading the good life but perhaps even of mere survival as an animal species.

I propose to set forth here a few of the reasons why I think a global superstate is such a practical necessity.

As we saw in Chapter VI, the reach of organization is set for politics by the range of communication and transportation—in short, by the achievements of technology. Communication by wireless and telephone is now almost instantly world-wide. Transportation closely approximates something like that same condition. The supersonic airplane will make it possible to get to any spot on the earth in, at most, a few hours. This brings the whole world population closer together. The recognition that there are common interests, if not common sympathies, is bound to follow from ease of access and the familiarity of proximity.

I am aware, of course, that all this sounds simpler than it is. Both access and familiarity can exist without producing common interests and sympathies. France and England have faced each other across a narrow channel for centuries without any visible results except intermittent conflicts.

Every great social advance has been accompanied by an increase in the size of political organization. The increases are made possible by advances in technology, not the least of which is the facile manipulation of the medium of exchange. The invention of gold coin was at one time a great step forward, but metals are too unwieldy to service the economic needs of international trade today. In its place we have paper money, at first backed by gold and now more efficiently by the economic strength of the government which issues it.

No doubt the "metallist" view of money did have to give way to the "chartilist" view. But now that technological advances are once again drawing the nations closer together, a newer and still more efficient medium of exchange appears to be coming into prominence. This is the simple system of computerized credit and debit records. Without the full development of the new system, no prospect of a global superstate would appear practical.

There can be no hope for mankind without the establishment of a global superstate, and there can be no global superstate until men learn how to reach beyond local organizations and affiliations, beyond the family, the community, the nation, the international hegemony, and on to the very boundaries of a common humanity. The tendencies in this direction which already exist: the hard actualities of international trade, the international appeal of the arts, the international exchange of information of the experimental sciences, must be interpolated and extrapolated and enlarged in general until it forms a common mass of human interests solid enough for the support of that world government which alone offers man the prospect of survival.

The global superstate has only recently been made possible. That there are cultural movements of which no individual is wholly aware is attested by the fact that developments which are logically correlated occur together. One cannot be understood as influencing the other when both are the result of deeper forces. Thus the medium does not determine the message any more than transportation determines travel. Both medium and message, both transportation and travel, come into existence at the same time in the existence of a culture. It is now possible to conduct affairs on a global basis, and this comes just at the moment in history when a global superstate seems called for.

The principle stated earlier as a political rule in the first section of Chapter VI that the state must extend further than any institution in it is violated in a number of ways. The work of artists, scientists, philosophers and international bankers extend beyond anything that can be controlled politically. This must make for difficulties both within the state and between states, and so it does.

What is to be done? Nothing that violates the political rule. It simply means that the state must be extended to include the reach of the work of its most gifted citizens. It must be a superstate.

There is gradually emerging from the shadows cast by conflicts the outlines of a world culture. It will substitute for the supernatural the human future as a primary if remote goal; it will prefer the external to the internal way of doing things when a specific technology offers the choice; it will seek to retain constructive aggression while getting rid of destructive aggression as the principal type of endorsed activity; it will cherish the richness of affirmative differences of a qualitative nature, such as is evident in the fine arts, while seeking contributive similarities of the kind found in the grounds of economic necessity; it will promote knowledge in the sciences without regard to their applications, while depending upon such applications to ameliorate the human condition; above all, it will preserve the individual in those of his freedoms which do not interfere with the corresponding freedoms of others.

The protection of the political autonomy of the individual in the midst of the currently largest possible collective is necessary because it rests on an indisputable fact: namely, that dependence relates to similarity while independence relates to difference. Every human individual is to some extent unique and therefore different, and it is to give this difference its due that his independence must in some measure be preserved.

The final goal of all politics, as indeed of all human endeavor, is to produce a happy man. And a happy man is a man who has an assured continuity of those materials which are requisite for the repeated reduction of all his needs. This means keeping things in proportion for him, supplying enough x and y, yet not so much of either that it interferes with the supply of the other.

But this is not a political problem, it is a cultural one. Eventually a society can accomplish politically only what it sets out to do culturally, and politics is not as broad as culture. In this way politics can never be the last word in human life, only culture can. But culture extends beyond the consideration of the individual and toward his species. Thus there is a built-in ambivalence to politics. What is the goal? Happiness for the citizen now? Or a better life for his remote descendants, a life to be based on a favorable mutation of the species?

We are learning fast that the state is not wholly accountable locally. It is the largest living representative of that type of organization which contains individual members of the human species. There are a number now in existence but there have been others and there will be others still. A "principle of type responsibility" could be invoked, one which states that "a thing is in existence in virtue of those others of its type which are not in existence and for which it is therefore responsible." If we consider that the thing in question is a state, we have another political rule: *for any state there are two sets of essential connections: (a) with the actual states of the past and present (a limited set), and (b) with the possible states of the future (unlimited)*. Those states of past and future are not actual. There is always the additional dimension in which are extended all those states of other societies on other planets, in this and other galaxies, which are actual.

To the extent that the state is unique, it is a whole to its parts, and, the extent to which it has connections with its contemporaries, it is a part of a larger whole. In both directions it can be held accountable and so is not entirely independent and without external obligations.

A population therefore can be self-governing only within limits, and those limits are strictly prescribed for it by the rules which prevail on more widely organized political levels: the international, global, and cosmic. The nation-state is a member of a class of nation-states and subject to its necessities, necessities which, as it happens for reasons already given, are becoming increasingly apparent.

Another way in which this fact is forced on our attention and the necessity for a global superstate made more urgent is the rapid increase in world population. The population explosion threatens to get out of hand. From wandering family to tribe to nomad to settled community to city-state to country to empire to United Nations—these are stages accompanied by sharp increases in population. The greater the population, the more necessary a tightly integrated political organization becomes. A sparse number of wandering tribes in a vast expanse of unoccupied country hardly poses a problem in this regard, but, in crowded areas where vast numbers of people live in proximity, it offers the only possibility of peaceful existence.

Two outstanding facts of our time are the rise of the great populations and the increase in technological efficiency. It happens that they dovetail neatly; for, without technology, it would not be possible to deal with populations. In size, the population explosion is more than matched by the atomic explosion.

We may now pause to look back from the lofty and comprehensive perspective of global politics upon the organ-specific needs of the single individual with which it starts. How far in his political connections does the individual have to extend himself in order to reduce his needs? This is the prime question of the reach of politics.

The answer, as we have noted a number of times in this book, is somewhat as follows. If the individual wishes to reduce all of his needs he will have to dominate all of his environment, for his needs include the need to survive permanently, and this can be accomplished only by a kind of superidentification with that largest and farthest of objects which is the cosmic universe. In more immediate terms, because he can anticipate need-reductions for himself and beyond these for his children and their children's children, his reach extends not only throughout the cosmic universe but into an indefinite future.

In more practical terms still, he must follow his own political extension as far as the technological developments of the day make it possible for him to go. Even as I write, two powerful nation-states are devoting an appreciable part of their material resources to a project for putting a man on the moon and getting him back again. If we consider all of the ramifications of the individual as set forth in the foregoing account, then his own nation-state is recognizable only as a local stage on the way to a global superstate, and, as we shall see before we leave this chapter, beyond even that goal.

What are a country's limits? If we consider peacetime tariffs and wartime expeditions, it becomes obvious that there always are activities which extend beyond the state, external activities which may be and often are essential to its internal peace and prosperity. We have long ago passed the technological immaturity which made it possible for the isolated primitive community to exist almost indefinitely without outside contact, on the assumption that its members constituted such people as they were. Even the members of a primitive tribe now may be at the scene of the expeditionary force of a great nation at war, and during the intervals of peace may look up casually at almost any time and watch strange men in airplanes flying over.

The isolation is ended and the policy which accompanied it outdated. Everyone must reckon with his neighbors, whether they be of another country or of another coalition of states. We are compelled to think, then, not in terms of the local unit alone but also in terms of the already existing combinations of units, until we get to the largest of all possible units. Nothing less than this is practical today.

The frontiers of the modern state are no longer situated near its periphery. The marches now are everywhere, thanks to a number of fast delivery systems. Messengers of culture and peace—such as the long-range civilian jet and soon to come the supersonic jet, the international television transmitted via satellite, and the high-powered radio that can pick up signals halfway round the globe—might make effective contact anywhere within a country.

The frontiers of a state exist all over the state. Every inch of the territory of a nation-state is now open to the world; its borders are world-wide. With the advent of modern technology, the exposure is omnipresent and pervasive, and this fact is destined to sweep away all provincialisms and localisms in favor of an international society and an international culture.

One result is that the tensions between the center and the circumference of a modern state have become matters of purely regional interest and hardly matter any more to the central government. Soldiers on the frontier are not sufficient protection against intercontinental ballistics missiles. Because of the prevalence of marches, everything points to the construction of a global superstate as a practical necessity. There is no effective isolation anywhere and hence no genuine independence. The only political protection henceforth will be to merge with others in a common political organization that is world-wide.

As we have seen, the politician presides over a vast network of cultural relations. About most of it he remains unfortunately ignorant. This is an age of increased knowledge and consequently high specialization. In mathematics the algebraist knows little about topology; there is even too much algebra for him to be able to assimilate it all. In physics, the specialist in atomic energy cannot afford to spend his time learning about the advances in solid-state physics.

But the politician finds himself in an even more awkward position, for where he formerly could imagine what was going on in the vast reaches of his domain of authority, he now can do no such thing. This would not matter if what happened in some remote specialty could not affect him, but it can and often does. The sudden development of space age science found him woefully unprepared to deal with it. There are many religions but there is only one science; science in this regard enjoys the degree of universality which every world religion strives for and none has attained. Since the problems of the politician in this respect are no different from the problems of his opposite numbers in other technologically advanced countries, he must seek for help in their company and in a coalition which would enable all of them to spread the knowledge and the responsibility.

Cultural geography holds the key to international relations in peace as well as in war, and for organizing purposes more importantly in peace. The ecological interface of cultural confrontation is sure to exercise a large determination upon the political structure of any single state. Geography, geology, even topography, must henceforth be included in the estimation of a nation's responsibilities. Its boundaries, for example, may contain the source of a river which is needed by a whole continent; its soil may conceal its monopoly of a rare chemical, such as uranium ore, which is essential to all industrial countries intending to avail themselves of the peace-time uses of atomic energy. In this sense, the space occupied by a state may define its responsibilities as a custodian of natural resources.

Section 2. Obstacles to the Global Superstate

States are like individuals, except for the restraints imposed on individuals by states. There are no similar restraints imposed on states except the loose, temporary and diverse ones offered by the possession of equal or superior force by another state or coalition of states. For just as the individual seeks to dominate all of his environment, since he needs all of it to reduce all of his needs, so does the state and for the same reason. The spoken or unspoken aim of every nation is the exploitation of all others. This aim has been the chief obstacle to world government and it continues to be one still.

The passion for any one political form stands in the way of the

progress to the largest of political forms. At the particular moment
in history in which we ourselves live, it happens to be the passion
for the nation-state. The attitude toward it was well expressed by
the novelist, Joseph Conrad, when he talked about "the spirituality
of a national existence." We can look backward in time now and see
it still in fossil form in Africa, specifically in Nigeria through "the
spirituality of a tribal existence." Where then is the spirituality of
human existence, of organic existence of whatever kind, or, better
still, of sheer existence? This is the goal-object upon which we shall
have to base our long-range ambitions.

The idea of a global superstate is not a new one. All great conquerors have dreamed of a world government under themselves, and
their ambitions in this direction were limited only by their lack of
knowledge of the extent of the world. The communist leaders in
the Kremlin and in Peking, like the earlier caliphs of Islam, do not
recognize the existence of any non-communist state as a permanent
political arrangement which they must accept and consider in planning the future of their own political state. Surely Alexander the
Great had such a dream, as had his father before him. The eighteenth century saw a description of a universal monarchy, but probably the idea was already by then many millennia old. Yet to date
no single nation has succeeded in imposing its rule on all others.

The approach to world domination, an ambition as recent as Hit-
lerian Germany, the Soviet Union and Communist China, is being
made more and more possible; yet it does not seem destined to succeed and indeed is the wrong approach. A free people under a free
government would seem to be what is wanted, for it offers greater
allegiance and therefore more security. Conquest is hardly the answer, and even the peculiar modern form of conquest through class
subversion will hardly be more constructive in the long run.

Some authorities profess to see in the concept of the coalition
of nations a halfway stage on the road toward the formation of genuine world government. But the coalition can survive only on the
basis of hegemony, for there must be a structure to a coalition, and
leadership provides the structure. The nations in the North Atlantic Treaty Organization form such a coalition, and so do their opposites in the coalition of Balkan and eastern nations headed by the
Soviet Union. Here a sort of equilibrium resting on the balance of

power concept has been established, and on the basis of this, it is argued, the collective security of the coalition is a step toward world government.

Perhaps so. But international relations of this sort have been good only where no aspirations of global influence or control are present. If each coalition thought of itself in defensive terms only, the arrangement might work. For coalitions can be looked at also as temporary power complexes which can come apart as easily as they were formed.

The willing combination of nations would appear to be the best way to seek a world government, but such lesser efforts in this direction as there have been do not lend much encouragement to those who wish to plan it on the widest scale. Shortly after World War II, many good Europeans had the vision that a United States of Europe could be put together from the existing nations of western Europe, and that it could operate as a third force to mediate between the United States and the Soviet Union in a way best calculated to preserve world peace. But this vision was shattered by the dour ambitions of France as expressed by de Gaulle who made it a condition that could be accomplished only under French hegemony.

How to achieve a world state without a world hegemony?—that is the problem. The size of a state is the extent to which it can extend its control and maintain that condition without the continual exercise of force. For instance, the central government had to exert tremendous force over the confederate southern states in order to maintain the union in the American civil war, but now it is no longer necessary. Franco led a rebellion against the duly constituted government of Spain, a rebellion which could not have been successful without the use of Moorish and Italian troops and German warships and planes; yet a quarter of a century later he was still in full and undisputed control.

The secret lies perhaps in the extent to which citizens can be made to feel that they have a stake in the government. The success of the Roman Empire lay in the fact that, despite the garrisons, people in the most remote colonies were made to feel that they were citizens too, and that the government was as much theirs as it was the government of the citizens of Rome.

Law without the provision for the mechanism of coercive re-

straints is meaningless. There is no law which is effective as a law
yet has no provisions for its enforcement when it is violated. Men
erect laws with a view to imposing penalties for their infraction.
This can be done within any political unit, no matter how large or
small. All that is needed is a sufficient degree of belief in the law on
the part of those who agreed to its establishment in order to have
them make arrangements for its enforcement. This has not yet happened on the international level.

Aggression rightly understood furnishes the energy for construction, and without it there would be no orderly government, no
society with its civilization, to regulate. And so we begin with this
order and add to it the channels provided for it by morality. There
is no change in the proportions of this arrangement when we move
from the nation-state to the global superstate. There aggression
still exists and with it the energy for construction, and a morality of
sorts exists also. Only, this time, the morality has not yet been promulgated by charter or constitution; it still remains in that nebulous
condition whereby it can be traced only through intuitions.

Clearly, the fundamental axiom of a morality suitable for a global
superstate is the one which declares that energy must be accepted
when it builds but rejected when it destroys. Everything between
the individual with his autonomy and the global superstate itself
must be strung along as between two poles, occupying lesser places
of importance. Steps in organization cannot be skipped but all are
only stages on the way. The greater whole is the aim of the lesser
whole in that long march toward unlimited harmony.

For a long time now the device has been well-known that men
control their actions best not by means of the individual will but
through the restraints imposed on them by institutions, of which the
state is one. It is part of that larger program of objectification
whereby everything human must be routed from man to man
through the intermediation of some external material construction.
Self-conditioning, whether by musical instruments or by books, is
the technique which the higher civilizations have employed to make
man over into an animal capable of supporting large areas of cooperation in which he has proved himself to have such immense resources. The pressures we exert upon ourselves issue from those
external and objective material elements we have been able to estab-

lish, from the building of roads, for example, to the custom of driving cars on their right side.

It is this very objectivity that enables the state to manifest the staying power which outlasts the lives of many generations. The intangibles upon which such objectivity depends in the last analysis can be spelled out as soon as we have become familiar enough with them. It is a serious mistake to suppose that intangibles are immaterial. Just because they enjoy a pervasiveness is no reason to suppose them ephemeral. Radioactivity is no less permanent or powerful than ocean waves although it is more difficult to detect. Anything strong enough to serve as the foundation of the global superstate will have to be very strong indeed.

But there will be no global state until there is a global morality, and there will be no global morality until there is a globally accepted set of values. Thus far, neither peace nor education nor material welfare has been globally accepted as a desirable goal. The concept of one world and of a single government for that world must be preceded by the establishment of a single morality. This does not yet exist. There is no global morality, only the law of the jungle in international relations. Every nation is tacitly presumed to be every other nation's enemy unless otherwise stipulated through a formal arrangement, such as a treaty. Since every state is founded on a morality and is merely an attempt to implement it and put it into effect, no steps can be taken toward the establishment of a global state until a global morality exists.

Individuals are capable of reaching a level where force is not the determining factor in social relations, but this is on the condition that there be a willing acceptance of the laws of the state. Since there is no superstate to keep governments on such a high level of intercourse, they behave the way individuals did before governments existed: naked power is their only form of speech. They command respect exactly in proportion to their ability to wage war. Still, the acceleration of international prestige is a factor in the international life of a nation. The more power it is believed to have, the more power it has. Thus nations need to lead from strength and not from weakness if they are to preserve their national identity.

There is a large and important step which has to be taken to move from the weak construction of international relations, such as the United Nations now represents, to a political organization of all terrestrial mankind in a global superstate. The assumption behind the United Nations—that all nations are equally nations, and that newly formed nations which have just achieved sovereignty will be as ready to surrender their sovereignty to a global superstate as an older and more secure nation to which sovereignty is nothing new —is obviously false.

Nations need to be confirmed in their integrity before they will surrender their sovereignty. There are instances where this has been done, and it can be done. At the present time such highly divergent regions as the northeastern and southwestern blocs of states in the United States work together in a common political effort.

The long-term trend is toward cultural uniformity. No other outcome can be expected when transportation and communication continue to improve in speed and efficiency. One can hope only that the uniformity can be confined to the economic and political sections of the global culture, and that local differences in all other respects can be preserved and emphasized. Morality lags behind art. There is already an informal but genuine international community of art through interchange and appreciation, but it is not based on uniformity. Uniformity in the arts, for example, would constitute a great loss and, if anything, a step backward. For there need be and should be no end of differences among peoples. It is the richness of differences which makes human life more intense and enjoyable. Who would choose deliberately, for example, to have everyone dance the same dances, perform or listen to the same music? But still a choice must be made in institutions where the differences lead to conflict. They lead to, or have led to, conflict in economic, religious, and political areas. We must eliminate all those differences which lead to violence and make an equal effort to preserve and promote all others.

Section 3. The Law of the Superstate

We have looked at the negative side of the law of the superstate often enough; first in the chapter on international politics and again above. Now it is time to look at the same prospect from the positive point of view.

International law, the law of the global superstate, would take its usual two forms. There would be the law of the superstate itself, its constitutional law, and the law administered by it; or there would be the laws establishing the superstate and the laws established by it. The structures of culture contain their own laws, which it is only necessary to extract and enact, and this is no less true of the global superstate than it was of states lesser in size and extent.

The global superstate is a state and not a relation between states. Its enormous size would not indicate a change of structure. In a sense, the global superstate would do away with the need for international law and would substitute its own internal law. Only on the condition, which is for the present some years removed, that other global superstates be discovered by communicating with other planets in other stellar systems, will it be possible to include the global superstate under international cosmic law as one among such states. For the present, the global superstate will have to be considered unique and all inclusive, and its laws the internal laws of a state.

International law can become the law of the global superstate only if it is possible to discover and to assemble those "general principles of law" which are "recognized by civilized nations." But such a concept, the Marxists argue, is bourgeois; they recognize no such international laws because they allow nothing to stand in the way of the advance of Marxism in societies, including the use of extreme violence. Agreements respecting international law with states they intend to overthrow seem to them, at best, mere expedients. The existence of Marxist states puts an end temporarily to the march toward the global superstate which lies through the organization and integration of international relations.

Those laws which facilitate the reduction of the needs of individuals or of societies, in so far as they do not interfere with the reduction of the needs of other individuals and other societies, may be considered legitimate. For what is desirable in this connection is the establishment of laws which can be determined by those necessities a terrestrial humanity succeeds in maintaining.

International law is possible only on the assumption that the law surpasses all lesser political organizations to root itself in the rights and duties of the individual. Put otherwise, it will be with the global superstate as it has been with all lesser organizations that the larger supersedes the smaller. State laws take precedence over municipal laws and federal laws over state laws, and so, in the same fashion, superstate laws will take precedence over state laws.

International laws lacking sanctions do not have the force of national laws, but they have the same moral force. International laws are framed within the limits of an internationally accepted though not formally established morality. Even when such laws are violated by nations acting in their own narrow interests, it is still against a background of international morality. Immoral acts deliberately performed are admissions that morality exists. The supreme court of the global superstate would function as an international tribunal based on the English concept of equity and including discretionary powers to modify any of the laws of lesser and subordinate political units.

Institutions by their very nature impose uniformity on individuals. This is true whatever the nature of the institution; it is as true of schools and colleges as it is of the armed forces, as true of churches and monasteries as it is of trains and airplanes and motor cars. To deal with people in the round, they must be handled alike so far as this is possible. The richness of difference about which I have spoken does not apply in the political domain where everything depends upon equality. In politics it is a cardinal principle that no distinction is to be made between one individual citizen and another with respect to anything concerning relations to the state. In the case of other institutions this is in many respects to be regretted, but in the case of the state it is a virtue, and every effort is made to preserve it.

In the superstate it will be necessary that all individuals acknowledge freely this absolute equality with regard to political status. Only in this way can the citizens of the superstate reach around lesser political organizations, such as particular nations, while preventing them from interfering with the aims of the superstate. In brief, it ought to be possible to convince a people of what they have in common without being under the necessity of demonstrating to them that there are properties they do not share with others. The bond provided by the similarities of the in-group should not have to depend upon the dissimilarities of the out-group.

Does it appear, then, that there exists an implicit international morality, a morality of the whole human species? If there is an international morality, there can be an international law through the process of enactment, provided always, of course, that law is established morality, as I have been maintaining throughout this work. The only missing element is the mechanism for law enforcement, provided by sanctions.

As we have noted, a hint at the possibility of constructing an international law based on the existence of an international morality is given in the universal prohibition against mother-son incest, possibly at the present time the only known "international law." It is pertinent to raise the question here of whether there is rooted in the human individual at this evolutionary stage of his development an unconscious crucial commitment common to all members of his species. It has been dreamed of by Jung and others. Its isolation and description, even if it exists, has not been undertaken successfully, and there is at the present only a revival of the cover term, instinct.

Finally, what might be asked of the global superstate is that it guarantee the civil rights of the individual citizen against any abuse of those rights by lesser political organizations. The global superstate is at once the largest unit of government and the protector of the smallest unit—the individual citizen; a global superstate therefore would function primarily as a magnificent ombudsman. For to speak of the collective organization of the greatest number of attainable members of the human species is to consider it the political representative of that species in so far as that species is terrestrial.

Section 4. Toward the Global Superstate

The global superstate and its world government can be understood only in terms of world-history, not the human history which Hegel meant by the term but literally terrestrial history. The global superstate would have the task of maintaining a terrestrial order, including the preservation for the individual of all of his rights. The destiny of the human species is, in the last and most cosmicallyoriented analysis, a part of terrestrial history. The human drama is played out on the stage of a single minor planet and must be viewed in those terms. Humanity has learned how to arrange things to suit itself, but locally only. The unbroken sequence of brief lived individuals constitutes a solid community, and nothing less than that is viable.

The proper size for a state is the smallest that it can be to function effectively. That is to say, there must be no elements omitted from the state which could threaten it from outside. It is possible that left to its own devices the city-state is the ideal, for then direct democracy could be practiced, every citizen taking his full share of responsibility for the decisions of government in which he would of necessity be involved. But the history of mankind contains too many examples of small political units which were destroyed by forces on the outside, even if only other city-states, as the case of Athens with Sparta. So long as there are human beings left out of the state, the safety of the state will be threatened. Therefore, the smallest political unit that will work in the long run is the global superstate which would include as citizens all human individuals on the surface of the earth.

Roughly, we can, by looking back, distinguish four stages of political organization, and they are strongly influenced by the size of the population participating. First stage: the settled community, second: the city-state, third: civilization, with the city still at the center, our present situation in process of change, fourth and coming: the civilization which is country-wide and which has no one general center but an administrative, a science and an art center, and so forth.

With fast communication and transportation, the idea of a center which is more important and more local than a generalized culture, must be abandoned as belonging to a more primitive stage. The situation in some respects reverts to an earlier corollary type when politics tended to lag behind culture. The Chinese have not often controlled politically, except in a nominal fashion, many of the people they influenced culturally, and this is as true today of European culture as it was centuries ago at the height of Chinese culture. The Indians have had somewhat the same history.

The ideal state, then, is the global superstate, *multum in unum.*
The richness of difference would be preserved and even its increase
provided for, but only under a system of laws outlining obligations
and privileges. The only hope for the total eradication of war lies in
the breakdown of political differences and the preservation of political similarities. In the past there have been unsuccessful attempts
at world political organization, evident in world religions and in
universal states, but these were not permanent. What has militated
against the voluntary surrender of national sovereignties to a global
superstate has been the wide variation in the degree of development
of nation-states, all the way from tribal surrender, as in Nigeria, to
solid tradition, as in Great Britain. It is possible to see the slow but
steady approach to a world government, through the increase in the
formalization of international relations. Some examples are: the
making of international laws, signing of treaties, establishing courts
specifically designed to settle disputes between nations (the World
Court), and recognizing different governments.

Politics should be taken emotionally only at the species level.
Local patriotism, such as intense nationalisms, will have to go.
Global politics is species politics, and the earth-wide superstate is a
species state. Nothing less will see the end of conflict and violence.
But we are not yet prepared for anything so large through education
or sympathy. We have not brought ourselves up to the level of species sympathies, and so the future is dark. The Christian brother-
hood of all mankind and the United Nations have been seen to fail
and even bring about results which were the opposite of those intended. There was no brotherly love in the savage religious wars
between Catholics and Protestants in sixteenth century Europe.
There is no cooperation between nations in the organization of the
United Nations which has become largely a forum for the propaganda attacks of one nation against another.

Two developments could conceivably bring a stable world government into existence.

The first could come about if all the small member states would
be brought up to a common large size through the voluntary combination of lesser units. The emerging countries of Africa and Asia,
some existed only at the tribal level, are making efforts to form nations, and the older and bigger states are endeavoring to help them

—clear evidence of strong internationalism moving in the direction of a global superstate.

It is not possible to have formalized relations between states, up to an international organization, and even beyond that to a global superstate in which the member states shall be lesser political units, until there is no geographical populated area which is not included in the territory of some state. A United States of Europe, for instance, could stand on something of a parity with the United States, the Soviet Union, and Communist China, and the same will be true eventually with Africa if the new African nations are successful in their efforts to take their place among the older nations. The fewer the national units, the greater might be the chances for their combination because there would be fewer politicians to deal with and fewer differences to reconcile.

Secondly, if the principle of dynastic legitimacy could be invoked for the larger units, it could be recognized that to deprive any one state of its sovereignty by force would mean to challenge the principle of which the rights of all others were founded, as with the principle of legitimacy which was recognized by the royalty of nineteenth century Europe. Here, instead of the few nations to deal with, there would be many; but for the many there would be a common principle at work in which they could easily recognize their common interest.

We have noted already that the balance of power and collective security are stages on the way to world government; stages such as the equilibrium of political power, partially-ordered global politics, and a totally-ordered global government, or state. But this end of the triadic process can be achieved only if all states agree that part of the education of its citizens shall include education looking toward global politics, for global politics is the goal for every terrestrial individual in the next stage of cosmic thrust.

I see connections between the large enterprises which characterize the current generation: between the formation of a powerful and operative United Nations and the conquest of space, between world communication and transportation and the formation of a central terrestrial economic organization to utilize to best advantage all raw materials and manufactured products. I see an inevitable cooperation among world nuclear powers in their own interest.

There are, then, three actions a state could take to move toward the formation of a global superstate. It could: (a) enlarge the coalition of which it is a member toward one which is world-wide; (b) engage with other states in constructing a common pool of economic resources, of raw materials and industrial capability, with a view to the equable distribution of material goods; and (c) as a start surrender at least a token sovereignty and with it some evidence of armed force to strengthen a central agency working toward global government.

The multistate system will have to prepare the ground for the global superstate in two stages, a stage of subordination and a stage of replacement. The United Nations at the present time has some 126 members. Many would like to forget that their origins were not lost in the mists of history. Canada and Belgium came into existence as the result of diplomatic discussions, for example. The state is an artificial contrivance, a political organization which was formed either through chance or design but never as an absolute necessity. It is genuine, but it can be replaced.

The global superstate would have to begin with the establishment of a common foreign policy for all existing states. The motivation would come from a competition for contributions: the most eminent state would be the one which had made the largest contribution to the global superstate, not in size, of course, but in social progress and achievement. And the nature of such a contribution would have to be of necessity international: an international language, an international mystique.

The sovereignty of the global superstate would be derived directly from every individual member of the human species on the planet earth and not merely by the delegation of powers from other sovereign states: not an international government but a global government, to be representative of the people—in this case, all of them. The decisions affecting them should be made by total representation.

There are three activities in which an individual could engage as his contribution toward bringing about the conditions under which it would be possible to establish a global superstate. He could (a) correspond with someone in a different culture with a view to making friends and understanding a different way of life; (b) follow the ancient Chinese model by cultivating a sense of shame at non-compliance; and, (c) give up the struggle to an antagonist in at least one local conflict.

We need to preach not a religious insight but a scientific one, for, whereas religions have been divisive because of their number, there is only one science. In scientific terms, all men belong to a common biological species, and differences which exist between them, such as nationality, race and tradition, are subsidiary and subordinate to the intra-specific fact of membership in a common organic species.

Except for the Roman Empire and a few central Asian empires of the past, all political units larger than nation-states have been made on the basis of a religious insight founding an international organization. The contemporary empires of Marxism come under this category also because they too are based on a pretension to absolute truth. But there is no reason to believe that wars can be avoided in this way. For an international organization to succeed it will probably have to be based on a common humanity and an interdependence. Fortunately such a one does exist, and it rests on the asymmetrical and disproportionate distribution of raw materials referred to earlier. Meanwhile, tiny steps toward the use of force at the international level have been taken; for instance, policing disputed areas, such as Katanga, Cyprus, the Gaza Strip in Egypt, the cease-fire line between Pakistan and India in Kashmir, and currently the Suez Canal.

A global state is impossible without a moral establishment from which its civil laws could be deduced, and an internal deterrent capability, as, for example, a standing army or air force to police the globe equipped with intercontinental ballistics missiles. But these are not all that is needed. We need to understand the method whereby we could construct some kind of global government, but not before bringing into existence a global patriotism, a sort of global nationalism of the spirit. Those who are divided by cultural differences must learn to find emotional satisfaction in their global similarities, their space sharing. States never come into existence as political units until something of the attitudes of patriotism are already there. When people take pride in what they are already doing together, then it is time to recognize this with the formal statement

of a morality, which, in turn, calls forth a state to establish and defend it.

The clue to the approach to a global superstate lies in the resolution of international conflicts. Is there any way to accomplish this
by means of computers? First, the problems would have to be solved
by objectifying political structures and by programming decisions
in order to make politics technical as well as professional instead of
arbitrary and impulsive. It should be possible to calculate political
decisions mechanically once the values are known, and the requisite
activities could then be deduced from the calculations. Computerized decision-making is not beyond the bounds of both the possible
and the practical. It will take the issues out of the hands of those
who rely upon popularity, instinct, and qualitative preferences
based on insufficient data.

The computer is the first of many machines that will make possible instigative behavior, a technique for having the environment
take care of itself with respect to certain alterations and the consequent continuous adjustments. The direction, at least, is clear. More
and more complex machines are being built, until the new generation of computers can be programmed in such a way that they are
capable of making at least some decisions, until computers become, so to speak, an animal with a brain stem but no cortex.

All along the front, with the environment and with man himself,
the operation will be self-determining and externalized. Abstractions
are essential parts of the external operations. The beginning is already
in sight here and there, and I have referred to it already. A new
condition of money, for instance, is about to be made functional.
In early primitive communities, the exchange of goods took place
by means of barter; then money in the form of coins and bills appeared in the city-states. Now there is, for the first time, as we have
noted earlier, the appearance of a new financial device: computerized credit, a fitting start for an efficient trade at the level of the
global superstate.

No doubt other capacities can be transferred to the state, all
representing, like the computer, an advanced and externalized
rationality. Looking beyond that, we are given glimpses of the
possible future afforded by developments in microbiology. It will

be possible to program human cells so that formulated goals in terms of an established global morality can be a common possession. Once individual man is able to instruct himself with truths, which are both based on facts and have the requisite consistency, a harmonic global superstate will be well within his reach.

I have just stated the positive element which constitutes the essence of the start of a new political unit, the state; but there is a negative element as well. For nothing welds a people together so much as a common enemy. This is now a larger question than it ordinarily is, for usually it is not necessary to look very far to discover the presence of a foe. But in providing a single government for the whole of mankind, we automatically eliminate the prospect of an enemy of the state. There are no other terrestrial peoples and no other states to perform that function. But just this was the plan, for we wished to eradicate wars, and we did so by eliminating the possibility of enemies to fight. So in getting rid of one problem, we have as usual uncovered another: where are we in such a case to find a common enemy for our global superstate? The answer to this question exists, but it is large and speculative and will have to be presented in another section.

Section 5. Toward a Cosmic Superstate

Whenever events in the cosmic universe seem peculiarly local, it may be because our limited projections of absent objects have disclosed no similarities among them. Yet they may all the same have a common origin, and the probability in its favor may be inferred from the statistical evidence of the enormous membership of most classes of events interpreted as overwhelming evidence against the existence of absolutely unique events.

Is man then terrestrially local? The odds are very much against it. Recent astronomy has disclosed that the probabilities of an abundance of life on other planets in this and other galaxies are exceedingly high, and high also the probabilities that such life has reached, if indeed not surpassed, that terrestrial evolutionary stage we refer to as the human species. Thus it turns out that the global superstate is not a political organization of the entire human species—that lies far beyond our present powers—but only of those members of that species which currently inhabit the planet earth.

The global superstate is the form taken by the state when it is faced outward. In this form it takes its place among those other institutions, such as art, religion and philosophy, in which the aspirations of the individual are categorically unlimited. For the first time in human history, it now appears that the confines of the human world reach the confines of the world, for evidence is strong that there is life on other planets throughout the universe. We have been reminded by thinkers as diverse as Hegel and the mathematician, Hermann Weyl, that there is a community of living organisms. They had in mind animals less complex than ourselves. But the argument is not weakened by the prospect now before us that there well may be on older planets throughout the universe animals more complex who would be obliged to include us in a single community. Such a probability is a product of the advances in astronomy which have been made in the space age and which will leave no speculative field exactly as it was before.

In these last pages we have been reading political projections entirely in terms of the human species as it is at present constituted, and after this brief discursus I shall return to that consideration. But it should be pointed out that evolutionary processes may decree otherwise. And this necessitates the mention of two points.

The first is that the biological evolution which led from the ape to man might still be going on, and therefore might lead in the future from man to moral superman. His newly found ability to construct the kind of artificial environment to which he would have to adapt through interaction has provided him with the ability to determine the form of his own species. If the human individual of the future should chance to be a moral superman, then the achievement of some kind of cosmic solidarity on principle would not be beyond his reach. The cosmic superstate would rest upon a formal charter of species-cohesion.

But let us return to our more immediate projection of the political future of man as he is now. The needs of the single human individual, we learned in Chapter IV, require that he control all of his environment for their reduction; but, as we also learned, this proved impossible and so his aggression was transferred to the state. The state can accomplish more in this direction than the individual yet not enough; so, as we see now, what is needed is the cosmic superstate. We shall have to deal first, however, with the global superstate, which, although only a stage, is still far beyond our current accomplishment.

It is not easy for those who have thought in more local terms, in terms of city politics, for instance, the politics of the ward heeler and the city council, to think of a cosmic superstate. Yet this exercise of the imagination is the final political requirement which will be exacted of us. Our present situation on earth with respect to the existence of human life on other planets throughout the metagalaxy is similar to that of the primitive tribes in western Australia, New Guinea, and the interior of Brazil before the coming of the Europeans, when each tribe, having no contact with other human beings, thought of itself as "we, the people."

In brief, what I am proposing is the recognition of a common universal humanity, an extension to the intergalactic cosmos of the concept of collective security. A government is an isolated system in which there is a tendency toward order. If we are prepared to concede that the aim of the human species is to restore order in the world, then it ought to become the widest order, a cosmic order, if possible. That same aggression which was handed on to the state because it was too large for the individual in a total terrestrial situation becomes too large for the global superstate as well, and has to be handed on again to a superterrestrial organization. Aggression cannot, indeed should not, be suppressed but it ought to be directed under the threat of sanctions toward maintaining order. I see in the accomplishments and hopes of the space age the possibility of an outlet for that aggression which currently prevents global politics from becoming an actuality. The assault upon the solar system, and possibly beyond, gives to humanity an outlet for its aggression as well as for its curiosity which should be not only harmless to the earth population but also a mechanism whereby its members might be drawn closer together.

Peace is inherently external to any social organization, and its continuance depends upon the demands made upon its members to work together for a common task. In short, an internal peace is

a function of an external war, or, at the very least, of the threat of
war on the part of an external enemy. Failing the enemy, there must
exist a common external and extremely dangerous undertaking
which has first to be proved absolutely essential to both survival and
welfare.

The conditions for permanence in government are supplied by
the isolation of the society. An isolated society is apt to be one with
stable institutions. The only way in which a global superstate could
be both ideal and desirable would be to have it both isolated and
challenged. The isolation would furnish the integration and the challenge would guarantee the interests of the members in working with
each other. It is well known that nothing draws people together
more than a common enemy. And so there must be an external society to challenge the global society. For just as the stage before the
United Nations was a stage of national antagonisms which did much
to facilitate the cementing of nationalisms, so the global superstate
would be organized quite easily if it could first be shown that other
inhabited planets contain hostile populations.

Populations from other planets would be apt to be hostile only
for one reason: that we would be strange to them. But with the limits of our present technology, the reach of politics does not extend
to such distances. The nearest star is Alpha Centauri, and it is 4.3
light years away, more than we could hope to visit without a vast
leap forward in our technological achievements. A mere radio contact would not quite accomplish what is needed. But the power to
maintain cooperation and mutual sympathy must always be external
to the unit in which such order is desired. Therefore, expeditionary
forces from the United Nations dispatched to a permanent station
on the moon could meanwhile act as an effective deterrent to international global aggression.

We are entering upon an age in which there has been an appreciable extension of the human reach and with it a new concept of
the ecosystem, that happy functioning of the community together
with its available environment. The interactions within the ecosystem run both ways: account has to be taken not only of what
part of the total cosmic environment is affected by the individual,
the political institution, and the whole society but also what parts

affect the human individual, the political institution, and the whole
society.

The expansion of vertical horizons is opening up vistas of tremendous new qualities and relations. For the first time, applied astronomy will make a contribution to the emotional life of man. But
more: orbiting equipment, military, weather, observational satellites, and space probes force a one world fact upon mankind. We are
all under the same orbit together, and together we shall benefit or
suffer. The concept is now with us in an urgent fashion of an increasingly large and comfortably modifiable environment. We have
the common problem for the entire terrestrial species of how large
the world is to be in which we choose to live.

This is not a vague picture of what will be the case in some remote future. The practical problems are with us now. The tasks
confronting an organization sufficient to preserve global peace
must meet the following requirements. They must be clearly external, or extraterrestrial; they must be constant; they must be in-
exhaustible; and they must be overwhelmingly large. All of these
requirements can be met by the space program. The costs involved
in the total space program are too much even for the great nations
of today. They ought therefore to be a charge against the total body
of humanity on this planet. The same can be said for the rewards
and penalties.

The United Nations ought to be the organization chosen to take
over the tasks of the National Aeronautic and Space Administration
and its Russian opposite, and the similar efforts of Communist China
when they arise. In terms of the space age goals, a superstate can be
erected and acts of legal construction arranged. The cooperation
of terrestrial mankind will be essential and obligatory; possible,
however, if, and only if, a majority goes along willingly out of deep
conviction and on the basis of the rule of law. The common language will have to be one which could be serviceable for cosmic intercourse. Such a one has, as a matter of fact, already been designed;
it is called "Lincos."

What I am suggesting is this: that the concept of a cosmos-wide
superstate be proposed and accepted as the goal which is to be set
beyond the goal of the global superstate if the global superstate it-

self is ever to become established and operated as a going concern. There is nothing half so magnificent as a towering thought, and the very prospect of a cosmic superstate is one. The idea that there could be a single government for an intergalactic common humanity discloses for the reach of politics a mechanism whereby mankind could dominate its entire environment not only for the reduction of all aggression but also for the restoration of that cosmic order which might, after all, be the end for which the human species had first been evolved.

APPENDICES

Appendix A

DEFINITIONS AND DESCRIPTIONS

The theoretical study of politics is best supported by means of a set of definitions and descriptions. Governments are conducted by means of language, and the political theories they undertake to apply are expressed in language. Precise definition, then, is a great aid to political order. A good political instrument recognizes this, a bad one does not, and that is one reason why a bad one allows for disorder.

The starting items will be the usual ones even though the definitions themselves may not be so in every case. I shall begin by defining culture, history, society, community, institution, politics, government, and state.

The first five will be treated in the first section, and the remaining three in the second section.

I adopt the method of multiple definition employed, perhaps inadvertently, by Aristotle. Accordingly, a number of other definitions of the same terms were found scattered throughout the book. This should have served to convey for each term the breadth of the concept which single definitions would leave out. Denotations are covered by single definitions, but for connotations the method is multiple; and I take it that for the analysis of the qualitative complexity of social and cultural entities the analysis supplied by multiple definitions is required.

Section 1. Culture, History, Society, Institutions

We begin, then, with culture. I use the term as synonymous with civilization and define it as the works of man and their effects, including their effects on man. It is thus an inclusive unit of social and material organization. Chinese civilization, European culture, are good examples.

By history I understand the chronological account of cultures, and by theory of culture those same cultures logically or structurally considered. In other words, history is chronological while theory of culture is vertical. The same entity is being understood in both instances.

A society is an organization of homogeneous members held together by principles of order. In the state the principles of order are defined by the common interests of the individual members. Thus society is that unit of culture whose boundaries are recognized by some peculiar modification of culture, language or some other. Thus France is a well-recognized society within Western or European culture. The distinction between culture and society is not absolute but vague. In the case of completely isolated societies the culture and the society are one and the same. A culture which has not come into contact with other cultures is apt to suffer no modifications sufficient to fracture it into societies. The culture of the natives of western Australia in the early nineteenth century would be a good example.

A community is a settlement of individuals living together in the kind of proximity which provides for immediate contact. A town is actually a community with political recognition, as was the Greek *polis*. The community, like the *polis*, is the first level of organization after the individual himself. Otherwise he turns inward and becomes subjective, as the Hellenistic people did, or leans toward the supernatural, as in the Christian Middle Ages. It is the sense of commonalty implicit in the community which makes it possible for the individual to relate to the environment in a way which develops the best achievement of which he is capable.

Within a culture or society, the first level of analysis discloses institutions as elements. I define institution as that subdivision of a society which consists of a social interest group together with its material tools, laws, customs and traditions, organized and established around a central aim. An institution is in fact a culture complex. Imbedded in it are a number of behavior patterns or traits. It has its own ambience, its special flavor; men who come within its purview are similarly marked and exhibit its personality effects accordingly. When we say that "Oxford University puts its stamp on its graduates," this is what we mean. The values which the university represents give rise to similar values in the men who have been exposed to them, and this may take place without conscious purpose or planning.

Marx and Engels called attention to a division of society which they considered more important than institutions: social classes based on economic interests, and they attributed such divisions to older political forms, to monarchies and capitalistic democracies, for instance. But the proletarian revolution thus far has brought about no classless societies. In the Soviet Union, party membership constitutes an aristocratic class, no less so because these words are not used in that connection. Except in a society in which there would be absolute economic equality of both opportunities and possessions, there are bound to be economic differences and with them social classes. But it could still be asked whether these are the fundamental distinctions. The place in society of a doctor who loves the practice of medicine intensely could hardly be explained on the basis of his economic rewards. And so there are important interest groups. While classes are the principal ones, there are others which cannot be neglected in the account. The struggle for academic freedom and the struggle for literary expression without censorship are surely not entirely motivated by economic considerations. Both university professors and literary artists constitute interest groups whose class identification is not sufficient to explain their actions.

All cultures or societies share the same set of institutions though the order of their importance within the society may and usually does differ. There are constitutive service institutions, such as the family, transportation, communication and economics, and there are regulative service institutions, such as the state, the military, the courts. Finally, there are higher institutions, such as the arts, sciences, philosophies and religions. In every society, there is always a superior institution which lends its basic value system, its sense of style, and its leadership to the society as a whole, by virtue of a general belief in the reality which it represents through its assumption of an implicit dominant ontology.

The primary purpose of an institution is the production, distribution or facilitation generally of whatever its aim provides: material goods (artifacts) or services. The secondary purpose of every institution is to survive as an institution. Obviously, it is possible for the second to be substituted for the first, or, in a lesser degree, to interfere with the first.

There are many possible dislocations of the institutional hierarchy and consequent bad effects. For instance, a service institution may be elevated to the position of higher institution, as when transportation occupies a disproportionate part of the available resources of a society, or, worse still, when the state becomes the reason for which the society exists.

Section 2. Politics, Government, State

We have seen that culture, society and institution, in that order, mark a decline in sheer unit size. Continuing that decline we now take up the definition and description of a particular institution, the state. But we have been describing actual social structures. Before considering the state in that manner, we must first examine the theory behind it. This will involve us in formulating a definition and description of politics. Before doing so, however, we might take a look backward and relate politics to culture.

Politics is committed to the theory of the social control of human culture by means of that institution within a society which is responsible to it for the establishment and maintenance of a moral order. The essence of politics is power in the physical sense over society in the cultural sense. It involves the control of activities and the disposal of property in a society through a definition of limits, backed by the presence and availability of force. It translates into action socially-held beliefs, and has the task of making decisions affecting the state or any part of it in the name and by the authority of the whole. Through the establishment of control, it has the responsibility for making and executing legitimate policy decisions with respect to the exercise of power. Such control can continue to be exercised as long as a majority of citizens or a minority possessing the machinery of power—the army or the weapons—is content with its effect. An extreme example of the culture-wide exercise of political power is the use by Stalin of the police to enforce his judgment of worth in the arts, for instance, to imprison or ship to Siberia those artists whose work displeased him.

We are now ready for a definition of politics. Politics may be defined as the theory of government, which is to say, the theory of the preservation of the established legal order through continual interposition and with the addition of the appeal to force, if necessary. The political domain is the institutional moralization of man. Politics exists by virtue of the attempt to establish by means of the institution the legal order which follows from a designated social morality. To ask whether there would be any political change if there were no conflict of interest is to ask whether there would be any politics. Governments do not exist only to settle differences. That is one of their functions, but they are needed because men cannot live together without social order; and, because they could not reduce their needs even to the extent that they now do without living together, some kind of government is essential.

The primary function of politics is the establishment and maintenance of a social order, and any order almost rather than no order, though some orders are greatly to be preferred to others. But what no individuals, living in that proximity to others which society requires, can endure is the absence of all social order. Social chaos quickly reduces men to animals entirely given over to sex and acquisitiveness, and deprived of all the amenities we have come to think of as human. Politics is thus a human necessity.

The theory of politics as the application by a government of a particular social morality is hardly new. There are many historical precedents, the oldest perhaps being that of Confucius. He said that men should be governed by morality (*Analects*, II, 1). Throughout that work we find references to "moral force" and "moral power." A considerable portion of the text is concerned with principles of morality for political reasons, for instance, the conduct of the ruler in connection with the state. Ritually correct behavior was especially connected with politics, for government, Confucius thought, should invoke the magic use of ritual (II, 3). Governments should operate naturally, as though the laws of human nature were not generically different from other laws of nature, and social behavior was as orderly as the forces of nature.

Politics has to do with all rules governing social behavior. Those rules concerned with the exercise of physical force as a compulsion belong to the state. But there are analogues in every institution where there is compulsion without physical force, and it is in this sense that men speak of the politics of an institution when they refer to the struggle for its control. Everything in the state depends upon the kind of organization it is, upon its form as an institution.

In all social relations between two or more parties the interposition of the political authority constitutes a third force external to those it relates. The political third party always brings with it the presence of force which exerts an effect even when not exercised. This presence is the source of the effectiveness of the political third party. What it facilitates is the preservation of itself, and, beyond that, of peace as a prerequisite for the other constructive cultural pursuits of the society. It should be noted that qualities are always present and effective at the interface of all encounters between material things. Thus, in politics, the threat of force is the quality at the interface of the encounter between conflicting or disputant parties.

Government is the control of human action to insure the moral use of persons and property. A government is a social instrument by means of which a given set of laws is enacted and enforced, and involves the application to a society of a practical political alternative. According to Marsilio of Padua, the function of government is to preserve the peace, and, according to Hobbes, it is to keep the peace and provide defense. But I should think that they were referring to one aspect only. There is more than the preservation of peace involved in the way in which the organization of power is employed to implement the established moral order.

A state is a collection of individuals and property organized in a single system of political order under a government which has the power to exercise sovereignty, i.e. supreme authority. The citizen

of a state is an individual having political rights. All citizens stand
in an energy-relation to property through control in some form or
in some contractual relation to those exercising control. The state
itself is a combination of government and territory, specifically, that
given territory over which a government enforces its laws. The
state, in other words, defines the geographical limits of the governmental exercise of force.

By state, then, I understand the body politic or supreme rule
exercised by a particular government over a given territory. The
range of the state is wide, so far as the degree of its possible participation in the society is concerned. This runs all the way from
merely being a superficial shell, or having little internal effect, on
the one hand, to controlling with absolute authority every aspect of
the lives of individual citizens on the other, from a very loose con-
federation to a rigid, monolithic totalitarianism.

The state is that kind of social institution intended to establish
and enforce a morality. The institution is society-wide and the morality socially accepted before being established. It is established by
some kind of charter, written or unwritten, and is enforced in the
form of enacted laws. State and government are correlatives: a state
is a government regarded statically, as a standing arrangement, a
structure; a government is a state regarded dynamically, as a going
concern, a function. (This last distinction, in which the state is an
arrangement of sovereignty and the government an exercise of
power, was anticipated by Jean Bodin.)

Every state exists on the basis of the legal order—the established morality from which its civil laws are deduced, and the police authority to maintain that order—an internal deterrent capability to insure that the laws will not be violated. The state can be
understood of course as the political organization of a society. Political relations are not confined to the state. They can in fact run
deeper and be less organized and still constitute a political force. The
Greek people had a sense of political membership even though it
rested on nothing formal, as in the archaic period of sixth century
B.C.

A culture is a larger unit than a state, although it may not be
politically organized. Cultures usually include more than one state;
they may, in fact, include many states having the same or different

political systems. The state does not influence the culture as much as the culture influences the state. For a culture involves a concrete philosophy of which the established morality which gives rise to the state constitutes only a part.

Before leaving the definitions of nation and country, less used terms ought to be defined also. By nation I mean a population together with its culture: its customs, institutions, artifacts, including, of course, its government. By country I understand both a nation and the land it occupies.

Finally, by political element, or just element, I understand human individuals, interest groups, institutions, properties, and also political subdivisions, such as departments, states, cities and regions.

Appendix B

THE POLITICAL INTEGRATIVE LEVELS

It will be among the assumptions of this study that politics is a construction erected over human nature; and, since human nature is part of nature, politics is natural enough. We would do well to locate it in nature before undertaking to examine it in detail. Before we are finished, we shall need to refer to the total background of nature because we shall need it in our final formulations. Man interacts with limited segments of his environment in his small enterprises and with his unlimited environment in his larger enterprises.

Section 1. The Structure of the Political Integrative Levels

We shall have to begin by placing politics among the other levels in nature. I ask you to look at nature with me from the point of view of its linearly structured character. What we see has already the ring of familiar names, only contrary to the usual practice we want now to consider them together. Nature is the collective term for a group of levels each of which is studied by a particular science, so we are justified in calling them scientific fields. Ordinarily, the integrative levels of the scientific fields are given as follows in order of decreased complexity: anthropological, psychological, biological, chemical, and physical. It is well known that each of these levels can

313

be subdivided into a number of sublevels, but we shall have to neglect that in order to keep our presentation in proportion.

We shall here be concerned with some of the subdivisions of the cultural level. Once again, in terms of decreased complexity we find: culture, the society, the nation, the community, the institution, and the individual. These six classifications we shall henceforth refer to as the political integrative levels.

It is possible at once to make a number of general observations concerning these levels. The first point to notice is the distinction between integrative levels and sublevels, which are not the same. The sublevels are levels of *analysis*. Analyzing downward from a given level, therefore, does not reach to the level below but only to elements of the given level. The political integrative levels are sublevels of the cultural and do not belong to any lower level.

I should hasten to point out that at no level should human beings be considered alone, for material tools, including languages, are always present. The organization to which the political integrative levels refer include both the human individual, or, at every level above the lowest, the individual and his tools. The material tools, it should hastily be added, are not merely material. A space may be a physical object composed of materials, such as wood and iron, but it is an ingredient of culture because it has a cultural function. Again, the political integrative levels are constructed stepwise so that each contains a number of items of the levels below plus further complexities and resultant emergent qualities. Reading up, for instance, an institution contains, among other things, a number of individuals, and, *mutatis mutandis*, a community contains a number of institutions, a nation a number of communities, a society a number of nations, and humanity a number of societies.

Each level is authentic, that is to say, it has its own values which it does not owe to any other level; it is at least semi-autonomous. Thus an individual is not merely a member of an institution but someone in his own right, and an institution is not merely a part of the community, but to some extent a self-contained unit, and so forth.

There are a number of similarities which can be found on all levels, also a number of differences between them. I shall discuss the similarities first, then the differences.

Section 2. Similarities of the Political Integrative Levels

For each of the political integrative levels it is true that the following properties are to be noted: (a) a certain degree of autonomy; (b) the normative and empirical; (c) rights and duties; (d) activities; (e) morality; (f) economy; (g) phenomenology; and (h) technology.

(a) There is autonomy on every political level. This means that as the levels are ascendant, the autonomy of the lower levels is preserved. Politics begins on the level where all human individuals are equal, and this is the lowest grade of value. It must be protected at all costs, for the entire hierarchy of values rests on it. To the individual belongs an intrinsic inalienable sovereignty. It can be delegated and, in this sense, fragmented, but only temporarily and never irrevocably. There is no possibility of there being an isolated individual without a society, and so the delegation of sovereignty is automatic, tacit, and always in process but never final.

Politics can be considered a game in which the stakes range from mere survival to prosperity—a game played for life and property. The game of politics is played inside the state and for the highest of contemporary stakes: to secure control of the society. (I say "contemporary stakes" because other games, those of the arts and sciences, for instance, are directed at control in the future and not only over society but over all of humanity.) It is seen at its best as a game in the contest for political office. Society here is meant to include not only all individuals, interest groups and institutions, but also all artifacts.

Thus politics, however ambitious in contemporary terms, is a limited game. There is the larger game of diplomacy, considered earlier; and the even more ambitious game played to dominate the environment—all of it, but more of this was considered earlier. Typical political games are those played for individual freedom and individual welfare, for collective material achievements, constructions or conquests, and for the advantage of the sovereign. Individual freedom, for instance, can exist only when politics makes it possible.

Individual freedom is the external relation of individuals and does not depend upon the individual but upon his society.

Those who argue with Rousseau that the individual is more important than the state and those who argue with Hegel that the state is more important than the individual make a common error. Both ignore the autonomy of each political integrative level. First and most important in this connection, then, would be the lowest level, the level of the human individual. For it must be carried upward through all the levels. Even at the highest level, for instance, which is the level of humanity—of the entire human species—the autonomy of the single and solitary human individual must be remembered. Give up the theory of the autonomy of levels, which accords to the human individual an ultimate status that cannot be challenged, and you have taken the first step toward corporate representation and the superiority of institutions and the state, a road which leads past Hegel's edifice to the fascist state. If, as Stalin declared, "Cadres decide everything," then there is no remedy for the abuse of the separate individual.

(b) In terms of the similarities of the political integrative levels, the normative appears as what man can change, and the empirical as what he cannot. The political levels exist and are empirical; his activities among them are normative. For each political integrative level, the one above appears as an environment containing *a priori* elements of order and providing for, but at the same time limiting, the number of degrees of freedom. In positive law theory all appears normative. Certainly a great deal is. The relative autonomy of the individual, the ready access of interest groups to political revolution, the arbitrary nature of social rules generally lend support to the view that men are free to determine everything about the nature of their government. That this is not entirely the case does not alter the extent to which it is true and sometimes forgotten.

It might be parenthetically remarked that the normative is, however, empirical from another point of view, the zone of silence setting the range of possible conditions for the zone of controlled violence. The choice of changes is one which the individual, at a given time and place and confronted with alternatives, was bound to make, and so his behavior is, viewed *a posteriori*, also empirical.

The empirical nature of the political integrative levels is the foundation upon which, in a sense, the entire argument of the book has rested. The meaning is somewhat as follows. Given a society consisting of a selection of each of the following elements: an available environment of nonhuman nature, a set of material artifacts into which part of that environment has been transformed, a human population with its customs and institutions, including its government, then all of the possible interactions between the elements are exhausted by membership in one of three sets: a set of enjoined interactions, a set of permitted interactions, and a set of prohibited interactions relevant to all three former elements. Imperatives in the form of laws consisting of selections from each of the three sets are established for the society and made explicit as statutes through the process of enactment.

It is here perhaps that we can best see how the scientific integrative levels cut across and condition the political. For if all of the political integrative levels exist as subdivisions of the cultural, and the cultural rests on a foundation through support by and inclusion of the others, then at any given political integrative level there are empirical conditions from the physical, chemical, biological, and psychological levels which, to some extent, determine both what is necessary, or empirical, and what is possible, or normative. For instance, from the biological level, humanity and all levels below it could be favorably affected by better techniques of crop improvement and adversely affected by new methods of germ warfare. Again, the cultural, which exists at the mesocosmic level of the physical, could be affected greatly by information concerning some of the details of the microcosmic level of the molecule and below, and of the macrocosmic level of the stars and planets and above. They support, for example, the "one world" concept which the Stoics introduced but which has never been genuinely accepted: one universe of astronomy, one common biology, one human society.

(c) Rights and duties exist at every political integrative level. Each of these is authentic and no one can preempt another. We are accustomed to thinking of these terms only in connection with the individual for whom they certainly do exist. But they exist also for other levels. Indeed, as we ascend the levels we find these increased, for at every level there are rights and duties. For communities, institutions, and even nations, have rights and duties—things they may do as well as things they must do to other social organizations at the same level.

(d) The normal condition of units within the domain of the human species is one of ceaseless cooperation and competition. This is the form of activity within the confines of the species. The political integrative levels are also levels of cooperation and competition: between individuals, between institutions, and even between communities, nations and societies. Cooperation sets the limits of the activities of competition. This is the form of the activities within the state. Individuals compete for many prizes: money, power, prestige, social position. Institutions compete for relative positions of importance as well as for the greatest possible share of the available resources. This holds true regardless of the type of government or the type of economic organization. How well such competition can be ordered without being too confined is an index of the degree of life and vitality in the state. Bargaining must not be too hedged about by restrictions if it is to be successful for all participants, yet there must be ground rules laid down and enforced.

The use of force between units of the political integrative levels is various, but the most common is physical force, the ultimate determinant of human behavior. Physical coercion can be and often is accomplished by other means. Brute force is physical but once again we have recourse to the analysis provided by the scientific integrative levels, for there is chemical force, provided by chemical "persuaders," biological force, as with the use of breeding proximity or contraceptives, psychological force, as with the use of argument, and social force, as conveyed by the type of political organization in their effects. Moral suasion, economic sanctions, psychological inducements, often substitute for physical coercion. Charisma leads, the gun compels; though in the end it is the same, for somebody has been made to do what somebody else wants done. Thus Plato's victory of reason over force simply means a preference for discourse over violence as a superior weapon.

(e) I have had much to say in this book about morality in connection with the state. It is sufficient here to point out that morality is an ingredient of every political integrative level. The individual has his morality in the unconscious or private retention schema as what appeals to his conscience. The institution has its morality in its charter or professional code of ethics, as with the code of medical ethics. The community has its morality in its customs and traditions. The nation has its morality in its publicly promulgated laws. The morality of a society can be located in a number of places: in the unconscious of the individual, in the hierarchy of institutions, and lastly in the myth of the leading institution. Finally, there is a morality for the human species, though here the outlines become rather vague and ill-defined.

(f) There is a conservation of resources, an economy, practiced on every political integrative level. The economy decides what resources are to be sought and developed, what proportion of the total available energy is to go into what pursuits, how the work load is to be divided and managed. The existence of a budget, of planned income and expenditures, is well known for every political integrative level from the individual to the nation. Beyond the nation it exists only in sketchy form for societies and the human species as the feeble attempts thus far to get international relations going. No utopian ideology would be complete without a blueprint for the exploitation and equable distribution of total global resources.   .

(g) The phenomenology of each of the political integrative levels is a function of its existence among other elements as a frame of reference providing a particular perspective, how the state or some part of it appears from the peculiar interests of some element from within. For the state is a whole which has the peculiarity that it cannot be viewed as a whole. Also, it is imponderable and invisible, and can be detected only through its workings. There is one way in which the individual views things for himself, and another when he functions through an institution, still another for the part he plays in his community, and beyond that others unique for his nation and his society. The human point of view sees its own species as more important than anything else on earth. The phenomenology, then, is the particular perspective understood as a perspective, a perspective on the perspective.

(h) Finally, and more easily understood than other similarities to be found among the political integrative levels, is the technology each possesses, the means at the disposal of its kinetics. The material relations of the state have hitherto centered around the claims of property, as in Locke's "life, liberty and estate." But there is an additional and, from the point of view of the welfare and progress of the state, equally important aspect of material relations, and that is how the artifacts function: not only who owns them but what they do.

Appropriate to every level is a peculiar set of material artifacts constructed for the purpose of facilitating the aims and executions of the entities at that level. There are individual tools, such as cooking pots and violins; institutional tools, such as public libraries or railroads; community tools, such as streets and drainage systems; national tools, such as flags and capital buildings; tools which are society-wide, such as languages and cigarettes; and cultural tools, such as the buildings and other facilities occupied and used by the managers of the European Atomic Energy Community (Euratom).

Enough has been said to show that the political integrative levels have much in common. It will next be necessary to distinguish them on the basis of their peculiar differences. Since many of these peculiarities and differences have been discussed at greater length in the book, they will only be listed here.

Section 3. The Differences Between the Political Integrative Levels

The differences between the political integrative levels are what enable political theorists to range them in a hierarchy. Each is a peculiar type, held in place by the similarities between types in the hierarchy. This can best be illustrated by a comparison of some differences which are ordered by means of common elements. We might choose for this purpose space and time.

Every political integrative level has its own space and time. Space is measured in terms of occupancy. The individual can occupy only a limited neighborhood, whereas humanity ranges over the entire earth and beyond. Every political integrative level has its own time scale. For each, time is measured differently. The life expectancy of the individual is of the order of thirty-five to seventy years, while for nations it runs into the thousands and for humanity into the millions.

In our discussion of the similarities between the political integrative levels, we considered the importance of the lowest, that of the individual. Here in discussing the differences, it will be well to consider the importance of the highest, that of culture. Just as the limiting unit at one end of the political spectrum is the individual, so at the other end it is culture. The state is a local hegemony of peoples under a social organizational segment of the culture. The autonomy of the individual is original and primordial, but the individual cannot maintain himself outside the culture, and it is this fact that makes the culture as such indivisible.

The differences between the political integrative levels will have to be specified for each level. It will be assumed that what is cited in connection with a level is peculiar to that level. It will be assumed, further, that from the phenomenological perspective of any level, all other levels can be neglected almost as though they did not actually exist.

The claims of each level rely upon the irreducible and irrefrangible nature of that level. The level of the individual includes problems of freedom versus enslavement, and of obligations and privileges. The level of the institution includes problems concerning the selection of just what values the laws of the state are to be given to codify and administer. The level of the community includes problems concerning conditions which are peculiarly local, such as the organization of services under special conditions of weather, terrain, available resources, special mixtures of populations, and so on. The level of the nation includes problems concerning peculiar forms of government to be adopted and modified, relations with neighboring states, and many others. The level of society includes problems concerning the growth and maintenance of the social order, with its beliefs, customs, and traditions. The level of culture includes problems of survival against other species and material threats from other integrative levels.

Section 4. The State as a Political Integrative Level

We are now in a position to understand a little more about the complex constitution of the state. Its ingredients can be read off from its position as one political integrative level among others. The state stands above the individual and above the institution and community, and below only the society and humanity.

The state is the political structure of the nation, and it includes many individuals, institutions and communities. It is more, however, than the sum of its parts, for this is true at each political level. The state is an entity well enough, but there are limits. It is not an organic entity having a "General Will," as Rousseau suggested. It is an entity of a different sort, a kind of superorganization in which the authenticity of the individual parts, individuals but also corporate institutions, preserve their separate identity. The identity of lower levels cannot be allowed to be lost in any organization, whether it be the organic individual or any other; to suppose that they can is to commit the logical fallacy of composition.

The state is an organization of its political elements intended both to serve those elements and to constitute itself as a stage on the way from the individual to the species, at once less important and more importunate than either individual or species. The values of the political integrative levels are clustered at both ends of the levels, hence the value to the individual of the whole of humanity and the value to humanity of every individual. Within the state no event is singly caused; all are multiply caused. Multiple causation, when properly specified, is the one concept capable of furnishing the explanation needed to account for any happening.

Much of the relations between the state and its constituent elements can be understood in terms of appropriately graded loyalties. Loyalty can be understood here as an emotional attachment to a political entity; sometimes to a people and sometimes to a territory, but sometimes only to an abstract ideal. Most Frenchmen do not like each other, but they are all fanatically devoted to something they describe as *La France*, which so far as anyone can tell is

neither a people nor a place but an esoteric meaning allegedly beyond the understanding of the foreigner—kith rather than kin.

There is a competition among loyalties: each level competes
with the others in terms of an exclusive attachment which every
level claims and none entirely deserves. For the individual, there
is always a graded hierarchy of interests and involvements. The
state remains a base of operations for the individual because it orders and facilitates his proper relations with the other elements
as well as with the state as a whole. The competition among loyalties is solved by proper grading.

Excessive loyalty to the state, as when it becomes an end beyond itself, is disastrous to the aims of humanity. The state as a
religion—superidentification—brings about a situation in which
the goal-object is unsatisfactory because it is too small and vulnerable. Men need something larger and farther away, offering the
security of total involvement and permanence. To this end, the
state will not do, and it is unfair to its proper grading to put this
heavy load on it, for under such a burden it is bound to fail.

The state, in the last analysis, is a means and not an end. Beyond the state lies humanity, and beyond humanity, those other
and higher organic species which may, and most probably do, exist
on other planets in the metagalactic universe; beyond them lies
the cosmic universe itself, so that loyalties as such exist in a graded
hierarchy which has no end except insofar as the universe has an
end. Politics bridges from the individual to humanity, and the
state has the task of facing both ways: upward toward the culture
and the humanity which lies beyond, downward toward the individual.

REFERENCES

I have included here the names of only some of the most interesting of recent works. There are no references to the classics of political theory which are easily available.

Andrews, William G. (ed.), *Soviet Institutions and Policies*. Princeton 1966, D. Van Nostrand.

Banfield, Edward C., and Wilson, James Q., *City Politics*. New York 1963, Vintage Books.

Barghoorn, Frederick C., *Politics in the USSR*. Boston 1966, Little Brown.

Beer, Samuel H., et al., *Patterns of Government: The Major Political Systems of Europe*. New York 1965, Random House.

Bentley, Arthur F., *The Process of Government*. Cambridge, Mass. 1967, Belknap Press of Harvard University Press.

Brecht, Arnold, *Political Theory*. Princeton 1967, University Press.

Cohen, Ronald, and Middleton, John (eds.), *Comparative Political Systems*. New York 1967, Natural History Press.

D'Entreves, Alexander Passerin, *The Notion of the State*. Oxford 1967, Clarendon Press.

Easton, David, *The Political System*. New York 1967, Knopf.

Ebenstein, William, *Political Thought in Perspective*. New York 1957, McGraw-Hill.

Ebenstein, William, *Modern Political Thought*. New York 1958, Rinehart and Company.

Fairlie, Henry, *The Life of Politics*. London 1968, Methuen.

Freudenthal, Hans, *Lincos: Design of a Language for Cosmic Intercourse*. Amsterdam 1960, North-Holland Publishing Co.

Greaves, H. R. G., *The Foundations of Political Theory*. London 1966, Bell.

Heren, Louis, *The New American Commonwealth*. London 1968, Weidenfeld and Nicolson.

LaPalombara, Joseph, *Bureaucracy and Political Development.* Princeton 1963, Princeton University Press.

Larus, Joel (ed.), *Comparative World Politics.* Belmont, Cal. 1966, Wadsworth Publishing Company.

Lasswell, Harold D., and Kaplan, Abraham, *Power and Society.* New Haven 1950, Yale University Press.

Laslett, Peter (ed.), *Philosophy, Politics and Society.* First Series. Oxford 1963, Blackwell.

Laslett, Peter, and Runciman, W. G., (eds.), *Philosophy, Politics and Society.* Second Series. Oxford 1967, Blackwell.

Laslett, Peter, and Runciman, W. G., (eds.), *Philosophy, Politics and Society.* Third Series. Oxford 1967, Blackwell.

Lucas, J. R., *The Principles of Politics.* Oxford 1966, Clarendon Press.

Miller, J. D. B., *The Nature of Politics.* London 1964, Duckworth.

Mitau, G. Theodore, *State and Local Government:* Politics and Processes. New York 1966, Scribner.

Morgenthau, Hans J., *Politics among Nations.* New York 1967, Knopf.

Oakeshott Michael, *Rationalism in Politics:* and Other Essays. London 1962, Methuen.

Olson, William C., and Sondermann, Fred A., (eds.), *The Theory and Practice of International Relations.* Englewood Cliffs, N.J. 1966, Prentice-Hall.

Pierce, Roy, *Contemporary French Political Thought.* London 1966, Oxford University Press.

Pye, Lucian W., *Aspects of Political Development.* Boston 1966. Little Brown.

Quinton, Anthony (ed.), *Political Philosophy.* London 1967, Oxford University Press.

Rogow, Arnold A., and Lasswell, Harold D., *Power, Corruption and Rectitude.* Englewood Cliffs, N.J. 1963, Prentice-Hall.

Rowat, Donald C. (ed.), *The Ombudsman.* London 1966, Allen and Unwin.

Schumpeter, Joseph A., *Capitalism, Socialism and Democracy.* New York 1962, Harper and Row.

Snow, C. P., *Science and Government.* London 1961, Oxford University Press.

Van Dyke, Vernon, *Political Science: A Philosophical Analysis*. Stanford, Cal. 1965, Stanford University Press.

Ward, Barbara, *Nationalism and Ideology*. London 1967, Hamish Hamilton.

Welch, Claude E., Jr. (ed.), *Political Modernization*. Belmont, Cal. 1967, Wadsworth.

Whitaker, Urban G., Jr., *Politics and Power*. New York 1964, Harper and Row.

INDEX

absolute truth, 96; and war, 269
absolutists, political, 10
actuality, theorem of, 11
action: man of, 12; principle of, 162
activities, political, 318
Adams, John, 15
administrative function, 203
administration, and institutions, 44
administrator, as enemy of genius, 169
agencies, regulative, 90
aggression (df.), 23; destructive, 187; older than institutions, 180; organically-based, 251; and social reprisal, 75; sublimation of, 224; total, 34
agriculture and animal husbandry, 31
Alexander the Great, 266
anarchy, international, 253
Angell, Norman, 259
animal husbandry and agriculture, 31
aristocracy, cultural, 168
Aristotle, 305
Aristotle's *Politics*, 4
artifacts, 77; corruption of, 136 ff.; and energy-interchanges, 53; importance of, 89; and the past, 28; artifacts as "properties," 38
artifactual environment, 273
artifactual relation, 104
Austin, John, 71

bad states, 131
belief in absolutes, 96
Bentham, J., 156, 172, 176
Bentley, Arthur F., 8, 9, 17, 186
Bergson, Henri, 180
Bismarck, Otto von, 222, 230
Bosanquet, Bernard, 32
bribery, 129

British power, ebbing of, 254 f.
broad-based revolutions, 207
bureaucracy: deficient, 130; excessive, 130; need for, 171, 188; recruitment for, 170 f.
Burke, Edmund, 15, 150
Burton, Richard, 257
business, 80
Bynkershoek's rule, 250

Caesar, 266
cannibalism, 32
capitalism, and state, 102
cargo cult, 246 ff.
Castro, Fidel, 244
causation, multiple, 43
Central Intelligence Agency, 133
ceremonies, political, 222
chance, as destiny, 153
change: challenge of, 188; persistence of, 178; and political minority, 60
change in state, source of, 59
changes, in institutions, 190 f.
Charlemagne, 46
Chen Yi, 222
citizen: average, 114; and decision-making, 125; and facilitative institutions, 38; and local contact, 113; and occasional politics, 115; and politics, 107 ff.; and state power, 124
citizens: protection of, 131; rights of, 67; short memories of, 174
civil disorders, and poverty, 127
civilization, as externalization, 28
civilizations, as largest social organizations, 181
civilized man, and tools, 28
civil liberty, 151